New Patterns in Old Mexico

En route to Oaxaca's market. Buses and even railroad cars are used for the purpose but burros and oxcarts are plentiful. In the background rises Monte Albán with ruins dating from 400 B.C.

New Patterns in Old Mexico

A Study of Town and Metropolis

Norman S. Hayner
University of Washington

in collaboration with

Una Middleton Hayner

COLLEGE & UNIVERSITY PRESS · *Publishers*
NEW HAVEN, CONN.

DRAWINGS BY UNA
PHOTOGRAPHS BY UNA, THE AUTHOR AND OTHERS
MAPS UNDER DIRECTION OF THE AUTHOR

MANUFACTURED IN THE UNITED STATES OF AMERICA BY
UNITED PRINTING SERVICES, INC.
NEW HAVEN, CONNECTICUT

To

SHERWOOD AND MARJORIE

Preface

Each of the five times I have driven south from the United States to that little hill (Tepeyac) just north of Mexico City and looked out over the churches and skyscrapers of this great metropolis, I have felt a surge of excitement. Here is a huge modern city that is more than six hundred years old. Its extraordinary recent growth and vivid problems offer an irresistible challenge. It was with the hope of gaining for myself and of giving others some understanding of this great capital and of the Republic which it dominates that the present project was undertaken. Seven months during the summers of 1941, 1943, and 1945, eleven months during 1948-49, and four months in 1960-61 were spent making field observations. The book that has grown out of these studies has been written primarily for seniors in the social sciences. It should, however, be useful to anyone who wishes to know more about Mexico's urban communities and social institutions.

I am under obligation to many people for help with this project. Only a few of the professors and friends who have influenced my thinking will be mentioned: Robert E. Park, for his counsel to "look for facts that are both interesting and significant"; Ernest W. Burgess, for his analysis of the processes in city growth; Roderick D. McKenzie, for his research on the metropolitan community; William F. Ogburn, for the idea of cultural lag; Clifford R. Shaw, for his studies of delinquency areas; Anita Brenner, for encouraging me to include data on all of Mexico before centering on two areas; and my colleague, L. Wesley Wager, for suggesting more attention to Mexican social values. In fact, to many of my colleagues at the University of Washington I am indebted. George A. Lundberg, Robert E. L. Faris, Stuart C. Dodd, and the late Jesse F. Steiner gave continued encouragement in this research; Calvin F. Schmid and his staff in the Office of Population Research assisted with the maps; Delbert C. Miller read critically the chapter on "Handicraft to Factory"; Charles E. Bowerman helped with the questionnaire study reported in the chapter on "Courtship and Marriage." Four members of the Romance Languages Department who drilled me in Spanish and cooperated in other ways are Hugo R. Alcalá, Carlos García-Prada, Clotilde Wilson, and William E. Wilson. Norman Sherwood Hayner, M.D., University of Michigan School of Public Health, checked carefully the chapter on "The Dream of Health."

Although Mexico City has no equivalent in Yucatán, the idea of studying communities that are changing at different rates came from Robert Redfield's classic treatise on *The Folk Culture of Yucatán* (Chicago: University of Chicago Press, 1941). It was Lucio Mendieta y Núñez, Director of the Institute for Social Research of the National University who suggested comparing Oaxaca, his home town, with Mexico City.

Great is my debt to Mexican intellectuals like Manuel Gamio, Alfonso Villa Rojas, and Mendieta y Núñez; also to specialists, such as religious journalist G. Báez-Camargo, engineer Claude B. Finney, psychologist and social worker Enelda Fox, lawyer Salvador Laborde, epidemiologist González Piñon, criminologist Alfonso Quiroz Cuarón, and architect Felix Sánchez B. They gave of their time and ideas more graciously, I believe, than would Anglo-American scholars who had not previously known me.

Since 1942 a Mexican and five Anglo-American sociological journals have published articles by me on Mexico. Parts of these, usually reworked in the light of later findings, have been incorporated in appropriate chapters of this book. Permission to do this has been granted by each of the journals. The articles so used are listed chronologically:

1. "Notes on the Changing Mexican Family," *American Sociological Review,* Vol. 7 (August, 1942) pp. 489-97. Copyright 1942 by the American Sociological Association.

2. "Oaxaca, City of Old Mexico," *Sociology and Social Research,* Vol. 29 (Nov.-Dec., 1944) pp. 87-95. Publisher, University of Southern California Press.

3. "Mexico City: Its Growth and Configuration," *The American Journal of Sociology,* Vol. 50 (January, 1945) pp. 295-304. Publisher, University of Chicago Press.

4. "Criminogenic Zones in Mexico City," *American Sociological Review,* Vol. 11 (August, 1946) pp. 428-38. Copyright 1946 by the American Sociological Association.

5. "Differential Social Change in a Mexican Town," *Social Forces,* Vol. 26 (May, 1948), pp. 381-90. Copyright 1948, University of North Carolina Press.

6. "Mexicans at Play—A Revolution," *Sociology and Social Research*, Vol. 38 (Nov.-Dec., 1953) pp. 80-83. Publisher, University of Southern California Press.

7. "The Family in Mexico," *Marriage and Family Living*, Vol. 16 (Nov., 1954) pp. 369-73. Copyright, 1954, by the National Council on Family Relations.

8. "La Ciudad de México: Su Estructura Ecológica Latinoamericana," *Revista Mexicana de Sociología*, Vol. 26 (Enero-Abril, 1964), pp. 221-31.

Grants-in-aid of this project were given in 1945 and 1948 by the Social Science Research Council of New York and from the Johnson Fund of the American Philosophical Society in 1961. A grant from the Agnes Anderson Fund of the University of Washington made it possible to employ twelve assistants for varying lengths of time during the two-year period, 1948 to 1950. Ten of these were Mexican, only three of whom could speak English, and two were American. All were specialists in some aspect of the field that was being covered. Credit is given to most of these assistants at appropriate places in the text.

My greatest indebtedness is to my wife, Una. Her patient and constructive editorial work accounts for the clarity of presentation. (She would not let me say more.) We are both under obligation to Geraldine A. Cox, an excellent typist.

NORMAN S. HAYNER

Seattle
October 1964

Contents

Photographs and Maps

PART ONE

MOUNTAINS AND A HIGHWAY

In a fertile valley near Tepoztlán a campesino cultivates his maize. Both wooden plow and oxen were introduced first by the conquistadores more than four hundred years ago.

1

Introduction

One of the reasons that Anglos fail to understand Latin America is that we are so different. We just do not think the same way as our neighbors to the south. Mexico experienced a violent revolution during the years 1910 to 1921. Growing out of that bloody struggle came some twenty years of "social revolution" which resulted in basic agrarian, governmental, and military changes. The generals, for example, slowly became professional soldiers rather than adventurers as in former years. In fact, the last three presidents have not been generals, but civilians. During the 1941 to 1961 period covered by this study, the country has experienced rapid economic and technological progress—often referred to as an industrial revolution. It is no longer an underdeveloped country but is in transition toward an advanced position among the nations of the world.

Hundreds of hamlets in Mexico, however, still use the oxcarts and wooden plows introduced in the sixteenth century by Cortés and his conquering soldiers. These same villages retain ancient and revered patterns of religion and family life. Even in the capital much of the old life remains. But tractors and steel plows are increasing in number, and in the cities skyscrapers and assembly-line factories appear. It is the purpose of this book to open a small window on the world of dramatic changes taking place in Mexico.

Part One introduces the country as a whole with a glimpse at a mountain hamlet. A detailed analysis of a provincial town and the metropolis follows. In Part Two the focus is on the quickening tempo in certain social institutions. How is the Mexican household responding to new inventions and techniques? What is happening to the roles of men and women in courtship and marriage? What adjustments occur when a peasant leaves his village to work in a large factory? In the sphere of religion how may Mexican social values be used to explain the alleged "weaknesses" of Catholics and Protestants? What relationship exists between type of delinquency or crime and size of community? Why do Mexicans permit conjugal visits for prisoners? In what ways may changes in recreation be described as revolutionary? Why do Mexicans consider health so important for happiness and what are they doing about it? And, finally, what progress are they making in the battle against illiteracy?[1]

Mexican mountains are rugged. Tucked away in fertile valleys between craggy peaks, the villages and towns of Mexico have preserved for more than four hundred years a culture fused from native Indian and Spanish-colonial elements. Following the shooting phase of the Revolution, inventions of modern civilization began to penetrate these mountain barriers. By 1932 a "black top" highway was completed by the Mexicans from Nuevo Laredo on the Rio Grande across the desert to Monterrey, on through the semi-tropical lowlands of the state of San Luis Potosí, and up through the sierras to the central plateau. Over this highway both from Mexico City and from the United States came trucks, movies, shoes, and loud-speakers.

At a point about two-thirds of the way from Laredo to Mexico City nestles the lowland town of Tamazunchale (see Map I). Surrounded by dense vegetation and tall mountains it was, in 1941, a winding string of primitive huts with thatched roofs and reed sides. By 1949 it presented a Spanish-style front. Hotels, auto courts, and gas stations had white stucco walls with red tile roofs.[2] Only a donkey-back ride away from the automobiles, however, folk life goes on very much as it has for centuries. Even a short distance behind its tourist front a town characteristically presents the traditional aspect. Highways bring contacts and facilitate changes, but the new traits are likely to be superficial. Especially in mountainous areas much that is old persists. An example of this was the arresting funeral procession for an infant, observed near Tamazunchale. One man held high the small blue coffin. Two others were playing guitars and singing. Perhaps seventy-five villagers, dressed in Indian-colonial costume, followed on foot along the highway and downward toward the village cemetery. Since a "little angel" is supposed to enter immediately into heaven, the burial is not a sad but a happy occasion.

More than one hundred years ago Madame Calderón de la Barca wrote of Mexico: "If anyone wishes to try the effect of strong contrast, let him come direct from the United States to this country; but it is in the villages especially that the contrast is most striking."[3]

Fifty-five miles south and east of Mexico City is the village of Tepoztlán where the anthropologist Robert Redfield spent eight months in 1926 and 1927.[4] At that time no wheels of any kind had bumped over its steep and rocky lanes, but in 1936 a paved highway was completed from the resort town of Cuernavaca, sixteen miles away.

There is a small central plaza and market place in Tepoztlán. A rough lane leads east past the great central church with both Aztec and Christian symbols in the stone carvings over the doorway, past adobe houses with their red tile roofs and protecting shade trees, past pigs that sleep peacefully in sunny spots, and on beyond the cemetery where cows graze unmolested. On the mountain top above the town there is a tiny Aztec pyramid which was the temple of a protecting god before the coming of Dominican priests in the sixteenth century. From its ruins one can look down on the faded roofs of the village almost hidden among the trees. Only the old church stands clearly above the green. In the sheltered valley to the east are the cornfields; beyond the village to the south, jagged cliffs.

In 1941 the most interesting example of social change was a mill on the central plaza, where a gasoline engine was being used to grind *nixtamal* into *masa*. Nixtamal is made by soaking corn kernels in limewater and removing the husks. It looks like hominy. Every morning women and girls bring their moist nixtamal to the mill to be ground. Returning to their homes they pat this masa with their hands into flat cakes, making a distinctive rhythmic slapping sound. Using a clay griddle (*comal*) they then bake the thin, flat unleavened *tortillas* which are an essential item in every Tepoztecan meal. When Redfield made his study each woman ground her own nixtamal. Kneeling behind her three-legged *metate* it took her an average of six hours to produce the daily supply of tortillas. It is easy to understand why the quick and economical machine-grinding of the nixtamal has become popular.

Wednesday is market day. Each vendor in the open-air market squats on his heels or sits on a stone displaying his beans, tomatoes, or medicinal herbs, scattered in neat piles over a cloth on the ground in front of him. The women, whether they come to sell or to buy, are barefoot and dressed in long skirts, aprons, blouses, and dark blue cotton stoles (*rebozos*); the men wear huaraches, white cotton trousers snugged in at the bottom, white shirts tied in a knot at the waist (sometimes the shirts are pastel blue or pink), and big straw hats with curved-up brims. Most of the merchants come from Tepoztlán itself or from five nearby hamlets.

The most incongruous sight in Tepoztlán that summer of 1941 was a Bayer-tonic sound truck moving cautiously over the rough cobblestone streets. Twenty-seven boys followed the truck which finally halted near the largest room in the six-grade school where the driver ran a 16-mm. movie featuring Popeye and his spinach. Older persons in the audience laughed, but the youngsters were quiet with wonder.

One day the neighboring hamlet of Santiago held a fiesta for its patron saint. In the outskirts of Santiago a group of men were putting the final touches on a section of the *castillo*, a castle-like array of fireworks, which would be set off in the evening. In the homes tamales and an elaborate hot sauce called *mole* were being cooked for the feast. With candles, wreaths of flowers, burning incense, and women on their knees, mass was being celebrated inside the tiny church. Worshipers who over-flowed the building stood beneath a white canopy before the doorway. Men were sitting and standing under the churchyard trees and even on the roof of the church itself. Occasionally some of the young fellows sent rockets into the sky. No Mexican fiesta is complete without them. Everything was so strange to an American family on a first visit to Mexico that it was hard to grasp the idea that this spot could be so near to the United States.

John Steinbeck in his beautifully illustrated book, *The Forgotten Village*,[5] pictures vividly the drama of modern Mexico, the epic struggle between ancient life and new ideas, which is occurring in places like Tepoztlán.

> Among the tall mountains of Mexico the ancient life goes on, sometimes little changing in a thousand years. But now from the cities of the valley, from the schools and laboratories, new thinking and new techniques reach out to the remote villages. The old and the new meet and sometimes clash, but from the meetings a gradual change is taking place in the villages.

Oscar Lewis did the field work in 1943 for a restudy of Tepoztlán. In 1956 he restudied the restudy and found some interesting changes. "The clothes of the young people were more varied, colorful, and citified," he reported. There was a resident physician and a free health clinic operated by the federal government. Over six hundred of the men, mostly be-tween the ages of twenty and thirty and from groups in the middle economic range, had gone to the United States as *braceros* and many had invested their savings in houses, land, or cattle. There were four rather than two elementary schools, a new secondary school, and students each year who attended the National University in Mexico City. Radios had increased from three or four to eighty, and a movie was operated every weekend.[6]

Electricity arrived in Tepoztlán by 1958; in 1961 a substantial power line was being extended to the village; part of the central market area had been roofed over; and there was a small hotel. A restudy in 1970 might reveal factories and labor unions in this once isolated center.

In the rugged Sierras of northern Oaxaca (wah-hah'kah) are the isolated Mazatecos, Chinantecos, and Mixe.[7] To guide them

in certain agricultural tasks the Mazatecos follow an eighteen-
month calendar with twenty days to a month plus an additional
period of five days.[8] The Chinantecos still boil water by placing
hot rocks in it, and the Mixe build hammock bridges of vines,
impassable for pack animals. Oaxaca City, the state capital, is
little more than a name to the people in these primitive villages.
Between their cultures and that of Mexico City there is a span
of fifteen centuries.

Robert J. Weitlaner, ethnologist at the School of Anthropology
and History of the National University, is bitter about what
happens to his Indians when they have contact with civilization.
The coming of a bus has a profound influence. Although in more
isolated communities an unlocked schoolhouse is a safe place for
storing equipment, in places accessible by truck he may have his
instruments stolen. And two years in that modern Babylon,
Mexico City, "ruins them completely." They become *pelados*
(bums—literally, "skinned ones").

Not all Indians who come to the metropolis, it should be said,
are demoralized by the experience. Benito Juárez and Porfirio
Díaz are classic examples of Indians who became great leaders.
Indian ancestry is not, in fact, a matter for prejudice in Mexico.
Cuauhtémoc, the last of the Aztec chieftians, is today a na-
tional hero.

The communities to be discussed in this book do not include
any that are truly primitive. The hinterland villages which were
studied give a first impression of being primitive but are
actually peasant communities like Tepoztlán. They are, of course,
more representative of Mexico.

There is, however, no Mexican "Middletown." The widely
varying Indian cultures, together with divergent elevations and
climates and distinctive communal histories, give the towns of
different sections of Mexico unique traditions. This study concentrates on social change in two areas: (1) the Spanish-Indian
town of Oaxaca plus certain hinterland villages; and (2) Mexico
City and its environs, with special attention to the village of
Atlapulco. These regions represent two aspects of Mexican life,
the provincial and the metropolitan.

The extent of social change differs sharply in the villages,
Oaxaca, and Mexico City. The isolated, agricultural village
shows the least change; the town, more; the large city, most.
Pre-Cortesian customs that are two thousand years old, such as
the use of the metate, persist most tenaciously in the villages,

less in the towns, and least in the metropolis. Likewise the proportion who eat meat or wheat bread and use modern technology tends to increase with the size of the community. That residential mobility is closely related to these changes is suggested by the clear-cut gradient for the percentage "born in the community": in the isolated agricultural village, 100; in the town of Oaxaca, 92; in Mexico City, 49 (1950).[9] A similar gradient is shown by the percentage of home ownership. Generally, hinterland villages, even those located near Mexico City, show great resistance to change; provincial towns like Oaxaca cling to much that is old but exhibit considerable urbanization; and the metropolis, with wide variations between privileged and underprivileged wards, shows the greatest extent and the most rapid rate of change.

The degree of social change differs also between social classes. It is greatest in the growing middle class, less in the small upper class, least in the lower classes. Even in the latter there is more change in the life of urban workers than in that of farmers. As a rule, the more skilled employees in city enterprises profit from new work contracts every two years and from the Institute of Social Security which is especially designed for their welfare.

Then too, among Mexicans of all groups, certain common social values influence the direction and nature of community and institutional changes in ways that are not easily understood by persons other than Latin Americans.[10] Five of these values will be described briefly:

1. *Dignity*. Each person has a certain inner uniqueness, a distinctive dignity, which deserves respect and which must be safeguarded. The *macho* or virile type of personality is, for example, highly regarded. He has self-confidence, sexual prowess, and a zest for action. In government, individual leaders who have these qualities tend to have more influence than any body of doctrine.

2. *Strong family tradition*. Even more than in the United States the family, and especially the kin group, is regarded as a fundamental institution. Anything that tends to destroy the group meets with opposition; anything that strengthens it is supported. Both within his immediate family unit and among his kin, a man feels that his uniqueness is understood and he can relax. However, the rising incidence of divorce and abandonment in the cities of the Republic and the growing problem of juvenile

delinquency in the larger centers suggest some weakening of the family controls under the influence of the urban environment.

3. *Esthetic values.* All sectors of Mexican society have appreciation for the beautiful in art and music. The slum dweller who grows pots of flowering plants on the crude bench in front of his one-room home, the artistic quality of many objects made by craftsmen, the policeman who refuses to arrest the misdemeanant when he discovers that he is a poet, and the many Mexican communities that support public band concerts—all give evidence of these esthetic values.

4. *Personal freedom.* Probably the greatest achievement of the Revolution of 1910-21 was an increase in personal freedom. After the centuries of oppression this was for the lower classes a positive achievement and is highly regarded. *Libertad,* as the Mexicans call it, is "a value in force."

5. *Education.* Under the leadership of José Vasconcelos, who was the first secretary of the federal Department of Education (1921-24), education became almost a missionary enterprise in Mexico. An active campaign has been waged against illiteracy. "Cultural missions" have helped the peasants in rural communities to improve their homes, health, agricultural methods, and recreational activities as well as their schools. Enthusiasm for the school is reflected in the expression "house of the people."

The emphasis in this book will, therefore, be on the changes in selected social institutions during the dynamic years from 1941 to 1961. From the Mexican standpoint, changes during these years reflect the continuing influence of the Revolution. In this period, also, the Republic increased in population from twenty to thirty-six million; the town of Oaxaca more than doubled; and metropolitan Mexico City almost tripled to an aggregate of five million. Differences in the rate and character of changes in the various social classes and in the roles played by important social values will be indicated where pertinent. First, however, it will be helpful to review a few points about the country as a whole.

A tractor in the northerly state of Tamaulipas suggests technical progress. Excluding the larger cities, as one moves southward in Mexico the incidence of modern technology and literacy decreases.

2

Ancient Life and New Ideas

Mexico is further advanced in economic and social development than most Latin American countries. It is the only one that has experienced a genuine indigenous social revolution extending over a substantial period of time. In Colombia, for example, there has been much turmoil and bloodshed for one hundred years, but as yet the basic social structure shows little change. In Mexico, the Revolution of 1910 broke the old structure, and fundamental social and economic modifications resulted. What

23

are the major features that have accelerated or retarded such an achievement?

The mountain range which parallels the México-Laredo[1] Highway from Monterrey to Tamazunchale, and through which the highway winds upward to reach the Central Mesa, is the Sierra Madre Oriental. On the western side of the great horn that is Mexico are the higher ranges of the Sierra Madre Occidental. Between these two Sierras stretch the dry, sparsely populated Northern Mesa and the less arid Central Mesa with one-seventh of the country's land area and almost half of its population. Still farther to the south, extending through the states of Guerrero and Oaxaca, are the jumbled ridges of the Sierra Madre del Sur. Thus, rugged land constitutes more than half the total area of the Republic. "This topography has made it difficult to communicate," wrote the late Dr. Manuel Gamio, "and to carry on commercial and other kinds of interchange between the several regions of Mexico, many of which still remain in the isolated situation in which they were centuries ago."[2]

Generally, rainfall is heaviest on the Gulf Coast, especially in the states of Veracruz and Tabasco, declines as the prevailing easterly winds move across the mountains toward the central highlands, and increases again along the Pacific Coast as far north as the state of Sinaloa. The average annual rainfall is 60 inches in Veracruz, 23 in Mexico City, and 40 in Guadalajara, four hundred miles farther west.[3]

Since mean temperature tends to drop one degree Fahrenheit for every 300 feet in altitude, the hot and cold seasons may be said to exist simultaneously in Mexico. The "hot country" (up to 3,000 feet) is always warm; the "temperate land" (3,000 to 6,000 feet) is a zone of moderate climate; the "cold country" (over 6,000 feet) is relatively cool. The Isthmus of Tehuantepec is in what Mexicans call the hot country; Oaxaca (elevation 5,000 feet), in the temperate land; Mexico City (elevation 7,300 feet), in the cold country.

The wet and the dry seasons are, by comparison with the hot and cold, more uniform and widespread. The rainy season begins in June and lasts until October. Mexico City has occasional rains in October and May and practically none in between. From this standpoint, the logic of having the longest public school vacation in December and January is obvious.

For Mexico City, January has the lowest average monthly temperature—54.3° as compared with 44.4° in El Paso, Texas.

May is the hottest month for Mexico City (65.1°); July, in El Paso (81°).[4] Since central heating is unusual in the capital, the old Spanish-style buildings used for many government offices become uncomfortable by morning and warm up slowly during the day. This is especially true in those periods when a norther brings a cold wave to the city. Apartments, homes, or offices into which the sun shines warm up quickly and need no other heat.

Wide diversity in altitude, rainfall, and temperature has produced many distinct climatic regions in Mexico. Thousands of years of struggle and survival in these isolated settings have selected and fixed divergent forms of plant and animal life and differing characteristics in the human inhabitants. Just as birds and lizards vary in different biotic provinces, so also do the indigenous populations in both their physiological and cultural traits. Perhaps the most advantageous biological characteristic developed by all Indians has been their relative immunity to such diseases as typhoid fever. On the other hand, the cultural diversity represented by fifty distinct language groups has been a handicap in the building of national unity.

The 1950 census showed that about 800,000 persons five years of age and over spoke Indian languages exclusively. In addition, at least an equal number had but a superficial knowledge of Spanish. Doubling the 800,000 therefore, this means that for one Mexican out of every fourteen in 1950 (one out of thirteen in 1960) the mother tongue was an Indian language.[5] In 1940 the ratio was one out of seven. More than half of those who speak Indian languages exclusively are included in four groups: the Aztecs who speak Nahuatl and live mostly in the environs of Mexico City; the Mixtecs and Zapotecs in Oaxaca; and the Mayas in Yucatan.

In contrast to the situation in the United States and Argentina the Indian, biologically considered, has survived in Mexico. Robert Redfield estimated that three out of every four persons are more Indian than white in ancestry and yet "in most parts of Mexico, Indians are not so defined."[6] The colonial use of the term "Indian" as identical with "sub-social" tends to persist and explains the unpopularity of the term. In comparison with the United States there is little color prejudice as such. A person with physical characteristics that are not European is looked down upon only if he lives like an Indian.[7] If he ceases to use objects and ideas of indigenous origin, learns to speak Spanish rather than his native language, and does not think of himself as part of an indigenous community, he is no longer regarded as an Indian.[8]

Most of Mexico's thirty-six millions (1961) are peasants, not primitives. About three-fifths of the economically active are engaged in agriculture (in the United States less than one-fifth) and a slightly smaller proportion of the total population lives in villages or hamlets of less than 2,500. About three-tenths dwell in cities of 10,000 or more, but many of these are not urbanites in the sense that they have acquired urban ways of living.

In *Rural Mexico*, the best sociological study of our neighbor to the south, Nathan Whetten uses an index of Indian-colonial culture which is based on the assumption that an individual should be included if he lives like an Indian. A person is placed at the Indian-colonial level if he speaks only an Indian language, or if he speaks Spanish but goes barefoot or wears huaraches, or even if he wears shoes but also wears Indian clothing.

Whetten's chart gives graphically for each *municipio* (a unit of government somewhat like a New England "town") the percentage of population whose standards of living are essentially at the Indian-colonial level. A study of this chart reveals an interesting series of cultural belts. Beginning with the northern tier of states, Indian-colonial standards present a sharply increasing gradient culminating in the southern tier. The northern belt, extending to about 200 miles south of the Border, shows a mean percentage of less than ten. The next 200 miles average about 40 per cent, the biggest variation upward being made by the Tarahumara Indians of southwestern Chihuahua. The next zone, this time 400 miles in width, averages about 60 per cent (not counting the Federal District which has a rate of less than ten). The percentage for the half of this zone which lies west of a north-south line between San Luis Potosí and Morelia is about fifty; for the eastern half, again excluding the Federal District, seventy. The southern belt—Guerrero, Oaxaca, Chiapas —averages close to 90 per cent. Whetten also found that "in those municipalities (*municipios*) in which a small proportion of the population is living at the Indian-colonial level and where, in other words, the more modern culture tends to prevail, there is also found a comparatively low rate of illiteracy."[9] The coefficient of correlation between these two percentages was +.76. Accepted statistical procedures recognize this as a significant relationship.

Two factors help to explain these gradients. One is the proximity of Mexico to the United States; the other is the strength of the early high cultures that existed in central and southern Mexico prior to the coming of the Spaniards.

One should not judge Mexico by Tijuana, Ciudad Juárez, or Nuevo Laredo. Although closer in distance, the "real" Mexico is farther from the United States in culture than the countries of western Europe. Northern Mexico is, of course, not an absolute break with the other side of the Border. Because it looks out on the neighboring country and is not truly characteristic of its own, Mexicans sometimes call it the "porch." "As one goes north in your country and south in mine," Dr. Angel de Garza Brito, public health pioneer from Chihuahua, declared, "people become more genuine."

Carey McWilliams points out that most of the Spanish-speaking people of the United States reside in a fan-shaped sector extending from the Gulf of Mexico to Los Angeles. "This territory is the fan of Spanish-Mexican influence 'north from Mexico' which spreads across the borderlands with the tip of the fan resting on New Mexico."[10] All of the latter and part of southern Colorado are included in this triangle of Spanish-speaking people. Since these borderlands were part of Mexico for some three hundred years prior to the American conquest, they "carry the indelible imprint of Spain and Mexico to the present day." Laredo, Texas, seems very American to the returning Anglo-American tourist, but the stores are nearly all bilingual.

A line showing the farthest extension northward of the so-called high cultures of pre-Hispanic Mexico begins at Tampico on the Gulf Coast, drops down close to Mexico City and Guadalajara on the Central Mesa, and swings upward to Culiacán on the Pacific Coast. The more primitive Indians to the north were referred to by the early Spaniards as Chichimecas. Paradoxical though it may seem, because of the weakness of these indigenous cultures and the sparsity of population, increasing contact with North American technology in recent years has brought about greater progressiveness of the material culture in these northern communities.

The most widely distributed modern convenience in rural Mexico fifteen years ago, for example, was the Singer sewing machine. Whoever promoted the sales campaign did a thorough job. A chart showing the number of sewing machines per 100 families gives 35 and over for the northern tier of states and less than 15 for the southern.[11]

Moreover, the strength of the early high cultures and the greater distance from the technical knowledge of the United States partially explain the persistence of certain antiquated and ineffective material traits in the South Pacific states. The 1940 percentage of wooden plows, appropriately called *egipcios* (Egyptians) by the Mexicans, was ten in Nuevo León and Tamaulipas on the northern border, 95 in Oaxaca.

A STRUGGLE FOR LAND AND LIBERTY

The Mexican agrarian problem had its origin long before the coming of the conquistadores. The Mayas, Toltecs, and Aztecs seized the best lands and made the weaker peoples toil as vassals or take refuge in isolated and barren regions. Within these dominant Indian groups small theocratic minorities monopolized the best resources and kept the masses in poverty. After the Conquest these monopolies were taken over by a handful of Spaniards. Repression was thorough. The peons were not permitted to carry arms of any kind or to use horses.

Social classes were rigidly defined in the colonial period. The Spanish clergy, public officials, and military commanding officers formed the aristocracy; the creoles born in New Spain of Spanish ancestry, and some educated mestizos, made up a small middle class; the rest were plebeians. The major change in this social structure during the first years of independence from Spain (1821-60) was that the creoles tended to take the place of the Spaniards and the mestizos the place of the creoles. The Indians remained isolated and neglected and continued to do the work that required physical effort.

Two outstanding personalities in the struggle for power between the liberals and the conservatives were Benito Juárez and Porfirio Díaz, both natives of Oaxaca. Juárez has been called the Lincoln of Mexico. Until he was twelve he was a shepherd, in what is now known as the Sierra Juárez. During that period he spoke Zapotec only. At twelve he ran away to the town of Oaxaca where he secured a position as servant to a priest. This religious man taught him to read and write Spanish. Juárez graduated from the law course at the Institute of Arts and Sciences and later served with distinction as governor of the state and finally as president of the Republic. He came eventually to feel that the temporal power of the church was too great, and initiated the laws abolishing clerical immunity (1855) and nationalizing all real property of the church (1858). Although Juárez wanted to distribute this church land to the peasants, the conservatives won out, and some 40,000 agricultural tracts, stripped from the church, went to those already rich.

Porfirio Díaz, most of whose ancestors were Mixtec, was at first a liberal, but later revolted against Juárez. After the latter's death (1872), Díaz became president of the Republic (1877). Between 1884 and 1910 he was re-elected president continuously. During this "Porfirian Peace" all foreigners were favored. Mexico was said to be "the mother of foreigners and the stepmother of Mexicans." French language, French architecture, French ways of dressing, and French medical practices became influential in Mexico. French and English names were symbols of aristocracy.

Finally came the great upheaval that is commonly referred to as the Revolution of 1910. Perhaps the most significant event during the fighting years of the Revolution was the framing of a new Mexican constitution at Querétaro in 1917. Its ambivalence throws much light on the recent political history of Mexico. "It is so written as to accommodate either capitalism or socialism," wrote Anita Brenner in 1943. "Which emphasis is applied depends upon who runs the government and so for twenty-five years Mexico's administrations have been in and out of crises brought on by the fight to apply or not to apply the radical clauses."[12]

One of the basic slogans of the Revolution was *Tierra y Libertad*, "Land and Liberty." The main method devised for giving land to the peasants was to break up the large holdings. During the period when Lázaro Cárdenas was president (1934-40) more land was distributed than in all the preceding administrations combined. During 1937 alone the total reached five million hectares or about 12,500,000 acres. Lands were expropriated without attention to the efficiency with which they were being managed or the methods by which they had been acquired. Properties of less than one hundred hectares—the minimum amount specified in the Agrarian Code for irrigated or humid land—were sometimes expropriated and in many instances the entire property was divided up, giving the owner nothing. In some cases local government officials used the agrarian program as a means of securing benefits for themselves. Land was expropriated and redistributed so rapidly that little time was taken to check the eligibility of recipients or to determine adequately the boundaries of the various parts—this last leading to many bloody disputes.

The *hacendados* (owners of haciendas) usually regarded the land-distribution program as wholesale robbery with the "stolen" property recklessly bestowed on ignorant, irresponsible peons. The liberals, on the contrary, felt that "there was no hope of ever developing the initiative and capabilities of the peon as long as he was in economic bondage to the hacendado."[13]

Three hundred miles north of Mexico City in the state of San Luis Potosí is the Ejido Guadiana, an example of the land dis- tribution program. It includes three hundred people and is one of eighteen *ejidos* in the municipio of Villa de Reyes. Since the land in an ejido actually belongs to the community, if the parcel assigned to each *ejiditario* is not worked for three years it reverts to the community. The idea that individual plots have to be tilled regularly to be retained comes from the pre-Conquest village. In 1948 a substantial number of the members of this ejido indicated to Robert C. Barnard and Ernest Lucero, in- structors in the School of Inter-American Affairs at the Univer- sity of New Mexico, that they would prefer to own the land privately rather than as ejiditarios.

Before expropriation this ejido was part of the 82,000-acre Hacienda de Gogorrón—one of the wealthiest in Mexico. At that time peons did not travel the forty-two miles to the city of San Luis Potosí because they did not have the money. They were paid the equivalent of five to fifteen American cents a day. Now[14] a considerable number make the trip regularly. If they hire help the pay is equal to a dollar a day in U.S. currency. Many go every week to Villa de Reyes, twelve miles away. The ejido president has been to Mexico City three times.

In the days of the hacienda they did not own animals. Now they have left the ground and "got up on a horse." It has done something for them psychologically. They did not own work- animals before. Except for two orphans, every ejiditario owns at least one animal. Many own a pair of oxen or mules.

The ability to purchase material goods has increased also. In hacienda days they made all their own clothing. Now several families do not make a single piece for members over fifteen years of age. They used to have no shoes—only huaraches. Now everyone has a pair of shoes. Whereas they wore only "whites" (white shirts and trousers of stout muslin), every man now has a zipper jacket and a pair of drill pants to wear to town. Previously, no one had a two-wheeled cart; now there are four *carros*. Two more, costing one to two thousand pesos and with spoke wheels, were to be purchased soon. Four families have victrolas. Practically every ejiditario has a steel plow. They make fun of oldsters who think the steel harms the seed. The fact that exactly half of the ejiditarios of the state of San Luis Potosí were reported in 1940 as having wooden plows suggests that this ejido is somewhat more progressive than the average.

On the basis of data from all parts of Mexico, Whetten concludes that "despite all the mistakes that have been made and the injustices that have been committed, there is still a net positive balance in favor of the revolutionary program. . . . The personal freedom enjoyed by the general population is probably the greatest achievement."[15] And writing about "Ejido Guadiana" in *The Pan American* (October, 1949), Barnard says: *"Tierra y Libertad?* Well, *tierra*—a little. *Libertad*—yes!"

A 1960 study by the Mexican economist Ifigenia M. de Navarette showed that during the years 1950 to 1957 the average real family income rose 23 per cent in Mexico, but was unequally distributed both geographically and between the various social classes. Whereas in the Federal District and the North Pacific Zone real income was 1.8 times as high as the average for the entire country and in the North (including San Luis Potosí) and Gulf states equal to it, in the Central region and the South Pacific (which includes Oaxaca) the real family income was only two-thirds of the national average. Further, while the richest 40 per cent of the population showed the greatest increase during these years, for the poorest 20 per cent real income actually declined.[16] This economic pressure among the lowest one-third of the peasants has caused many of them to move into the cities in search of better conditions or has made them eager to procure jobs as *braceros* in the United States.

It is clear, then, that a jumble of mountains and distinctive climatic regions have made for great cultural diversity in Mexico. But recently highways, railroads, steamships, and planes have helped to break down this isolation of two thousand years or more and bring Mexico in touch with the ideas and modern technologies of Europe and the United States. Increasing contacts have encouraged the struggle of the masses for "land and liberty." As an outgrowth of the Revolution, the standard of living for most of the peasants has risen.

The kitchen utensils in rural areas of southern Mexico are simple and ancient. Note the metate for grinding nixtamal into masa, the clay griddle for baking tortillas and the olla for beans.

3

Hamlet in the Highlands

People of the United States are accustomed to farmers who live in isolated houses scattered over the land. Our villages, and even our hamlets, are primarily trading centers, not communities of active farmers. But Mexican farmers, like their European prototypes, usually live in aggregations, traveling daily between clustered homes and scattered fields. A Mexican village of as many as 2,500 inhabitants rarely has more than a half-dozen families who are clearly non-agricultural.

Consider, for instance, two Zapotec villages of the valleys which unite at Oaxaca City. San Francisco Lachigoló, ten miles east, and San Agustín Amatengo, fifty miles south (see Map II on page 70), each have five persons engaged in trade. In Lachigoló the 677 residents (1950) live in the village and travel forth to their fields and back; in Amatengo most of them live in the village, although in the adjacent area there are, it is true, some scattered ranchos.

When the number engaged in trade or industry increases in a village, the standard of living seems to rise. In Santa Catarina Cuixtla, for example, seventy miles south of Oaxaca, 82 out of the total population of 1,500 were reported in 1950 as engaged in trade. Some of the villagers are traveling merchants. They take a string of burros loaded with knives, machetes, and guns from nearby Miahuatlán to some such place as Puerto Escondido on the Pacific Coast[1] and bring back a product like coffee. Many residents of Cuixtla sell fruit and vegetables in Miahuatlán. Such activities have made it possible during the past twenty years for a number of people to change from huts with *carrizo* sides and thatched roofs to adobe houses with tile roofs or in several cases to sturdier dwellings of stone and mud.

For Teotitlán del Valle, fifteen miles east of Oaxaca, the 1950 census reported 615 out of a total population of 2,831 engaged in industries—most of them weaving colorful serapes—and 19 in trade. Only 401 were reported for agriculture and stock raising. This situation helps to explain the high proportion who eat wheat bread and sleep in beds.

FIVE MILES FROM THE HIGHWAY

Santo Domingo Nuxaá (pronounced noo-sah′) is a mountain hamlet fifty miles northwest of Oaxaca City. The municipio[2] includes a total of 14,000 hectares (35,000 acres) divided into 570 holdings of land. Most of these are good only for raising brush and trees. Even the tillable soil produces little. Contrary to the usual pattern, the majority of the people live in isolated ranchos on their holdings. Although the 1950 population of this small "county" was 2,385, the hamlet itself would be hard pressed to number two hundred.

From La Joya, a tiny charcoal-distributing center on the Inter-American Highway, Luis—a servant—and the author had taken a steep zigzag footpath down into a canyon. For some four miles we had followed a stream. We inquired of a man on horseback whether we should turn left to reach Nuxaá. He answered in the affirmative. About halfway up the precipitous slope to the village he overtook us. "Why are you going to Nuxaá?" he asked. "To see Sr. Cruz." "I am Sr. Pablo Cruz." "Then this letter is for you." The missive was from Hugh Nelson, Presbyterian missionary in Oaxaca, who had expected to make the trip. Upon reading the message, Sr. Cruz insisted that the visiting stranger ride his horse. A welcome respite after a five-mile hike at an elevation of 7,000 feet.

Above us, half ruined by the earthquake of 1931 and only partially repaired, was the Catholic church. Extending along the ridge of the mountain were many *jacales*. Soon we were ushered into the guest jacal with its thatched roof and dirt floor. Two narrow tables pushed together were to be the author's bed. Guadalupe joined us. He was a seminary student from Mexico City who had been preaching in this region for two months. He and Luis were to sleep on planks placed across two benches. All that Luis had with him as protection against the cool night air was a thin red blanket.

For supper we went to Don Pablo's jacal just below the Protestant church. The thatched roof extended low over the entrance. The sides of the hut were of crooked tree limbs set upright with substantial openings between them. Chairs were brought in for the occasion and the three of us as guests were seated at a small table covered with a clean white cloth. Using pitch sticks, Don Pablo's daughter coaxed the wood fire which was smoking badly. The upper part of the hut was black with the soot of many fires. The traditional three rocks held the pots for rice and beans. Don Pablo, his daughter, and young grandson squatted in the customary way on the tamped earth floor. Two shy children, who regularly stayed with this family during the week while they attended school, hovered near the open doorway. When dogs or chickens from outside the hut ventured too close, the animals were shooed by the grandson.

Guadalupe said grace before we ate. The rice, which included an herb that gave it a pleasing flavor, was something special. Usually the family eats tortillas and beans only. The tortillas were large and delicious; the beans, small, black, and as flavorful as nuts. The coffee was watery and sweet, made with a little *café* and much brown sugar.

After supper a service was held in the tiny church. There were seventeen men on the wooden benches at one side of the room. Many of them wrapped their serapes around them to offset the chill of the evening. Seventeen women on partly decorated benches on the other side wore their blue rebozos over their heads. The mud walls were painted white. A table on the platform had a white cloth with white flowers. Guadalupe was the preacher.

There are five congregations of Presbyterians in this municipio alone, and more in Inés de Zaragoza several miles away. The movement started in 1907 and at first met with strong opposition. Don Pablo was one of the first to leave the Catholic church and become an Evangelical. He was driven out of the village and lived as an exile in Nochixtlán for several years. By 1916 two of his six brothers had been killed by the Catholics and the first Protestant church had been burned. The present church was built in 1936 and since that time the two groups have been at peace. In the municipio the 1949 proportion of Catholics to Protestants was about two to one. Don Pablo had been president during the preceding year, and the president who followed him was also a Protestant.

One of the brethren, Sr. Angel Reyes, invited us to have breakfast with him. Luis and I accepted. We found that Rancho Buena Vista was located at the southern end of a mountain ridge, about a mile and a half from the hamlet. The land dropped steeply in three directions. A thousand feet below, skirting the edge of a small river, were scattered jacales. Huts, fields, and trees were to be seen on other ridges. Truly, this rancho had been well named *buena vista.*

Don Angel helped us wash our hands by pouring over them a *jicara* bowl of water from his own well. A new, attractive *casita* was the dormitory for the daughter and two younger girls who were living with the family. It had a thatched roof and walls of hewn planks set on a foundation of rocks held together with mud. There was the usual tamped-earth floor. In this "little house" we were served a breakfast of excellent tortillas and black beans. As a special gesture of hospitality the author was also given scrambled eggs. There was no fork; and the only spoon was in a dish of chile, the piquant hotness of which Luis enjoyed. In the Mexican way, therefore, tortillas had to be used for scooping up the beans and egg. The absence of knives or forks in a city household is generally regarded as one index to a low standard of living.

The mother, father, and two sons slept in an older casita, where the cooking was done in the same primitive way as in the home of Don Pablo. During the rainy season, the spaces between the crooked logs that form the sides of this older jacal permit the entrance of wind-driven water. The hewn planks of the new casita were much better, they said.

Machine technology was practically nonexistent in Nuxaá. There was at this time a sewing machine out in one of the ranchos. The director of the school had a typewriter, and there was another in the office of the municipio. There were no telephones, bicycles, phonographs, radios, flush toilets, electric lights, motion pictures, nor power-driven mills to grind the nixtamal for tortillas. A few hand mills were used for this purpose. No automobile had ever arrived in Nuxaá. A jeep employed by the hoof-and-mouth disease campaign had made it to Santa Inés, a neighboring village, but not to Nuxaá. Mail came from Santa Inés once a week. Few changes, if any, have occurred since 1949.

The ruling group of the municipio is composed of the president and four property owners, who make up what is called the *síndico*. Each has a substitute who serves when he cannot. The president is the attorney for all governmental affairs. Another public official is the chief of police, who has one assistant. The period of service for all is one year and the work is done without compensation. Eight men seen leveling an area for a new school were in this way doing their *gratuito* (free service), three days of work a year.

Nochixtlán, about twenty-five miles away, is the nearest center for health services. It is also the closest market town. Few of the villagers travel farther.

Two hundred and twenty-three students were registered in the Nuxaá public school; 180 actually attended; only fifteen had reached the fourth and top grade. There were three teachers. Thirty-one students in the third and fourth years gave written answers to a few simple questions. Several interesting points came out clearly. All of the children, for instance, were born in Nuxaá and all of them lived in casitas owned by their parents. Most of the places known to the students were small villages nearby. Fourteen of the thirty-one knew Nochixtlán; ten, Etla (ten miles north of Oaxaca); and eight, Oaxaca. The three daily meals were practically identical and very similar in the different families—tortillas, beans, and chile. Sometimes there were no beans. Only five mentioned meat; three, wheat; one, vegetables. None of the mothers worked outside of the home for money. Significantly, the occupation given for the mother was corn grinder (*molinera*). All of the fathers were farmers. Boys wore huaraches; girls went barefoot.

The principal, Rodrigo Vásquez López, explained that school opens at 10:00 A.M. and closes at 1:00 P.M. It reopens at 3:00 P.M., closing at 5:00 P.M. This allows for the distances between school and homes. No privies are provided for the school children. Like everyone else they use the out-of-doors.

At planting time, Sr. Vásquez continued, women do some work in the fields. Although much charcoal is made in this region, wood is here the cooking fuel. All charcoal is sold. The people manufacture candles for sale also, but do not use them. The sterile quality of the soil is an important factor in the poverty of the community. Oxen are the people's bank accounts. If the corn runs out before the new crop is harvested, they can sell their animals to buy food. These oxen pull wooden plows exclusively. Sr. Vásquez was experimenting with watermelons, tomatoes, and squashes in a large school garden. He regularly spent the vacation months of December and January attending Normal School in Oaxaca. When his studies were completed, he hoped to teach in a city.

No Mexican village is completely typical for the country as a whole. There are too many regional variations in language and tradition. In Nuxaá the background is Mixtec; in Lachigoló it is Zapotec; in Atlapulco near Mexico City, Aztec. Here in Nuxaá is a large group of Protestants which is unusual. Again, not more than 15 per cent of the population of this municipio live in the village itself. The rest are scattered on more or less isolated ranchos. This pattern of settlement is close to that in the more primitive communities of Mazatecos, Chinantecos, and Mixe in the rugged sierras of northern Oaxaca. It is different from the Spanish-inspired, compact village which is customary in most of Mexico.

Santa Cruz Etla, a hamlet half the size of Nuxaá and nearer to Oaxaca, is a little more representative. It is delightfully described by Helen Miller Bailey in *Santa Cruz of the Etla Hills* (University of Florida Press, 1958). The residents live within a small radius. There are no Evangelicals. A bus gets near enough each Saturday to take people to the market in Oaxaca. Fiestas are colorful and Catholic.

However, Nuxaá is representative of other small Mexican villages in being exclusively agricultural and in having all of its population born in the "county." The predominance of the jacal; the Indian-colonial clothing; the use of tule mats (*petates*) for sleeping; the method of supporting cooking utensils on three rocks and of working up the corn masa on metates; the dominance of tortillas, frijoles, and chile in the diet; the paucity of modern inventions; the poverty combined with gracious hospitality—these are characteristic.

Carrying her wares and her baby she is on her way to the Porfirio Díaz market in Oaxaca City. Each week many natives of the state walk long distances to participate in their local markets.

4

Oaxaca, Town of Old Mexico

Among the attractive old towns beyond the Rio Grande, visitors rank Oaxaca near the top. Located in Mexico South at an elevation of 5,000 feet, it was in 1945 a compact cluster of patio-centered homes for about 42,000 people. The town was built for a walking rather than a riding economy. Seven to twelve blocks from the Zócalo, or central plaza, one came to the open country. Almost every house is of Spanish architecture. Stucco walls that come flush to the narrow sidewalks are tinted blue, green, pink, lavender, or yellow. Enter the large doorways and you see the patios, some of which have flowering shrubs, fountains, and singing birds, while others near the market or on the periphery are used for burros, cows, or oxen. There are thirty churches, two of which, Santo Domingo and La Soledad, are tourist attractions. By routing the recent traffic of the Inter-American Highway around a hill to the northwest, the town has preserved the leisureliness of its center.

There is an aura of history and prehistory about Oaxaca. Archeologists say that civilizations centering on Monte Albán, six miles west of the city, date back to about 400 B.C.[1] It is certain that six years before Columbus discovered America Aztecs from the north established a military post on the valley site now occupied by Oaxaca City. The Spaniard Francisco de Orozco was the next conqueror of the region. That was in 1521. By the following year about 120 Spaniards had settled in Oaxaca. The population of the town reached 2,000 in 1626, 14,000 in 1790. Since so many earlier structures have been destroyed by earthquakes, the more important colonial buildings of the town date from the eighteenth century. The Chapel of the Rosary in the Santo Domingo church, for example, was begun in 1731 and completed in 1738.

As the capital, Oaxaca is the political focus of a state whose inhabitants numbered 1,750,000 in 1962. This state is divided into eight natural regions. To the northwest is the Mixteca where the village of Nuxaá is located. Moving clockwise around the state one comes next to the Cañada through which the train puffs and snorts on its way to Oaxaca. Far to the north in the lower reaches of the Papaloapan River system is an area economically tributary to Tuxtepec. This region includes the President Alemán Dam, largest dam in Latin America. Between it and Oaxaca City, in the southern headwaters of the winding Papaloapan, is a very mountainous district called the Sierra. Southeast of the Sierra is the Mixe region centering in rain-drenched Zempoaltepec which rises to a height of more than 11,000 feet. This isolated Mixe country slopes abruptly eastward to the Isthmus of Tehuantepec, the highest point of which has an elevation of exactly 660 feet. The Istmo, as the people of Oaxaca call it, is the geographical dividing line between North and Central America. Along the Pacific to the south is the Costa. Because of the three valleys that center in the town of Oaxaca —one from Etla, a second from Mitla, and the *valle grande* of the Atoyac River to the south—the central part of the state is usually referred to as Los Valles (the valleys). Thus, due to the state's jumbled topography and to difficulties in transportation, less than one-third of the total territory was economically tributary to the capital even in 1961.

Oaxaca's 1945 trade area (then about one-fifth of the state) is shown by an inset on Map II. As would be expected from the high mountains that rise abruptly to the north and northeast, penetrated at that time only by horse trails and a very rough "truck road" as far as Ixtlán (twelve miles), and from the size of the *valle grande*, Oaxaca's greatest commercial influence was and still is to the south. Within this region of dominance only a few stores are to be found in the small towns and none in the villages. The village market, a pre-Columbian institution, is held in the larger places on a traditionally established day of each week—sometimes for the morning or afternoon of that day. It serves the valuable function of bringing producer and consumer face to face. In the Oaxaca trade area, market days are coordinated. Tlacolula has its market Sunday morning; Teotitlán del Valle, Sunday afternoon; Miahuatlán, Monday; Ayoquezco, Tuesday; Etla and Zimatlán, about thirty miles apart, Wednesday; Ejutla and Zaachila, also thirty miles apart, Thursday; Ocotlán, Friday; and Oaxaca, Saturday. Milta, twenty-six miles east, has a rather weak market on the same day as Oaxaca's. Actually, the latter has some market every day. This coordination of at least eight markets makes it possible for traveling merchants to move from one to another in a weekly cycle.

One can sit in a Oaxaca hotel lobby of a morning and see barefooted Zápotec women balance baskets on their heads as they walk with dignity to and from the central market, or a *cargador* carry a trunk down the street on his back, or a serape vendor with his colorful products. One day a vendor came into the lobby and, with the aid of three other natives, spread out a Teotitlán-del-Valle blanket which measured about eight feet by fourteen. It was gorgeously decorated with idols and other pre-Cortesian designs. A retired manufacturer from Detroit, F. W. Woolrich, showed some interest. He had lived in Oaxaca for several years, early in the century, and knew the bargaining folkways. The vendor wanted two hundred pesos (forty dollars); Woolrich offered one hundred. There was much talk about how long it had taken to weave the serape and about the pure wool that had been used in making it. Woolrich got up from his seat, wandered over toward the hotel desk and feigned loss of interest. Finally after at least a half-hour of good-natured higgling it was bought for 150 pesos. Both Woolrich and the vendor knew in the beginning what the outcome would be.

Construction of highways has brought sharp changes in the time-cost distance between Oaxaca and its hinterland. Five days on horseback following the most direct trails, or three days by train with overnight stops at Tehuacán in the state of Puebla and at Córdoba in the state of Veracruz, were formerly required in order to visit Tehuantepec. On the new highway the trip can now be made easily in four hours. Miahuatlán used to be two days south; now it is two hours. Mitla was a day's journey on horseback when Woolrich owned a mine in the mountains north of there. Today one can drive a car to Mitla in less than thirty-five minutes. Engineer Annuar Abdala, who has been in charge of constructing 1,300 miles of highways in the Papaloapan Basin (1948-61), now drives home each week over the new road from Tuxtepec through Ixtlán in the rugged sierras to Oaxaca in order to spend Saturday and Sunday with his family. This would have been impossible earlier.

Oxcarts still lumber into Oaxaca on market days, however. Some have solid wooden wheels and attractive petate-covered tops. In Oaxaca City they are competing unsuccessfully with trucks and buses. To protect the new pavements from the ruinous wear of the huge iron-rimmed wheels, oxcarts are permitted on certain peripheral streets only. In Ocotlán, twenty miles south, oxcarts are still the predominant type of transportation, as they were in Oaxaca City fifty years ago. Long lines of them move clumsily over the rutted side roads into Ocotlán on market day. Often the whole family enjoys the trip.

In spite of the improvement in transportation, there is as yet little decentralized control of the retailing function either in the state or in the capital. The big market in Oaxaca City (Mercado Porfirio Díaz—see Map II), which regularly occupies two full blocks, spills over into adjacent streets on Saturdays. It is one of the largest and most colorful markets in Mexico, but it has no branches.

Perhaps half of the population in this market on a Saturday is from outside the city. On that morning Oaxaca's trade area is picturesquely marked by an influx of human and animal traffic. People walk, ride burros, and, especially from the greater distances, use the buses that distinguish the new era in rural transport. Articles for sale are brought in trucks, slow-moving oxcarts, and probably to the largest extent on burros. From every direction burros can be seen carrying such items as black pottery from Coyotepec, green-glaze pottery from Atzompa that withstands fire, charcoal and wood from the sierras, petates with colored designs, sugar cane to be cut in pieces and sucked for its sweet juice, a surprising variety of vegetables and fruits, ropes made from maguey fiber, shopping bags and hammocks from the same material. Frequently an Indian woman will ride in from one of the hinterland villages, sitting on her burro with the dignity of a queen. Beside her in baskets will be the live chickens or turkey, eggs, butter wrapped in corn husks, vegetables, or fruits that she plans to sell at the market.

SPANISH CENTER; ZAPOTEC MARGIN

In the cities of Latin America the better homes were in the past characteristically located near the central plaza, and the least desirable residential areas were on the periphery. This conclusion is supported by nine sociological and anthropological studies beginning with Hansen's description of Mérida in 1934, continuing with the author's articles on Mexico City (1945) and on Oaxaca (1948), and ending with Whiteford's ecological comparison between Querétaro, Mexico, and Popayán, Colombia, in 1960.[2] In small towns like Oaxaca's Ejutla, Miahuatlán, Tlacolula, and Mitla the adobe houses with tile roofs are located near the center; the thatched huts with carrizo sides and earthen floors are on the outer edges. The centers of these towns tend to be Spanish; the margins, Zapotec. Families living in the center are more likely than those on the margin to have a kitchen separate from the dining room and to wear shoes rather than huaraches. They are less likely to use stagnant water and probably spend twice as much for food as those on the outskirts.

In Oaxaca City the amount that citizens were willing to pay for a residence in 1945 declined steadily as one proceeds toward the periphery. The one exception was due to the establishment of an American colony (now greatly reduced) on the northeast edge of the city. These North Americans did not hesitate to build separate houses on the outskirts, whereas Mexicans had always wanted a house in a central location with at least one wall shared by a neighbor. By 1961 there was a slight trend among Oaxaqueños with comfortable incomes to establish homes eight or more blocks northeast of the Zócalo. With an increase in population to 78,000 in 1960 it took from ten to seventeen blocks from the center to reach open fields. Yet, to corroborate the continued preference for a home close to the center, there is the 1958 study of fourteen peripheral hamlets by a Oaxaca lawyer, Pedro Yescas Peralta. He classified only one of the fourteen as "rich" (San Felipe del Agua on the mountain slope two miles north), whereas eight were listed as "poor" and five as "miserable."[3]

A rough index to the distribution of "privileged" and "underprivileged" families in Oaxaca (1945) is shown on Map II. Using the telephone directory as a source—only privileged families could afford to have their own phones—the *spots* represent a sampling of either rich or at least comfortable private homes.[4] The *circles* indicate the addresses of children enrolled in the one kindergarten that provided three meals a day free. Each of the "underprivileged" families from which these children came had been visited by a social worker to validate the economic necessity of this assistance. The line drawn through the mid-points of the spots in each sector is an average distance of about two blocks closer to the Zócalo than the line drawn through the mid-points of the circles. This demonstrates graphically the preference on the part of people who could afford it for living near the center. The fact that the two lines cross on the east and come close together on the north suggests the beginning of an outward movement by the "privileged" families.

"THE DIRT CAME UP"

In terms of housing, occupation, and source of income,[5] the percentage of the population in each of the major social classes differs in Oaxaca City, the smaller towns, and the agricultural villages. The upper class makes up about 5 per cent of the total population in the capital, a smaller percentage in the towns, and is usually not present at all in the agricultural village. It is composed of the more successful merchants and industrialists and some of the more prosperous professionals. Its members live in substantial houses and have "better customs." Those who have lost the money they once had—some of the former hacendados, for example—still regard themselves as belonging to this class although others may refer to them as *mencionados* ("has-beens").

The middle class comprises 20 to 25 per cent of the population in Oaxaca City. The proportion is much smaller in the towns of the trade area and may be represented solely by the school-teacher in the strictly agricultural village. Even he is usually regarded as belonging to the lower class. The middle class includes most of the professional and government employees, small shopkeepers, white-collar clerks, police officers above the lowest ranks, and city teachers. The 1940 census lists 947 government employees of various types in the municipio of Oaxaca de Juárez and that number has since increased substantially.[6] As would be expected, members of the middle class are lower in material level of life than those of the upper group—with poorer houses, for example—but they are often better educated. Almost all of the students in the Institute of Arts and Sciences (recently renamed the Benito Juárez University of Oaxaca) are from this class.

The lower class includes 70 to 75 per cent of the population in the capital, more in the smaller towns, and almost everyone in the agricultural villages. Craftsmen, servants, *campesinos,* and beggars, in that order, make up successive strata. In Mexico *artesanos,* such as carpenters, plumbers, tailors, and handicraftsmen making articles for sale to tourists, occupy the upper ranks of the lower class. This position reflects the early Spanish disdain for manual labor. Due in part to tourist demand, the income for this group has increased and some of them have been able to give their children short courses in obstetrics, pharmacy, or commerce, and in a few cases they have been able to provide complete professional training in teaching, law, or medicine. These young people have an advantage in that they are accustomed to a simple life including scarcity of food and sleeping on mats.

A servant will say to his master: "An Indian wants to see you." Although he may have an "Indian" background himself, he considers the visiting campesino inferior. Ninety-five percent of the employed population in small agricultural villages are campesinos. Ordinary policemen and soldiers and the majority of rural school-teachers are also plebeians.

Lawyer Yescas, cited above, concluded on the basis of a questionnaire that 3 per cent of the employed population of Oaxaca City and its immediate environs had incomes of more than $75 American per month; 28 per cent, $25 to $75; and 69 per cent, less than $25. He classified the first group as living in "riches"; the second, in poverty; the third, in misery.

Upper, middle, and lower classes may be represented in a single Oaxaca home. The roles played by the members of such a household and their attitudes toward each other will illustrate the social structure of the town:

The mistress of the household, her daughter, and a son home on vacation are members of the upper class; a boarder who has lived with this family for three years belongs to the middle; the three servants, a cook, a maid, and a houseboy, are members of the lower class. They live in a typical Spanish-style home with 15 high-ceilinged rooms enclosing a patio. In the patio there are flowering shrubs and potted plants around a playing fountain, a macaw which chatters raucously and is especially noisy when the maid's baby cries, and canaries that twitter when the sun shines on them.

Before the *señora* lost her husband this was a leading family in Oaxaca society. Although less prosperous economically at present it is still regarded as belonging to the *gente decente* or "nice people" of the community. The *señora* is a devout Catholic and a jolly, considerate hostess. Her culinary activities are limited to the preparation of special *pasteles,* cakes or pies, every Sunday. All other cooking is done by the *cocinera* trained by her, the most intelligent of the three "Indian" servants.

The 19-year-old daughter is less religious than her mother, breaks with the old Spanish tradition by working in a local business house, likes movies and dancing, may often be seen with her *novio,* or boy friend, in a restaurant near the Zócalo, and is very fond of her brothers.

The handsome 21-year-old son is a student at the National University in Mexico City. He is home on a 10-day vacation to celebrate the Sixteenth of September, Mexico's Independence Day.

The middle-class guest is a specialist with the Oaxaca state department of agriculture. He gives skilled assistance to farmers in many parts of the state. He complains that it is difficult to work with "Indians" because many of them are very dumb. His attitude toward the houseboy's mistakes is harsher than that of the upper-class members of the household.

In addition to cooking a delicious sequence of gastronomic adventures, the *cocinera* accompanies the *señora* on the Saturday shopping expedition to the central market. The houseboy goes along on this weekly trip to help the cook carry home the purchases. To get the best prices they must haggle over every transaction.

The maid is less alert than the cook, but gains status as the mother of a cute year-old boy. From the *señora* and the servants the baby receives enthusiastic attention and affection.

The houseboy of 13 years who seems a bit slow, perhaps because he doesn't yet know Spanish well, compensates for this with a happy personality. About a month ago he left his Zapotec-speaking home in a village of thatched huts twenty miles away and obtained this job in the city. His father is an old-fashioned *indio* who kisses the hands of visiting members of the upper class.

Common sounds in the household are the sweeping of the patio at dawn by the houseboy and his singing, at other hours, of the *Cucuracha* song made famous by Villa's soldiers. There is also the pitter-patter of the tiny sandals worn by the baby, the quiet shuffle of servants' bare feet over corridor tiles, and the clatter of upper-class high heels.

Social change in Oaxaca has varied markedly in the different social classes. Many of those who had become rich during the rule of Porfirio Díaz—hacendados, owners of urban property, professionals—having had their power weakened by revolution, expropriation, and earthquakes, moved to Mexico City. The same insecurity forced others of the old upper class to move from the outlying districts of the state to the city of Oaxaca where they occupied, with the new ruling group, the places of those who had left. Those who remained in Oaxaca City and those who come in from the districts still regard themselves as *gente decente*, in spite of the fact that their old economic power is gone. They will do business with such newcomers as the large group of government employees, but they will not accept these "intruders" into their inner social circles. Some swallow their pride enough to seek refuge themselves in these poorly paid government jobs or in positions as retail clerks. Money means little in their analysis of class lines. "If your parents were upper class, then you are upper class," they say. It is natural for them to idealize the period prior to 1910. In the nostalgic words of an ex-hacendado:

I was the *amo*, a kind of spiritual father to the 1,200 Indians who lived on my place. They came to me with their troubles. I treated them pretty decent. Relations on the hacienda were something like those in the Old South of the United States before the Civil War, but the Indians were free to move. When the mines were opened, they worked in them part of the year and then returned to the hacienda. The Indians during those times were dumb but honest. With 25 or 30 armed men I kept the bandits away from my hacienda during the Revolution. We killed a few, but that was a good thing.

The earthquakes of 1928 and 1931, especially the latter, destroyed many buildings in the Oaxaca region and hastened the dispersion of Oaxaqueños. The impact of this factor, and of expropriation and revolution, is measured objectively by population statistics. During the prosperous decade from 1900 to 1910 when the land was producing more than in the 1940's and many mines were operating in the state, the population of Oaxaca City increased from 35,049 to 38,011. With the disturbances incident to the Revolution of 1910-21, the count dropped sharply to 27,792. By 1930 the municipio of Oaxaca de Juárez, which includes six small villages, four haciendas, and four ranchos in the immediate vicinity of the city, had increased again to 35,074. After the severe earthquake of 1931 and the expropriation of agricultural lands the inhabitants dropped to an estimated low of 22,000 and numbered only 31,839 in 1940. By 1950, however, the population had risen to 49,953. The 1960 census showed another substantial increase to 74,765.

An excess of females over males seems to be normal in Oaxaca City. Women come in from the villages to work as servants; men from the town leave to work elsewhere or to study. The ratio in the marriageable years of males to females is striking. For ages 15 to 19 (1940) it was .78; for those 20 to 29 it was .70; and for those 30-34 it was again .78. In 1950 these three ratios were sharply lower: .55, .57, and .54. Truly, as one *señorita* expressed it, "the struggle for a husband in Oaxaca is terrific."

There is a saying in Mexico, which obviously reflects the bias of the "old aristocracy": "In the whirlwind of the Revolution the dirt came up." Some who were "only Indians" became generals. The middle class in Oaxaca is largely a product of the Revolution and of the changes that came afterwards. Its number and importance have increased sharply. Most of its members have risen from the ranks. During the decade from 1940 to 1950 the clothing worn by this new middle class changed to the type that was formerly used exclusively by members of the upper class. The women exchanged the long cotton skirt and blouse for the rayon dress and rarely wear the rebozo, while the men wear ordinary business suits. They can now go to dances and mix with upper-class groups unnoticed. They are eager for education and are more willing than other groups to accept new ideas.

The most outstanding feature of the lower class is the persistence of old ways. The plebeians of the state of Oaxaca are predominantly either Zapotec or Mixtec in both ancestry and culture. According to the 1930 census Zapotecs and Mixtecs in the state numbered about 390,000. The former live mainly south and east of Oaxaca City; the latter, north and west. Although some of the "Indians" in the suburbs and a few in the outlying villages have helped their children to advance through education, most of them retain a substantial proportion of pre-Columbian culture traits. Attitudes are so strong against fellow campesinos who change their ancient apparel or improve their living conditions that they are regarded as traitors to their class and are forced to leave their native villages. It is only in the towns that men of the lower class have been able to wear shoes, drill pants, sack coats, or European-style felt hats.

The 1940 census showed that in the municipio of Oaxaca one person in five slept on the ground, using a petate, and that more than one person in every four went barefoot. Almost twice as many women went barefoot as men. The proportion of the population that slept on the ground or went barefoot was greater in hinterland communities. In the state as a whole, two persons out of five slept on the ground; in the small towns of the Oaxaca trade area one person in every two went barefoot.[7]

The Mexican government is coming more and more to the view that the "Indian" is the Mexican, that the long-term welfare of the country is the welfare of the "Indian," and that the only way to develop initiative is to give responsibility. Before expropriation the campesino was like a servant to the hacendado. He can now work for himself. The government is trying to improve the use he makes of his parcel of land. There was by 1960 more production under the new system than there was under the old, but this is true for Mexico North rather than for Mexico South. The ejiditarios of Oaxaca live in the same type of jacales as before. The same small percentage have adobe houses. Partly because of inflation, they eat the same food. On the other hand, they have a little more confidence in themselves. Elections among ejiditarios to choose the head man for a given group are said to be the only truly democratic elections in Mexico.

Besides farming, two supplementary types of work have been

available in recent years for men of the lower class: (1) as laborers on the Inter-American Highway until its completion through Oaxaca State in 1948 and on other highways since, and (2) as braceros in the United States. Of these experiences, the latter has been the more significant. Those working on the highways continued to live in the same way. Usually they did not work more than sixty kilometers from their villages. When the highway went farther, they quit. This was not a trip into an industrialized country like the United States. Some of the eight thousand braceros who went out from the state of Oaxaca in 1949 came back better dressed, with money in their pockets. Some of them sent money to their families while they were away. Usually they had lived better, had eaten better food, and had learned how to do new things. However, many of them were unable to employ in Mexico the skills they had acquired. Those who had become mechanics could get jobs of that type. Still, the majority of braceros possess at least some tangible mark of material progress as a result of their work north of the Rio Grande.

In general, it is clear that this small, provincial, Spanish-Indian city of southern Mexico clings to much that is old. Its community life continues to center in the Zócalo and its family life in the patio. People go out to do their shopping, they attend movies, they take a walk to the park at night and then shut themselves up in their houses, isolated one from the other. In the past all efforts to establish clubs, permanent places of social gathering for families, or intellectual societies have failed. Except in times of crisis, there has been little interest in civic enterprises designed to improve the community. By 1961, however, there was some evidence, such as the development of lunching clubs, that these traditional attitudes were beginning to give way.

The trend in recent years has been toward a decline in the power of the upper and an increase in the importance of the middle class. The latter shows greater freedom in marriage, education, and the work of its women. Surely the greatest hope for the future of the plebeian class, and of Mexico, lies in the expansion of educational opportunities. In Oaxaca old Mexico is awakening, not as West Germany has done with a leap to the feet, but with a stirring, a stretching, a yawning. In the metropolis she really moves!

This was the skyline looking north-east along the Reforma in 1948. Since then many additional skyscrapers have been built in the booming capital—on the Reforma, on Avenida Juárez, and on Insurgentes.

5

The Capital: Its Growth
and Configuration

For almost six hundred years Mexico City grew slowly. Most of that time residential desirability declined with distance from the central plaza. But in recent years under the influence of rapid growth in population, many new industries, and some improvement in the means of transportation, the metropolis seems to be shifting toward a basic structure similar to that of large cities north of the Border. Yet it retains certain important differences.

Anglo-American cities usually develop their worst slums in a zone just outside the central business district.[1] As business expands outward, land values for commercial purposes rise, but

51

homes deteriorate and rents go down. Better residential areas are most frequently located a considerable distance from the center. Until recent decades, Latin American cities have grown very slowly over a long period of time. In a city that is not growing there is naturally no "zone in transition." The central business district is not expanding into surrounding residential areas. Where this is true it is more desirable to have a home within easy walking distance of the central square. Less favored sites for homes tend to be farther away, and the least desirable on the outskirts. Ordinarily the band plays for a *serenata* in the plaza two evenings a week. For smaller cities like Oaxaca or Querétaro, this public square is still the social center. But Mexico City today shows an interesting shift from this older pattern.

Since 1900, when its population was only 345,000, the capital's central business district has expanded outward, creating a "horseshoe" of high-land-value slums immediately to the north and east (see Map V). Then too, one of its best residential areas (the Pedregal Gardens) is located a full ten miles southwest of the Zócalo. In spite of these facts, its tendency to develop a circle of low-land-value slums on the outer edge of the metropolitan area has persisted for more than 440 years. In this respect it is similar to other large Latin-American cities but different from the larger cities north of the Border. A 1957 United Nations *Report on the World Social Situation* concludes that in Latin American cities "peripheral slums are frequently displaced and pushed farther out by the expansion of the city proper."[2]

AZTEC SETTLEMENT TO MODERN METROPOLIS

To understand the present configuration of Mexico's capital, it is helpful to think in terms of four major periods in its development. First, there was the ancient Aztec city of Tenochtitlán (1345-1521). Then came the Spanish-colonial city (1521-1821) founded by Hernán Cortés and his followers. With independence came a century of French influence (1821-1920). The present city combines a rich heritage from the past with an increasing infiltration of ideas from the United States.

Most archeologists agree that Tenochtitlán was founded about 1345 on islands in the salt sea of Texcoco.[3] The name "México" was at that time used for the high valley in which Tenochtitlán was located. In the beginning, this Aztec settlement was a small village of reed huts with thatched roofs. By 1398 the earliest stone houses were built. When Cortés first saw Tenochtitlán and adjoining Tlaltelolco (1519), it was reputedly a city of more than 500,000 people,[4] perhaps larger than any other in the world. It had narrow canals as in Venice and three main avenues, two spear-lengths in width. The pink stone dwellings of the nobles included courtyards with fountains, birds, and flowers. An aqueduct brought fresh water to the Aztec capital. Since these structures were almost completely destroyed by the conquistadors, few vestiges of the ancient city remain.

Map III is helpful for understanding the growth of Mexico City. The central area, a block roughly one mile on each side, is the section planned for occupation by the Spaniards in 1521, but actually not used until 1524. During the period when the city streets were being reconstructed in the form of a grid, the seat of government, the home of Cortés, and that of his captain, Alvarado, were in Coyoacán, a suburb just south of the present city limits. It is significant that even at this early date the native population was largely accommodated outside the limits of the Spanish city, their humble huts "scattered without order—as is the ancient custom among them."[5]

During the next three centuries Mexico City grew slowly from perhaps thirty thousand, after the destruction of Tenochtitlán, to more than one hundred thousand. At the beginning of the nineteenth century it was again the largest city in the Western Hemisphere.[6] A century later the capital had grown to more than three hundred thousand; by 1921, at the end of the revolution, its population had passed the six hundred thousand mark, finally exceeding the size Tenochtitlán is alleged to have reached four centuries earlier.

As Map III shows, growth during these four centuries has been primarily westward. During this long period the area occupied by dwellings expanded only one-half mile to the south and about a mile east and north, but three and one-half miles to the west. Until 1903 further expansion eastward was blocked by Lake Texcoco. At that time this lake was partially drained by a gigantic canal and tunnel project, but the establishment of new residential neighborhoods to the east was still discouraged by the alkaline character of the reclaimed soil. During the major portion of these four centuries, the least desirable areas for residence were those beyond an easy walking distance from the Zócalo and the Alameda.

Throughout the colonial stage in its development, Spanish

influence was of course dominant. The official language, the Roman Catholic church, the burros, the siesta, the patio, paintings, public administration, were all heritages from Spain. Buildings in the older part of the city, whether governmental, ecclesiastical, educational, or residential, are still predominantly Spanish in architecture.

The oldest official panorama map of Mexico City, dated 1737, shows the largest and best residences in the center, the smallest and poorest on the periphery. Cortés had ordered the Indians to move out of the center and had divided up the more desirable section among his retainers. The house used by Cortés himself is still to be seen near the Zócalo. Canals came as far as the Zócalo from the east and almost connected with the oldest plaza in the Americas from the west.

After Mexico gained its political independence from Spain in 1821, Spanish cultural patterns continued to be important. Of the other European nations, probably the dominant influence through the next century came from France. During this period, French was the preferred foreign language in the schools. Up to the 1950's, it still was in Oaxaca's Institute of Arts and Sciences. It was not until after the Revolution of 1910-21 that English came to lead other foreign languages in the metropolis. Maximilian, emperor of Mexico from 1863 to 1867, designed a Boulevarde Imperiale patterned after the Champs Elysées of Paris. This magnificent avenue—later renamed the Paseo de la Reforma—extends as a fourteen-lane, tree-lined boulevard from the equestrian statue of Charles IV of Spain[7] about two miles southwest to Diana the Huntress at the entrance to Chapultepec Park. In the Díaz regime (1876-1910) many pretentious *palacios* were constructed along the Reforma. It is significant that the two older *colonias* (neighborhoods)[8] north of the Reforma, Santa María (1869) and San Rafael (1891), are predominantly Spanish in architecture, whereas in the newer colonias south of the Reforma, Juárez (1902) and Roma (1906), the homes are distinctly French in style—many recently replaced, however, by modern commercial and residential buildings.

Before the Spaniards came the capital city was Indian; during the next four centuries it was predominantly Latin; recently it has been moving toward a fusion of these two elements supplemented by a growing influx of ideas and artifacts from the United States. Since the opening of the México-Laredo Highway (1932), followed by construction of three other highways from

Mexico City to the Border, increasing streams of American tourists have poured into the capital. World War II accentuated the flow. Many travelers, who could not visit Europe, turned to Mexico. By 1960 the tourist trade was generating 23 per cent of Mexico's foreign exchange earnings.[9] At the same time, *norteamericanos* not only had invested a billion dollars in Mexico's expanding industries but also had provided much of the technical know-how for their development.

The impact of this North American influence may be seen both in the business center and in the newer colonias to the south and southwest. Many of the office buildings of the central business district and along the Reforma are now as modern as those in large cities north of the Rio Grande. In fact, Mexican engineers have recently overcome the handicap imposed by the spongy lake bottom on which the city is built. As a result, by 1961 many skyscrapers of more than ten stories had been completed and numerous others were under construction. Beginning with the 44-story Latin American Tower just south of the center of highest land values (see Map IV), these tall buildings tend to form a row extending west along Juárez and southwest along the Reforma. Such a development spells centralization.

Another influence from the United States and an index to decentralization of services, combined with centralization in control, is to be seen in the well-organized *supermercados*, located in better residential districts, such as the Lomas, Polanco, Anzures, Condesa, Roma, and Del Valle. These supermarkets sell a wide variety of both Mexican and foreign groceries. As in similar institutions north of the Rio Grande, prices are marked for every item, carts are available to carry purchases, and everything is checked over and paid for on departure. In the Spring of 1961 the Mexico City supermarkets celebrated their fifteenth anniversary. None of the supermarkets, however, had parking lots for automobiles. In fact, at that time the writer saw no automobile-oriented shopping center of the type that has developed in the United States.

Externally, the city's upper-class residential district, the Lomas de Chapultepec, is very similar to certain sections of Los Angeles. All houses in the area must have gardens extending around the outside in repudiation of the patio of the Spanish-style home.

There is another way in which the Mexican capital can be compared with Los Angeles, and that is in its recent growth. In 1930 the population of Mexico City was over a million and that of the Federal District (comparable from a legal standpoint to the District of Columbia in the United States) about 1,250,000. By 1960 the city had almost reached 3,750,000, and the Federal District was approaching five million. In the period 1930-60 the population of the Republic doubled; that of the capital tripled; that of the Federal District quadrupled.[10] The Mexico City "metropolitan area" as determined by International Urban Research had a population of 2,960,120 in 1950[11] and 4,816,393 in 1960—an increase of 63 per cent.[12] This growth rate is faster than the 54 per cent increase for the Los Angeles-Long Beach metropolitan area during that decade and almost as rapid as the estimated 67 per cent increase for the metropolitan area of São Paulo, Brazil.

Heavy in-migration to the capital, and to cities like Guadalajara (with 734,346 persons in 1960) and Monterrey (601,085), has been stimulated by such factors as the persistent low real incomes among peasants, and industrial developments fostered by the government's policy of "Mexico for the Mexicans." Up to 1926, for example, all makes of cars were imported. Beginning in that year automobile companies willing to assemble their cars in Mexico were favored. By 1961 importation of expensive cars, such as Cadillacs, was stopped while corporations willing to use a large proportion of parts manufactured in Mexico were encouraged. It is probable that eventually all new cars purchased by Mexicans will be manufactured within the Republic.

Along with the growth in Mexico City's population, there have been improvements in transportation, but nothing comparable to the subways or commuter trains of New York or Chicago. This fact has prevented the star-shaped spread of the metropolis along lines of fast transit. But wherever burgeoning cities are found, transportation has difficulty in keeping up. Two-fifths of the passenger automobiles of Mexico are registered in the Federal District[13]—three times its quota in proportion to population, but still only one privately owned car registered as of 1958 for every 36 individuals (1960). During the past decade improvements have been made in the highways leading into the metropolis and in arterials within and around the city. With the exception of jitneys which operate along major avenues for a flat one-peso charge per person and the slightly more expensive taxis, the use of passenger automobiles is largely limited to the middle and upper classes. For the masses, transportation is by streetcar or, increasingly, by the clumsy, crowded "ubiquitous bus." And the buses, which do seem to go everywhere, are neither rapid nor dependable.

The expansion of the city, at first largely to the south and southwest (see Map III) and more recently in all directions, has pulled the business district westward along the Avenida Juárez and southwest along the Reforma. The old French-style houses in the northern part of Colonia Juárez and the "palaces" along the northeastern end of the Reforma have been replaced by hotels, apartment houses, governmental and commercial establishments including automobile agencies. Apartments have increased greatly in number. In 1941 the huge Arch of the Revolution, on an extension westward of the Avenida Juárez, stood alone among vacant lots; now it is surrounded by apartment and office buildings. The area near the Caballito (equestrian statue of Charles IV of Spain) is perhaps the clearest example of the process so common in North American cities in which a neighborhood of individual homes is "invaded" by apartments or commercial enterprises. Old buildings in this area have, in fact, been sold for the value of the land.

A similar process of invasion and succession has been taking place during the past two decades along Avenida de los Insurgentes south of the Reforma. The success of Sears Roebuck de México in Colonia Roma, the congestion and parking difficulties for a major department store still located near the Zócalo, and the fact that most of its upper- and middle-class clients lived to the southwest, encouraged the Palacio de Hierro to establish a large branch a few blocks west of Roma. Changes such as these have resulted in sharp increases in land values in the areas invaded.

As is true to a greater or lesser extent for many capitals in progressing countries, and demonstrably so for Latin America,[14] the metropolitan area of Mexico City had in 1960 six times the population of the metro area for the next largest Mexican city, Guadalajara. From this standpoint the capital ranked ninth in a list of 39 such areas having an estimated population of over one million in 1955 and may, therefore, be described as a "primate city."[15] This growing metropolis is the dominant center of the political, business, and intellectual life of the Republic. Here is the largest center of manufacturing, the focus for transportation facilities, the financial hub of the Republic, and here are the managerial headquarters for many enterprises. It attracts leading professionals from all the states and territories. In the words of Hubert Herring, it "devours the leadership of the country. Every politician, doctor, and lawyer nurses the ambition to live in the capital—draining the states of their leadership."[16]

Data on personages listed in *Who's Who in Latin America*[17] indicate the extent to which this was true in 1946. The occupations represented most often among these *intelectuales*, in order of frequency, were: lawyer, engineer, writer, physician, army officer, businessman, professor, painter, newspaperman, and banker. Although only 148, or 18 per cent, of the 808 listed for the whole of Mexico were born in the Federal District, 672 or 82 per cent lived there, a ratio of two to nine. It is assumed that the ratio between the number of distinguished persons born in a given state and the number who live there provides a rough measure of the relative drawing power of the Federal District as compared with the state. This ratio was twenty-one to one for Oaxaca and eight to one for Puebla; but two to one for Jalisco where Guadalajara is located and four to three for Nuevo León, where Monterrey is the capital.

The distribution of Mexico City and local newspapers serves also as a rough measure of the extent to which the metropolis actually dominates the social and economic life of the country. Where the number of Mexico City papers drops below that of local papers it may be assumed that the capital has ceased to be dominant. If this index is adequate, the capital's social and economic pre-eminence is felt most on the Central Mesa with a substantial share of the western part of this great plateau controlled by Guadalajara.[18]

In addition to the natural attraction which the metropolis offers, even to people from Guadalajara, there is the insecurity created by the governmental policy of expropriation of agricultural lands. In 1937 under President Lázaro Cárdenas this reached the peak of five million hectares (about twelve and a half million acres). Whatever one's personal opinion on this fundamental question, it has produced an insecurity among landowning classes that has caused many to migrate to the city.

PALACES AND SLUMS

The best available index to the ecological structure of the metropolis proved to be land-value gradients. Estimated commercial land values for 1943 and 1948 are shown on Map IV. They were based on actual sales, offers, or demands.[19] A map prepared by Professor Edmundo Flores of the National University, using what are presented as "approximate commercial values" for 1958, shows a similar pattern with the most notable increases along the Reforma.[20] The center of highest values is occupied by the Guardiola Building on San Juan de Letrán between Cinco de Mayo and Madero avenues. Values decline slightly as one moves east from this building to the Zócalo. Westward on Avenida Juárez and southwestward along the Reforma, values remain high as far as the intersection with Avenida Insurgentes. They are slightly lower from Insurgentes to Chapultepec Park. In general, values drop as one moves north or south from this Zócalo-Caballito-Chapultepec Park axis with the longest continuation of high values south along Insurgentes. The center of population in Mexico City gradually shifted from the Zócalo southwest so that by 1940 it reached La Garita at the intersection of Bucareli and Avenida Chapultepec (southeast corner of Ward VII). A panorama of the city as it was in 1856 shows this intersection three or four blocks beyond the built-up portions.[21]

As the city grew, factors determining the southwestward movement of the middle and upper classes included: the more fertile soil, higher elevations, and greater scenic beauty to the southwest; railroad yards little more than a mile to the north and northwest of the center (moved three miles northwest in 1958); city sewers that flow eastward and then, without covers, northward on a natural gradient; and prevailing winds from the northeast which, just before the rainy season starts, stir up alkaline dust storms from the dried-up bottom of Lake Texcoco northeast of the capital. This shift of people, together with the fact that the streets are wider, has helped to make Avenida Juárez and the Reforma more important than Avenida Madero, long the stronghold of real estate values.

Two phenomena seem to be correlated roughly with socioeconomic status in the metropolis. For one of these, the sex ratio, the correlation is negative; for the other, the number of distinguished persons, the correlation is positive. As the number of men per one hundred women decreases, the socioeconomic status of an area, within certain limits, increases. Two wards (*cuarteles*) with high average financial standing had in 1940 a sex ratio of 68.5 males to 100 females (76.5 in 1960). These wards (VII and VIII) include the prosperous colonias north and south of the Reforma. The ratio for the city as a whole was 83.3 (88.4 in 1960).[22] In the three poorest wards (I, II, and IX), which include the Morelos, Merced, and Tacuba neighborhoods, the percentage stood at 90.6 (95.3 in 1960). This difference seems to be due to the larger number of women servants in the wealthier districts. Interestingly enough, when one studies the very wealthy Lomas, the sex ratio rises again. Chauffeurs and gardeners have been added to the servant group. The fact that between 1940 and 1960 the sex ratio increased 1.6 times as much in the rich wards (8.0) as for the city as a whole (5.1) suggests that the higher wages offered by factories make it more difficult now to retain female help in the homes.

In contrast to large Anglo-American cities like Chicago, this Mexican city contains no area of homeless men. Women and children share with men life in the worst slums. This is probably best explained in terms of family mores. Women put up with more in Mexico.

The spots on Map V show the "homes" of distinguished persons as revealed by the above-mentioned study of *Who's Who in Latin America*. Cases where only office addresses were given are not included on the map. It will be noted that Colonia Juárez, the Lomas, and Del Valle, with about thirty personages each, have the largest number in *Who's Who*. San Angel, Roma, Hipodromo (west of Roma) and Cuauhtémoc came next with about fifteen each. The low number in Polanco (3) and Nueva Anzures[23] (4) is to be accounted for by the newness of these colonias and the predominance of the *nouveaux riches*. The north-south avenue, which is named Guerrero on the north and Cuauhtémoc on the south,[24] divides the land area occupied by dwellings and the population of the metropolitan area approximately in half, and yet there were only 22 spots east of this line as against 225 west. In fact, using the same line as eastern boundary and an imaginary extension westward of Avenida Juárez as northern, the southwest sector of the metropolitan area contained 202, or more than four-fifths, of these distinguished persons.

An interesting housing map prepared by the National Urban Mortgage Bank showed for 1932[25] the exact distribution of various types of housing in Mexico City. *Vecindades*[26] and other types of homes for workers were most frequently present in the congested areas of "Old Mexico" north, east, and south of the Zócalo (Morelos, La Merced, Obrera), whereas west of the north-south line of Guerrero-Cuauhtémoc mentioned above there was a preponderance of residencias and very few vecindades. In

1947 the National Urban Mortgage Bank continued its studies of Mexico City's housing problem with an investigation by Architect Felix Sánchez B. The slum areas on Map V are based on this report.[27] One-fifth of the land area of the city (1946) was covered by these slum zones, and one-fourth of the estimated population—about half a million persons—lived in them. One hundred and thirty thousand individuals lived in dwellings whose destruction was recommended.

As was mentioned earlier, when the boundary of the Spanish city was established in 1521 the huts of the Indians were built outside. Architect Sánchez points out that this hodgepodge of *jacales* outside the Spanish city was the beginning of the present high-land-value slums. Areas of greatest density of population— from 1,000 to 2,500 persons to the acre—and some of the worst present-day slums form a "horseshoe" around the north and east sides of "México Viejo," the older, central part of the city.

Northeast of the Merced district is the neighborhood called Moctezuma studied by the author in 1948 (see Chapter VI). Here in 1961 the pressures from the expanding city could be seen. An earlier population of manual laborers (*obreros*) had been replaced by white-collar workers (*empleados*) who could pay higher rents. This increase in rentals, however, has made it necessary for many newly married couples to live in the home of the husband's father. Schools that operated two shifts in 1948 had four in 1961.

One answer to these problems is the construction now in process (1963), on the northern edge of the inner "horseshoe," of the largest housing project in Latin America. This project extends from Insurgentes Norte on the west to a proposed prolongation of the Reforma on the east—about one and a half miles. It will average three-eighths of a mile in width. Extensions northward of Guerrero and of San Juan de Letrán will divide it into three semi-independent units. Here, eventually, in buildings that are two, three, and seven stories high, ninety thousand people will be housed. Markets, playgrounds, and schools will be included. Apartments will range in size from one to four bedrooms and will rent for 12 to 40 dollars per month. They are planned for workers who earn from 32 to 96 dollars monthly. The construction is being financed by the same government-supported institution that has been making some of the housing studies—the National Urban Mortgage Bank. The location was made available by the moving of railroad freight yards (nationally owned) three miles to the northwest. It gets its hyphenated name, Nonoalco-Tlaltelolco, from two ancient communities that once occupied the site. A nine-level pyramid discovered here convinces archeologists that Tlatelolco (*sic*) was at least four hundred years older than Tenochtitlán.[28]

At some distance outside the "horseshoe" Sánchez found a broken circle of low-land-value slums. These slums seem to develop in vacant areas between or peripheral to established communities. Such clusters may be initiated by so-called "parachutists," squatters who just "fall" into these open spaces. In the beginning at least, these aggregations of makeshift huts and substandard houses lack transportation, lighting, water, and sewage disposal. Eventually such services tend to come in and the shantytown achieves the status of a "proletarian community."

If for the Federal District data on recorded offenders against the law consistently covered the geographical distribution of their homes rather than merely the place where the crime was committed, probably they would fail to show the same degree of concentration in a transitional belt near the center as in North-American cities. In addition to the outer circle of slum zones outlined on Map V, smaller slums are often to be found near the best residential neighborhoods. In some instances these have been started by a few jacales where poorly paid quarry workers and their families lived.

About three-fourths of Sánchez' half million slum dwellers lived east of the Guerrero-Cuauhtémoc line. These poverty-stricken people were for the most part crowded into the older, more congested sections or into the new proletarian additions to the east and northeast.[29] In "Old Mexico" every sidewalk and every entrance to the numerous vecindades seem to be teeming with humanity. Due perhaps to better facilities than in the spot that is called home, eating and even sleeping on the street are commonplace. The other one-fourth of the city's slum dwellers lived in the Tacubaya, Tacuba, and Pro-hogar (north of Santa María) zones. But between Tacubaya and Tacuba the magnificent residences of the Lomas rival anything in Hollywood.

Comparison of air photos of the metropolis and its vicinity for 1936 and 1959 plus field observations of 1941 to 1961 indicates a large increase in homes for workers in the area north of Morelos outside the city limits, in the flat lands northeast of La Villa extending into the State of Mexico, and in the industrial suburbs of Atzcapotzalco and Tlalnepantla to the northwest. New proletarian colonias have sprung up to the east along the Puebla highway and to the southeast in the Ixtapalapa delegation. A 1958 report on *Colonias Proletarias* locates 300 such areas and concludes that by the end of 1955 they covered 30 per cent of the land area of the city. These neighborhoods make an almost complete circle around the outer part of the city with a two-mile break on the west and another two-mile break on the south.[30] There is also an increase in homes, some of them palatial, in new subdivisions west and southwest of the city's legal boundaries.

Between 1940 and 1950 the tier of delegations in the Federal District immediately outside the political city grew four times as rapidly as the city itself, and from 1950 to 1960 eight times as rapidly. The remaining delegations in the Federal District, farther from the city, grew in the earlier decade a little less rapidly than the political city but between 1950 and 1960 2.4 times as fast. Actually, the four central wards of Mexico City declined 4.6 per cent between 1950 and 1960. This decrease at the center is, of course, to be found in other large cities. In other words, the Mexico City metropolitan region is growing most rapidly on the fringe of its built-up area and not in spatially independent suburban towns.[31]

"Short Breath and Quick Heartbeat"

More than in New York or London, life in Mexico City is hectic. The capital has been described as a city of "short breath and quick heartbeat." The elevation (7,349 feet) is no doubt a factor but probably not the most important. Toluca, a Spanish-Indian city of 77,124 inhabitants (1960) 40 miles to the west, is higher but has a much slower tempo. The terrific struggle for a livelihood is a more basic explanation. To earn an adequate income many men of the upper-middle class must carry two, three, and even four positions.

Perhaps in no other aspect of its life does the feverish tempo of the metropolis reflect itself more vividly than in its traffic. This is especially noticeable when driving in from a leisurely place like Oaxaca. The number of cars and trucks increases long before the city limits are reached. In the city itself the individualism of the drivers is rampant. It is customary for taxi drivers to stop in the middle of a busy street to haggle with a prospective customer over the amount he will pay. If, as often happens, a traffic officer leaves his corner, it is every man for himself. This may lead to a tangle of cars in which each individual inches along as best he can. When traffic is blocked completely, there is a clamorous honking of horns. Red and green lights are obeyed rather well, but *alto* (stop) signs for avenidas "don't mean a thing." Driving with a definite purpose and conviction seems to pay off. Lanes are not kept if there is any advantage in weaving. Mexicans are very courteous in direct personal relations, but behind the wheel of a car only the exceptional driver is polite. The pedestrian, on his part, is apt to cross highways at any place, any time. He seems to have a kind of toreador psychology. He dares the car to come as close as possible without permitting the bumper to "gore" him. In fairness, it should be added that Mexican drivers are skilled at squeezing through tight places and excellent in the use of brakes. It is astounding that there are not more accidents. This was the situation in 1949.

By 1961, Mexico City traffic had increased in volume but seemed to be directed more efficiently. Schools had been established for training the new traffic officers. The greater number of red and green lights were obeyed fairly well. On a few new highways a speed of fifty miles an hour was mandatory. There was less honking of horns but weaving continued. Although by then they could meter the distance traveled, taxis still stopped in the middle of the street. Pedestrians still crossed any place. But in general there was progress in traffic control.

In conclusion, the following observations have been emphasized: (1) the slow and more recently the rapid growth of Mexico City; (2) the shift in basic configuration from the plaza-centered structure of the older Mexican cities toward certain characteristics similar to Anglo-American urbanized areas, including a "zone in transition"; and (3) certain differences between Mexico City and the latter. The absence of an area of homeless men, and of better-class residential suburbs with matricentric families, the tendency for low-land-value slums to form a zone on the periphery, and the greater tendency to be the political, business, and intellectual center for an entire country are features of the Mexican capital which differ sharply from the ecological patterns presented by larger cities north of the Border. Reflecting as they do distinctive aspects of modern Latin-American family and community life, these structural differences are apparently characteristic also of most of the larger urban aggregations south of Mexico.

MEXICO

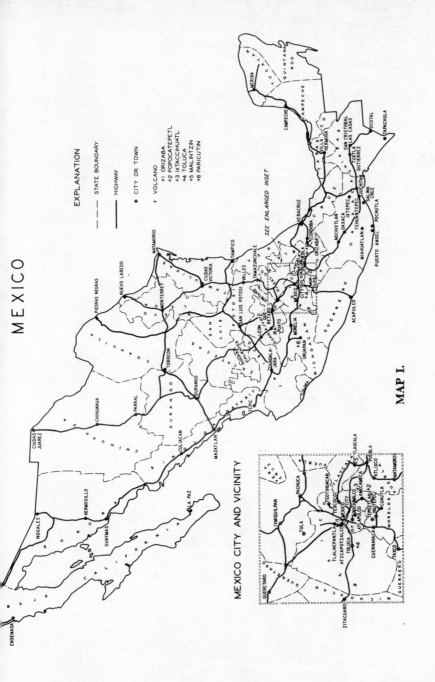

EXPLANATION

---- STATE BOUNDARY

—— HIGHWAY

● CITY OR TOWN

+ VOLCANO
+1 ORIZABA
+2 POPOCATEPETL
+3 IXTACCIHUATL
+4 TOLUCA
+5 MALINTZIN
+6 PARICUTIN

SEE ENLARGED INSET

MAP I.

MEXICO CITY AND VICINITY

Photo by author

A peasant group on the way to market

Oxcarts with solid wooden wheels about to cross the Inter-American Highway

Feather dancers at Teotitlán del Valle with designs from
the Mitla ruins in two background rugs

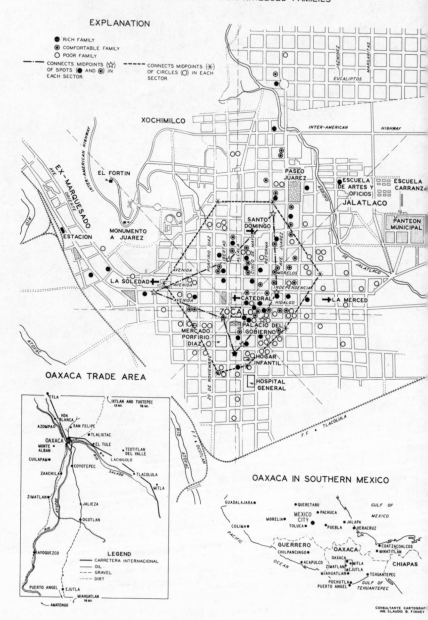

OAXACA CITY

PRIVILEGED AND UNDERPRIVILEGED FAMILIES

EXPLANATION

● RICH FAMILY
◉ COMFORTABLE FAMILY
○ POOR FAMILY
— · — CONNECTS MIDPOINTS OF SPOTS (●) AND (◉) IN EACH SECTOR ☆
— — — CONNECTS MIDPOINTS (✳) OF CIRCLES (○) IN EACH SECTOR.

OAXACA TRADE AREA

OAXACA IN SOUTHERN MEXICO

CONSULTANTE CARTOGRAFI
ING. CLAUDIO B. FINNEY

MAP II.

Maid's baby with toy

Three Oaxaca beauties
From left: two Zapotec, one Mixtec

Photo courtesy of Räúl Bolaños Cacho

Native athletes at a Oaxaca track meet

Ejutla from bell tower of the church, showing Spanish center
and Zapotec margin

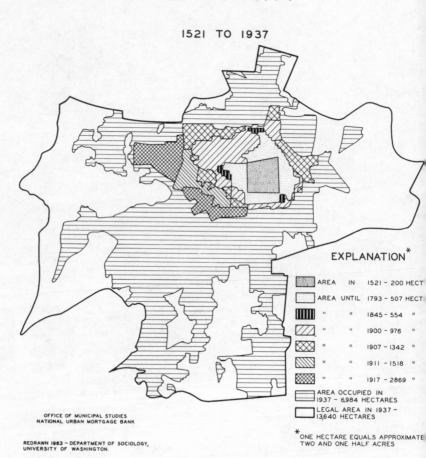

GROWTH STAGES

MEXICO CITY

1521 TO 1937

EXPLANATION*

AREA IN 1521 - 200 HECT
AREA UNTIL 1793 - 507 HECT
" " 1845 - 554 "
" " 1900 - 976 "
" " 1907 - 1342 "
" " 1911 - 1518 "
" " 1917 - 2869 "
AREA OCCUPIED IN 1937 - 6,984 HECTARES
LEGAL AREA IN 1937 - 13,640 HECTARES

*ONE HECTARE EQUALS APPROXIMATE TWO AND ONE HALF ACRES

OFFICE OF MUNICIPAL STUDIES
NATIONAL URBAN MORTGAGE BANK

REDRAWN 1963 — DEPARTMENT OF SOCIOLOGY,
UNIVERSITY OF WASHINGTON.

MAP III.

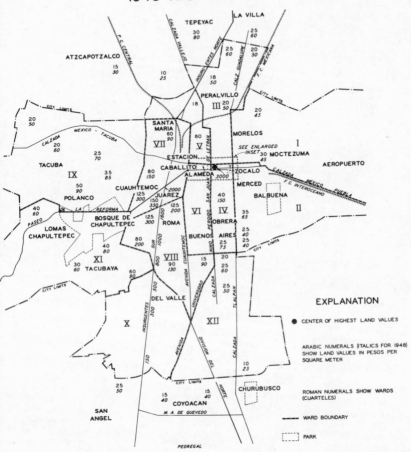

MEXICO CITY
LAND VALUES

1943 AND 1948

TEPEYAC — LA VILLA

ATZCAPOTZALCO

PERALVILLO

III

SANTA MARIA — VII

MORELOS — I

ESTACION — SEE ENLARGED INSET

MOCTEZUMA

TACUBA — IX

CABALLITO — ALAMEDA — ZOCALO

MERCED — AEROPUERTO

POLANCO — CUAUHTEMOC — JUAREZ

BALBUENA

BOSQUE DE CHAPULTEPEC — ROMA — VI — IV — II

LOMAS CHAPULTEPEC

BUENOS AIRES

XI TACUBAYA — VIII

DEL VALLE

X — XII

COYOACAN — CHURUBUSCO

SAN ANGEL

PEDREGAL

EXPLANATION

✴ CENTER OF HIGHEST LAND VALUES

ARABIC NUMERALS (ITALICS FOR 1948) SHOW LAND VALUES IN PESOS PER SQUARE METER

ROMAN NUMERALS SHOW WARDS (CUARTELES)

━ ━ WARD BOUNDARY

☐ PARK

CENTRAL BUSINESS DISTRICT

ALAMEDA — ZOCALO

CENTER OF HIGHEST LAND VALUES

MAP IV.

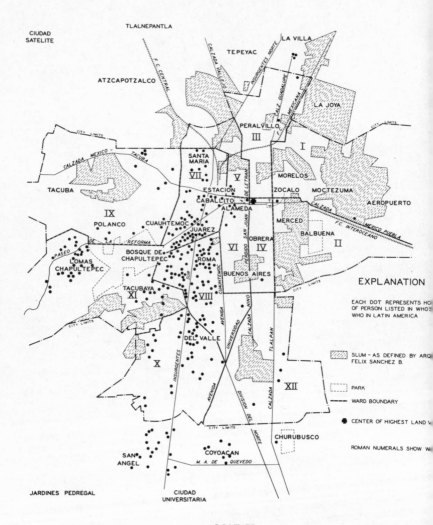

MEXICO CITY

HOMES OF INTELLECTUALS
AND THE POOR

CIUDAD
SATELITE

TLALNEPANTLA

LA VILLA

TEPEYAC

ATZCAPOTZALCO

LA JOYA

PERALVILLO

III

I

SANTA
MARIA

V

VII

MORELOS

ESTACION
CABALLITO

ZOCALO

MOCTEZUMA

TACUBA

IX

ALAMEDA

AEROPUERTO

POLANCO

CUAUHTEMOC

MERCED

JUAREZ

BOSQUE DE
CHAPULTEPEC

OBRERA

BALBUENA

II

LOMAS
CHAPULTEPEC

ROMA

VI

IV

BUENOS AIRES

EXPLANATION

TACUBAYA

XI

VIII

EACH DOT REPRESENTS HO
OF PERSON LISTED IN WHOS
WHO IN LATIN AMERICA

DEL VALLE

SLUM – AS DEFINED BY ARQ
FELIX SANCHEZ B.

X

PARK

XII

WARD BOUNDARY

CHURUBUSCO

CENTER OF HIGHEST LAND V

SAN
ANGEL

COYOACAN

ROMAN NUMERALS SHOW W

M. A. DE   QUEVEDO

JARDINES PEDREGAL

CIUDAD
UNIVERSITARIA

MAP V.

A patio in the slums

A view of Nueva Anzures in Mexico City, looking south toward Chapultepec Castle

Photo courtesy of Antonio Ruiz Galindo, Jr.

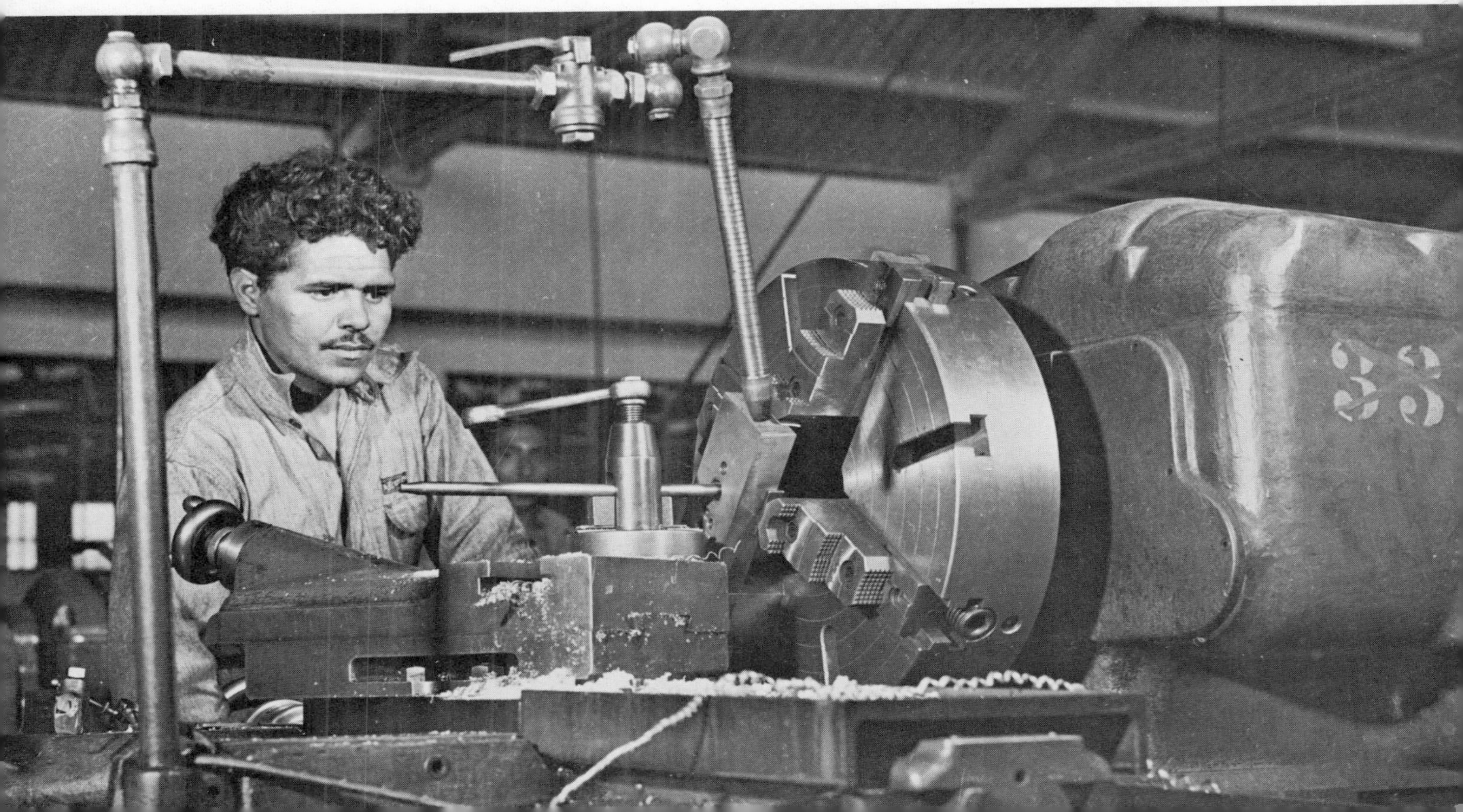

Assembling in the capital for the parade on the Day of the Revolution

THE TEMPO QUICKENS

This cocina in a Mexico City apartment has running cold water, a gas stove, a refrigerator and a few pieces of pottery. The wood-burning water heater serves the bathroom thirty feet away.

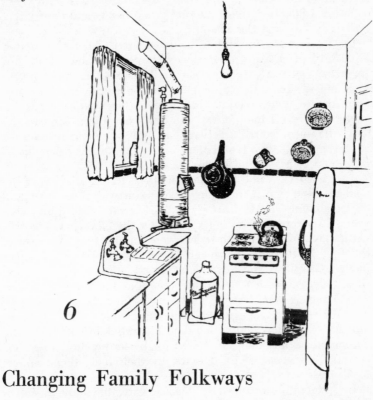

6

Changing Family Folkways

Institutions as well as communities alter at different speeds. Spheres of activity such as health and education change more rapidly than long-established institutions like the family and religion. In Part Two, the slower tempo of change in family life and marriage will be discussed first, the quickening developments in health and education last.

Usually people cling to tradition in family relationships like ivy vines to a clapboard wall. The accepted roles of husband

and wife, parents and children, change slowly. In contrast, the material culture of the household, not regarded as involving human welfare to the same extent, may be altered with alacrity. The use of certain types of cooking utensils, clothing, or home furnishings, or the family means of transportation and communication are traits in this material culture. It is with these superficial folkways, these external group habits and their effect on family life, that this chapter deals.

In Mexico, most inventions have appeared first in the capital. Even city people are often slow in accepting new ideas. But there has been greater time lag in the spread of these inventions outside the city. Table 1 shows the dates, in some cases approximate, when certain machines or techniques were introduced or came into general use in Mexico City, Oaxaca City, and Atlapulco. Nuxaá in 1949 had only three innovations—a sewing machine, two typewriters, and a "municipal police force" composed of a *jefe* and his assistant.

The first train came to Oaxaca in 1892. Before that event the median difference in time between the arrival of an invention or a technique in Mexico City and in Oaxaca was thirty-three years; afterwards, it was eight years. Of the eleven more recent items, gas stoves and flush toilets were the last to reach Oaxaca; the first three were passenger buses, automobiles, and silent movies. Gas stoves must overcome the prejudice of servants; and flush toilets necessitate a sewage system and a supply of water. The Oaxaca sewage system did receive a thorough renovation by an American contractor in 1948, but water was, even then, available for only a few hours each day. The rapid acceptance of the automobile is no doubt accounted for by its practical uses plus the status it gives; of the movies, by their recreational appeal to all classes.

In spite of its nearness to Mexico City, the only invention which managed to arrive in Atlapulco before the coming of the electric streetcar in 1910 was the Singer sewing machine. The transition from a bridle path to a paved highway in 1927 seems to have been even more significant for cultural change than the coming of the streetcar. Although the first movie projector was brought to the pueblo in 1918 on the streetcar, it was not until 1932 that exhibitions became regular. But even in 1950, movies, which were a source of delight to young people, were still disgusting to the old. Adults regarded them as an efficient means

TABLE 1. *Arrival Dates for Selected Inventions and Techniques in City, Town, and Village*°

| | Date of arrival in: | | |
Inventions or techniques	Mexico City	Oaxaca City	Atlapulco
Aqueduct for drinking water	1620	1727	1928 (piped)
Oil streetlights	1790	1824	1911 (electric)
Municipal police	1825	1882	1928
European-style clothing stores	1850	1888	....
Telegraph	1851	1883	....
Sewing machines	1858	1885-1890	1900
Mills for grinding *nixtamal*	1864 (gas)	1922 (gasoline)	1932 (gasoline)
Telephones in public offices	1865	1895	1913 (this year only)
Horse- or mule-drawn streetcars	1869	1887	....
Radios of galena (crystal sets)	1882	1922 (electric)	1930 (electric)
First train arrived from Mexico City:	....	1892	....
Bicycles	1893	1898-1899	1920
Flush toilets in general use	1902	1927	....
Silent movies	1908	1912	1932
Women as stenographers in public offices	1908	1916	....
First electric streetcar arrived from Mexico City:	....	....	1910
Automobiles	1910	1912	1928
Electric irons in general use	1912	1923	1930
Permanent waves	1915	1927	....
Gas stoves	1920	1944	....
Passenger buses	1923	1923	1929
Electric refrigerators	1925	1932	....
Neon signs	1927	1938	....
Paved highway from Mexico City:	....	1944	1927

° Data derived in 1949 from documentary sources by Sra. Isabel H. de Pozas, Mexican anthropologist.

for corrupting youth and often refused to let their children attend.

In the middle- and upper-class homes of Mexico City there had been a marked trend by 1949 toward electric refrigerators, gas stoves, and other modern conveniences. The custom of employing untrained girls from Indian-colonial villages as servants in these homes had, no doubt, retarded the speed of change. Dr. Manuel Gamio found that 40 per cent of the material traits in the culture of the impoverished Otomí Indians of the Mezquital Valley north of Mexico City were pre-Columbian in origin. He discovered also that 5 per cent of the artifacts in his own modern household in the capital were pre-Columbian. His cook not only insisted on using a metate for grinding peppers but also, preferring the traditional charcoal burner, opposed the use of a gas stove. For a long time Gamio had in his home a "museum" of up-to-date mechanical devices. Included, among other items, was a washing machine which his servants refused to operate.

Conversations with key officials in Sears Roebuck de México revealed trends in the sale of household equipment. The demand for electric sewing machines and vacuum cleaners was in May, 1949, greater than the supply. Although a Mexican company was making a good-quality flush toilet, production was exceeding demand and prices had dropped. Mexicans were also putting out a good electric iron which sold well. The electric "liquidizer" was a "tremendous" item. Although introduced for the first time in Mexico just after World War II, more liquidizers were being sold by this one store on Avenida Insurgentes in Colonia Roma than by all the Sears stores in Texas combined.

Keeping House in Nueva Anzures

Rudyard Kipling says in *Something of Myself*: "I had known a corner of the United States as a householder, which is the only way of getting at a country."[1] He was right. And just as they differ between nations, housekeeping equipment and techniques differ markedly in various types of neighborhoods. This is especially true south of the Border.

What was it like living for six months of 1948 in a furnished apartment in Nueva Anzures, one of the better colonias of Mexico City? The living room-dining room in this fourth-floor apartment was twenty-seven feet long, its south wall completely of glass. From it was a view of imposing stucco homes with Chapultepec Castle and high mountains beyond. The kitchen, planned for a maid, was small and near the door into the outer hall. Gas for the stove was bought by the tankful and piped up from the first floor. There was a General Electric refrigerator. The two bedrooms and bath were at the opposite end of the apartment from the kitchen, properly separating master and mistress from maid.

The biggest handicap to the functioning of the bathroom was due to the fact that, even with the aid of storage tanks on the roof, water was usually exhausted by six in the evening. Once unwittingly we went to bed, when the water was off, leaving a sink faucet wide open. Early next morning the maid from the neighboring apartment banged on the door. Our living room was flooded and the overflow was running through the hallway into the neighbor's kitchen.

Elena, the attractive daughter of the janitress (*portera*), cleaned the apartment and did our laundry. On the flat roof, directly above our floor, each apartment had a maid's room and a screened locked cubicle for drying clothes. The roof was consequently a servants' world with a life and atmosphere of its own. The portera and her family of five children and three grandchildren considered themselves superior to the others. Elena, for example, did not wear an apron like the regular maids. Occasionally a party was held on the roof. There would be music, tapping and dancing. Men's voices could be heard in what was ordinarily a community of women. Usually these high jinks occurred between 1:00 and 3:00 A.M.

In the better colonias of Mexico City it is cheaper to rent an apartment than to maintain a house. More children are found in Mexican apartment houses than in comparable multiple dwellings in the States. There was an average of one child for each of the twelve dwelling units in our apartment building. The occupations of fellow "cliff dwellers" indicated middle-class status.

In contrast to these families, those living in the pretentious mansions to the south were mostly upper-class. The residence catercorner was rented to a lawyer. To the left, in the house with the Christus in the stained-glass window, lived the owner of a cement factory; to the right on the far corner was a *casa grande* owned by an architect. On the far side of the circular *glorieta* with its statue and fountain was the showy home of Sr. Gamboa, head of the combined departments of Health and Welfare in the federal government. A fashionable wedding in this palatial dwelling was attended by President Alemán.

The roof of the residence just opposite us was a little below the level of our apartment. It was there that the well-dressed children of the family played with their wagons, tricycles and pets. There also was the work place for the laundress. According to Elena, whose contacts with the maids of the neighborhood gave her information about each household in the vicinity, the father in this elaborate house owned clothing factories in Guadalajara and Mexico City. We will call him Señor Avila.

The Avilas had eight children. The oldest son, who was studying chemistry at the National University, honked the horn of his red car demandingly when he returned, signaling the *mozo* to unlock the garage doors in a hurry. The younger children were in private schools to which they were taken in one of the family cars. The two smallest attended a private kindergarten. The family had seven servants: a cook, two chambermaids, one *nana* who watched the children, a chauffeur, a mozo, and a *lavandera de planta* who washed the clothes and, like all the others, lived in the house. The mozo looked after the flowers and lawn of the small garden, which was outside the house rather than inside as in Spanish-colonial mansions. He also kept the upstairs patio clean and daily helped the chauffeur polish the three cars. Sr. and Sra. Avila went out together to mass once a week and to occasional social gatherings in the evening. The entire family made a weekly trip to the country.

A low wall along the sidewalk gave the Avila home a semi-privacy which was characteristic of this colonia, but not of older neighborhoods. All windows and doors on the ground floor were protected by wrought-iron bars or grillwork against the city's numerous thieves. That beggars were not so much a problem in this household as an opportunity for gracious charity is attested by the following observation:

> Two neatly dressed children carrying a basket were attempting to ring the bell on the garage. The larger girl lifted the little one but not high enough. The baby cried and tried to climb the ironwork of the doors. Hiding around the corner of the wall was a hard-looking woman, with dirty feet, tattered black skirt, and dun-colored shawl. She seemed to be watching the shops across the street, although actually she was with the children. Just then

the chauffeur drove up, saw the girls, unlocked the door, and entered. Soon a servant appeared with a pan of clean food which she scraped into their container. With *"muchas gracias"* the children left, the waiting woman joined them, and they proceeded down the street. (Although probably not the situation in this case, the kidnaping of children in order to use them for begging has been frequent enough in the capital to keep young mothers on the alert.)

The French windows of the master bedroom on the second floor of the Avila residence opened onto small balconies. Opened wide during the day while the maid worked on the room, the windows were tightly closed at night. Since screens are a rarity, closing windows is a way of keeping out mosquitoes.

Truly, one never knows a country until he tries to keep house in it. This was the author's fourth and his collaborator's third stay in Mexico, but never before had they realized that Mexican maids wash dishes in cold water. That fact alone explains some of the poor health. There was a wood-burning water heater in one corner of our kitchen, two and a half feet from the sink, but piped hot water was available only in the bathroom thirty feet away! Water for dishes had to be boiled on the stove. Furthermore, one does not drink water from the tap in Mexico City. It may have been harmless when it left the purifying plant, but uneven settling of the ground[2] plays havoc with water and sewer pipes and sometimes they get mixed up a bit. It is the custom in better neighborhoods to buy Electropura or some other brand of allegedly sterilized water. Fresh vegetables are boiled, and fruit is either carefully peeled or cooked. Pasteurized milk is widely available, but tops are so frequently tampered with that a second cooking is recommended.

On the positive side of the food ledger there were epicurean delights like bananas with tree-ripened richness; succulent five-pound papayas; hot crusty loaves of bread almost as satisfying as can be bought in France or Italy; and from a shop on the Reforma, chocolates tastier than any in California.

"What I would like most, though, before I get all my fingertips fried," complained Una, "is just a five-cent box of American matches." There was no lighter on the stove; the gas was slow in igniting; and Mexican matches are short and brittle. "No wonder the maids shy away from gas stoves!"

On one of her first trips to the supermarket six blocks away, Una had the following experience:

> Down the center of the street toward me came an "Indian" doing the strangest running dance, his face so serious that he looked comical. With a roll of the wrist he was ringing a musical bell. He would walk a bit, hand clapped over bell, then he would start the running dance again and the ringing. At first I thought he must be a hawker, but he had nothing to sell. Then I noticed the maids peering out. By the time I had reached the end of the block they were sallying forth with containers of garbage. And, sure enough, at the corner I could see the garbage truck, a block away at a right angle. A small neighborhood fiesta seemed to be taking place. Like the heralds of medieval days, my dancer was announcing the arrival of the garbage truck!

We had never seen anyone go out from our apartment house when the garbage truck came by, so we asked Elena about it. "We collect the *basura* in a big container," she explained. "Then we dump it over the back wall." "But doesn't anyone object?" With a sly smile she said, "We always do it at night so no one will see us."

A revealing index to life in any country is the daily cycle of sounds. In Mexico, sounds emphasize the juxtaposition of old and new. To announce the coming of day, roosters crowed from adjacent housetops. Sometimes the gobble-gobble of a turkey could be heard from the roof of a pretentious home to the southwest. By dawn the sweepers were at work cleaning up the streets with that characteristic swishing so often experienced at daybreak in Mexico.

At 6:30 A.M. and again before and after seven o'clock came a variety of factory whistles from the belt of heavy industry that divides Ward IX into large underprivileged and small privileged sections, including our colonia. These whistles marked the end of the night shift and the beginning of the day in big factories like the Euzkadi Goodrich Fabrica de Llantas, the Mexican affiliate of the Goodrich Tire Company. By this time in the morning there was much life in the servants' quarters. Something would be dropped on the floor. The portera would call down the ventilating well or the one winding stairway.

Between 8:00 and 9:00 A.M. there were many kinds of toots from automobiles, buses, and trucks. The morning traffic rush was beginning. A big bus for a private school honked three times and, since there was no answering blast, pushed rapidly across the blind intersection at the apartment-house corner. There was the clank of milk bottles in the bicycle basket and the toot of his horn as the delivery boy approached the crossing. Twice a week at about eight o'clock there was a pleasant clattering of hoofs when the Avila sons and their friends came back from a morning canter.

Throughout the day a series of vendors passed along the street. The man with oranges to sell called out *"Nara-a-anjas."* The knife grinder and the toy balloon salesman had distinctive whistles. A purveyor of cotton dresses, looking like a walking clothes closet, had his special cry, and the flower hawker shouted *"Flo-ores."* Other calls were: *"Hay nueces"* ("Here are nuts"); *"Limo-ones"* ("Limes"); *"Uvas"* ("Grapes").

Frequently one heard a boom-boom-boom like an African tom-tom. This meant there was a group of gymnasts or a dog show in the street. Then there was the urgent clanging of a bell for mass in a new Catholic chapel not far away.

Best of all was the organ grinder who came by in the late afternoon giving excellent numbers on his German-made instrument. He played to certain balconies where there were small children who liked his music. He was on the city payroll, but unless encouraged by tossed coins would move along rapidly to the next corner. One afternoon three chubby little girls, about four years of age, took hands spontaneously and danced on the sidewalk to the rhythm of the music.

Between six and seven in the evening one of the three cars across the street would come home with a loud, demanding, long and three shorts, long and three shorts. The door to the garage must be opened at once.

Aside from Saturday nights, things quieted down early. After ten, one occasionally heard the shrill, high-low, low-high whistle of the private watchman as he made his rounds on a bicycle. Cynics suggested that the whistle was to warn thieves he was coming. Theoretically, at least, it was to assure his employers, the residents of the neighborhood, that he was on the job. Late in the night the Cuernavaca train, en route through Tacubaya, the Lomas, and the industrial belt, would wail through the darkness. And occasionally in the hush of the early hours there was a distant clock chime or a lion's roar from Chapultepec zoo.

Twelve years later we rented a similar apartment in the same neighborhood.[3] This time the gas stove did have a pilot light, and hot water from an automatic gas heater was available in both kitchen and bath. It was still important to be careful about water, milk, and the preparation of vegetables and fruits. Nearly identical was the cycle of sounds, even to the gobble-gobble of a turkey across the street. There were, however, two additional distractions. One was the roar of jet planes as they circled overhead before landing at the airport six miles away; the other, the increase in noise from traffic.

⟍ Home Life in a Working-Class Colonia

Colonia Moctezuma is located about a mile and a half east of the Zócalo. Most of the houses in this neighborhood have been built, not too well, since 1940. It is somewhat higher in economic status and less crowded than those parts of Ward I which are nearer the center. The community (about 20,000 in 1949) is composed of people who have moved outward from more densely populated sections and of migrants from many parts of the Republic.

To determine the occupations of the residents, Sra. Isabel H. de Pozas, an experienced field worker and advanced student in the School of Anthropology and History, interviewed briefly 150 boys in the fifth and sixth grades of the Moctezuma Ilhuicamina primary school. These interviews revealed the following parental occupations: federal employee (37); worker, usually in a factory (33); chauffeur (24); merchant (17); craftsman (16); private employee (15); proprietor of industry (5); professional (2); campesino (1). The one farmer lived and worked on his land outside the city limits. The industry owners were clearly at the top financially with an average monthly income of $183 American. Chauffeurs and merchants were next with $81 and $80. Workers averaged $68, federal employees $46. The latter ranged from a cashier in the Banco de México at $129 to a collector of garbage in the Merced Market at $21. The average monthly income of the families from which these boys came was about 450 pesos or $64 American. This places the neighborhood in the upper level of the lower class.

Twenty boys in the fifth grade were interviewed further with a battery of fifty questions. A majority of the fathers and mothers of this group had moved to the city from outside. The fathers were predominantly craftsmen and workers—not a representative sample[4]—with monthly incomes averaging $86 and ranging all the way from $23 earned by a floor polisher to $259 by the kind of taxi driver who cruises the streets in search of business (*chofer de ruleteo*). The chauffeur owned two cars, had earnings from both. Five of the mothers were working for income. Of these, in one case the husband was dead; in another, he had gone to Texas and had not returned; the rest had husbands with very low incomes. This suggests that work by married women outside the home is largely due to necessity.

A visit was made with Sra. Pozas to one of the twenty homes which she thought typical. Probably the boy's mother had had no warning of the visit, but she received us graciously, ushering us out of the pouring rain into the living room-bedroom with its wood floor, brass-posted double bed, wardrobe, china closet, Singer sewing machine, and two chairs.

The father, Sr. Suárez Aguilera we shall call him, had left his rural home near Texcoco twenty years before at the age of twenty and had come to Mexico City where he secured a job as fare collector on a bus line at 2.25 pesos daily. After three years he returned to Texcoco to marry Ana María by both civil and religious ceremonies. The couple moved at once to the metropolis, renting a room and small kitchen for ten pesos a month in the less desirable western section of Moctezuma. Sr. Suárez was ambitious to be a chauffeur. He took a job at one peso daily in order to learn mechanics. During this period the maternal grandmother helped the family by sending beans, corn, lard, and meat. He finally secured a position, which he still held, as chauffeur on a cooperative bus line. His earnings were irregular but probably averaged about $57 a month. He was giving $9 a week to his wife and keeping the balance. Formerly he had given her everything.

From savings at the rate of $4 a month the Suárez family bought a lot which was eight meters wide on the street and thirty-seven meters deep. There were still $43 to pay. At first they lived in an improvised room with walls of brick, roof of asbestos sheets, and dirt floor. This was being used at the time of our visit for the kitchen. In addition to the usual assortment of pottery and some porcelain, it contained a three-burner oil stove. Charcoal was used also for cooking in emergencies. Except on fiesta days all meals were cooked and eaten here.[5] Eventually more shelter was needed and two rooms of brick and cement were built by hired labor. Windows and doors were still lacking. The second of these rooms contained two beds, one for the schoolboy, Emilio, and his uncle, the other for Emilio's sister, Ester. The household also included an older son, another uncle, and, temporarily, in order that she might get medical treatment, an aunt. These three persons slept somewhere in the two bedrooms or kitchen, perhaps on the floor.

Ana María Carillo Rodríguez de Suárez was born in the town of Texcoco. Following Mexican custom she keeps the family name of both father (Isidoro Carillo) and mother (Francisca Rodríguez). When she married she added the name of her husband. He had also retained the names of his father (Suárez) and his mother (Aguilera). Both Ana María and her husband attended school as far as the third grade.

Sra. Suárez had never worked for money outside the home. In characteristic Mexican fashion the husband was boss in this family and had not permitted his wife to go to work. Her older son, Renato, was also opposed to the idea. The thirteen-year-old daughter, however, wanted to be either a dressmaker or a hairdresser. "Times have changed," said the señora. "A girl who works outside of the home is not a bad sight (*mal vista*)."

Renato, at the age of fifteen, was an apprentice in a machine shop. Although he had been receiving only $1.50 a month, soon he expected to be paid $8.50. Obviously, apprentices are exploited in Mexico. Emilio wanted to be a doctor. He probably had the intelligence (ranked third in his class at school); but would he, even with help from his family, be able to finance the long period of training?

On Sundays the Suárezes might go to Chapultepec Park, attend a ball game, visit the Villa de Guadalupe, or go to Texcoco. They made these jaunts as a family. Emilio, with his sister, brother, or mother, went to the "Mundial," a local movie, about four times a month. Only when the show was expensive did they sit in the gallery where fleas and bedbugs distract attention from the picture.

CAMPESINO CUSTOMS

Outside of Mexico City the Federal District is divided for governmental purposes into twelve delegations. One of these, famous for its canals, is Xochimilco. Less than half of its 69,000 people live in the town of the same name; the rest are scattered in thirteen villages, among them Atlapulco.

The more interesting statistical items for Mexico City and its environs are available only by wards and delegations. Assuming that Nueva Anzures is roughly comparable in socioeconomic status to Ward VIII, that Moctezuma is at least crudely represented by Ward I, and that the characteristics of Atlapulco are reflected in data for the delegation of Xochimilco, Table 2 makes a comparison between the three communities possible.

The sharpest differences between Wards VIII and I as shown in Table 2 are in the percentage of servants and in the sex ratio. The former appears, in fact, to be the most satisfactory item in the census for measuring differences in socioeconomic status. Privileged wards (VIII and VII) are high for this percentage and underprivileged wards (I, II, and IX) are low. The large number of unmarried female servants has, of course, a significant relation to the unbalanced sex ratio in the more prosperous wards.

The most striking contrasts between Xochimilco and Ward I, as indicated by the statistics for 1940 and 1950, show in the percentages employed as farmers, born in the Federal District, eating wheat bread, sleeping on the ground, and wearing shoes. Quite appropriately, most of the men in the area around Xochimilco (place of the flowers) raise vegetables and flowers for Federal District markets. Their fertile islands, called *chinampas,* once floating rafts of sticks and earth in Xochimilco Lake, have long since been anchored with willow poles and filled with mud from the canals around them. Today graceful willows that are tall and slender, keeping out little sun, hold fast the chinampas.

Although most of the inhabitants were truck gardeners in 1950, a few raised cattle. Since these animals were not carefully tended, they crossed dried-up canals and got into the vegetable plots, a source of many complaints to the mayoress[6] of the delegation. Sometimes complainants wanted five centavos for every stalk that had been nibbled.

The data that are given in Table 2 for 1960 (data not available until October, 1964) show some trends that influence all three census divisions, others that are more noticeable in two jurisdictions and several that are definitely greater in Xochimilco. The percentage engaged in industry has increased in all districts, but especially in Ward VIII and Xochimilco. All units have experienced an increase of single men as compared to single women. Probably there are now more jobs available for single men. Persons united by religious marriage only or living in free unions, both illegal in Mexico, are declining relatively while the percentage of persons united by civil and religious marriage is

Table 2. *Percentage of the Total Population, or of an Indicated Part, in Three Census Divisions of the Federal District, 1940, 1950, and 1960*

Item	Ward VIII 1940	1950	1960	Ward I 1940	1950	1960	Xochimilco 1940	1950	1960
Born in the Federal District	36	43	46	44	51	58	97	93	87
Catholic	91	92	91	95	98	96	99	99	98
Servants	16	*	*	2	*	*	1	*	*
Eat wheat bread	98	96	94	93	92	93	73	77	87
Sleep on the ground	3	*	*	6	*	*	52	*	*
Sleep on *tapexcos* (platforms of boards or poles off the ground)	0	*	*	0	*	*	13	*	*
Sleep in beds or on cots	97	*	*	94	*	*	35	*	*
Wear shoes (*zapatos*)	+	97	95	+	95	92	+	50	78
Population 6 years of age and over who cannot read or write	12	11	11	22	19	16	38	24	20
Males to females	65	67	67	93	94	95	98	98	96
Single men to single women	44	49	66	105	108	119	100	108	117
Widowers to widows	11	12	15	15	18	24	27	31	33
Farmers, cattlemen, foresters, fishermen, and hunters to total employed population	+	1	1	+	1	1	+	55	38
Persons engaged in industry to total employed population	+	8	19	+	43	45	+	9	18
Person united by civil marriage only to persons living together as man and wife	13	14	15	18+	21	22	13+	20	20
Persons united by religious marriage only to persons living together as man and wife.	5	4	3	13+	10	5	21+	14	8
Persons united in free union to persons living together as man and wife	10	8	6	29+	24	16	13+	13	9
Persons united by civil and religious marriage to persons living together as man and wife	72	74	76	39+	45	57	52+	53	63

* Not available for 1950 and 1960.
† Data for 1940 not comparable to 1950 or 1960.
‡ Because of rounding, these percentages do not add up to 100.

increasing. The wards show an increase in those born in the Federal District; Xochimilco, a decrease. Probably many of the migrants from states noncontiguous to the Federal District have settled in peripheral areas like Xochimilco.[7] Ward I and Xochimilco have clearly made progress in the battle against illiteracy. Xochimilco is unique in its sharp decline in the number of farmers and cattlemen, and in the increased percentage of those who eat wheat bread and of those who wear shoes. In fact, several indices point to a recent urbanization of the way of life in the Xochimilco region.

Five miles east of Xochimilco town is the agricultural village of San Gregorio Atlapulco. Like many Mexican communities, its name includes the original Indian designation (Atlapulco) and the name of a saint (San Gregorio) added by the Spaniards. There are five crude quays (*embarcaderos*) in Atlapulco to which, in the afternoons, farmers bring flat-bottomed canoes loaded with vegetables. The produce is transferred to trucks or streetcars to be transported to the capital. Mexico City's Zócalo is, in fact, only twenty miles away. Early in the morning, village women go out to sell these vegetables in the widely scattered markets of the big city. This gives them contact with outside ideas but, since they do not visit the homes of city dwellers, it has changed their housekeeping habits very little.

In the winter of 1949 Sra. Pozas made an intensive study of ten Atlapulco families. The outstanding impression that one gains from studying these cases is the conservative character of the people. As in Nuxaá, all used the pre-Columbian method of cooking on three rocks. The houses were jacales with thatched roofs and dirt floors. Sanitary facilities were lacking. Forms of social and religious organization that date back before the Conquest were predominant.

These points and others were seen in the family of a man we shall call Joaquín Apango Fuentes. In addition to the data given by the twelve-year-old daughter, Luisa, we visited the home with Sra. Pozas to take photographs. While we were his guests, Sr. Apango poled us in a canoe for a mile or so along the main canal that parallels the village. The willows, the other *canoas*, women in native dress kneeling over their washing on the banks, men laboring on their chinampas, made a photogenic sequence. Nothing here was commercialized as on the canals nearer Xochimilco.

Joaquín Apango and Gregoria Rodríguez, thirty-nine and forty-two years old, respectively, both natives of Atlapulco, had four children. Juan, the oldest, fifteen, was deserting the chinampas. With ambitions reminiscent of Renato Suárez, he was studying mechanics as an apprentice in a Mexico City factory and was paid *"ni un centavo,"* "not one cent," for his work. He left at 7:00 in the morning and got back at 9:30 in the evening. His mother gave him two pesos daily for transportation.

All of the family members, except Eva, who was in the first grade, knew how to read and write. Even the lively sixty-year-old grandmother was literate.

The house was owned. The site was the property of the mother who received it as an inheritance from her mother. The walls of the one 12-by-15-foot room were of rock, the floor of tamped earth, the roof of thatch. The kitchen was a separate small building of similar construction. The beds were planks placed on the ground and covered with petates.[8] The father, mother, and youngest child slept together. The two older sisters slept with the "little grandmother" (*abuelita*). The family had six benches, a chair, a soap-box for storing clothes, and a table. The table was not for meals, but for the saints. The principal *santos* on the table were the Virgin of Guadalupe, the Archangel Saint Michael, the Lord of Chalma, and the Virgin of Perpetual Aid. Every day a candle burned for them and fresh flowers were brought from the chinampa. As in Nuxaá the members of the household ate in the *cocina* with plates on the petate-covered earth. Tortillas were used in lieu of teaspoons or forks.

The masa for their tortillas was ground in a neighborhood mill, but was worked up on a metate and baked on a *comal* over the wood fire of the *tlacuil* (three rocks), just as in Nuxaá. Dishes were of pottery and serving spoons of orangewood. A charcoal brazier was available for heating flatirons. There was no watch or clock, but they did have scissors. Candles provided light. Water was carried in a shiny galvanized bucket from a public tap just outside the yard. Wheat bread had never been eaten in this household nor had tortillas ever been bought ready-made.

Sr. Apango had four chinampas where he cultivated lettuce, spinach, cauliflower, corn, and beans. He employed four workers (*peones*) to aid with planting, hoeing, and harvesting. The children helped at harvest time. He himself worked from 5:30 in the morning until 6:00 in the evening. Both Sr. and Sra. Apango went to the market at Jamaica (about two miles south of the Mexico City Zócalo) to sell their produce. In fact, the mother in this family kept the money, bought the clothes, paid the peones.

Luisa prepared the dinner on several Saturdays because her mother had been busy bringing dishes from the Xochimilco market for the fiesta to be held on the twelfth of March. Sundays she helped with the ironing and sometimes washed with her mother at the public washing tubs installed in 1940. Every day she took a small pail of nixtamal to the mill for grinding. She also went to the store to buy the best quality of pulque, for which she paid 15 to 25 centavos a liter.

Juan was the only one in this family to use shoes. He wore them when he worked in the city but not when he helped his father in the waterbound chinampas. Most of the children in Atlapulco go barefoot. They wear shoes on Sundays or when they go into the Sierra. For work in the chinampas and canoes bare feet are better.

Sr. Apango was soon to be a *mayordomo* in a religious fiesta for the third time. This meant that he would have the major responsibility for the expenses at this fiesta. It developed later that the cost of food for the free dinners, the new clothing purchased for members of the family for the occasion, the hiring of musicians and other disbursements came to the substantial total of 1,300 pesos ($185).

No one in the family had been to see a doctor. The Apangos had always been cured by home remedies. When little sister Eva was sick with a stomach-ache, she was "cured" with chamomile tea. Luisa had never gone to a movie. Her father did not permit it because, he said, she would only learn bad things. She cheerfully complied. Luisa constantly showed for her parents an affection and respect which was not common among the children in Colonia Moctezuma.

The questions raised by these ten cases were so intriguing that Sra. Pozas was asked to gather additional data concerning the material culture and social organization of Atlapulco. Her final report—about 180 typewritten pages, received in February, 1950—brings out clearly the many ways in which Atlapulco differed from Moctezuma.

Colonia Moctezuma was a community in which the needs of the population were satisfied by a series of individuals and services characteristic of a great city. It was, for example, supplied with running water, sewage and garbage disposal, electric lights in both streets and houses, mail and phone service, bus lines, and with shops and stores to supply food, clothing, and household furnishings. But in Atlapulco satisfaction of needs required few individuals beyond the family and few public services. Atlapulco lacked the sanitary facilities, telephones, and mail deliveries considered essential by most city dwellers. For food its people stored the corn and beans from their own reapings, buying only such outside products as sugar, coffee, rice, and pulque.

If she wished to have a dress, the *atlapulqueña* bought cloth in Xochimilco or Mexico City and made it at home. Since people rarely used shoes, there were no shoe-repair shops. Household furnishings were so simple there was little need of a special place for construction or repair. When houses have no plumbing, one does not call a plumber.

In Moctezuma the type of clothing worn might be described as modern European. It varied with occupation, economic position, and change in fashions. In Atlapulco, although changes were a little more rapid in the small group of *ricos* (persons richer than other villagers), the major factor explaining differences in clothing was age. Grandfathers tended to wear Indian-colonial whites; and grandmothers, like the *abuelita* in the Apango family, continued to use the indigenous *chincuete* and *quexquémetl*. The chincuete is a pleated white cotton skirt with a yoke around the hips of homespun wool. The quexquémetl is a sleeveless double triangle of cotton print slipped over the head like a poncho. The second generation wore a mixture of indigenous and European clothes. The fathers were likely to have trousers of drill for work and of lightweight wool for fiestas; the mothers, a blouse buttoned down the front and an ankle-length skirt. The oldest son added socks and shoes, shirt with tie, and a felt hat to the wool pants when he decked himself out; the daughter substituted a dress for the blouse and skirt of her mother. Both young men and young women wear sweaters when it is cold, but the rebozo was used on some occasions by all women regardless of age or economic condition. The changes taking place in the clothing of Atlapulco have been hastened by the requirements of certain teachers in the school and by the opening of the highway.

In Moctezuma the trend of housing was toward facilities as good or better than those of the Suárez family. Most of the houses in Atlapulco, and especially those in the older central *barrio,* are similar to that of Sr. Apango, i.e., one room, dirt floor, thatched roof, no windows, with separate building for a kitchen. Not even the ten ricos had modern bathrooms. There was no running water inside the houses, and there were no sewers. Defecations were made in part of the yard and left to the sun and air. The houses of the ricos usually had but one large room, with thick high walls, roof of tile, and very small windows. Although Moctezuma had a high proportion of home ownership, in Atlapulco practically every family owned its house. A few lived in abodes that were loaned to them rent free. The renting of houses was not in the mores.

The bed in Atlapulco seems to have followed certain stages in its evolution. From the petate on the ground which is the most primitive, it gives way to the petate over boards or planks, as in the Apango household. Next, the boards with the petate are placed on wooden horses (*burros*). These first three forms are the most common in Atlapulco. Later comes the wooden bed with the same boards and petate and next the bed with metal springs and a petate. The first bed with springs arrived in 1930. Finally comes the bed with springs and a mattress. There are a few families in Altapulco who use this type. The inner-spring mattress had yet to appear in 1950.

The kitchen is the most important part of the home. Here the family assembles at mealtime. Here problems of major importance, such as the future of the children and the use of income, are decided. The honor of serving as mayordomo (keeper of the saint's image and fiesta-maker) is received here. The sewing and mending of the clothing, the planning of chores for the children, learning the important news of the day—all these occur in the cocina. Xochimilco's mayoress, Señorita Guadalupe Ramírez, was correct in arguing for a large kitchen, a place where the older members might chat and work and the younger play and learn. Most kitchens, however, continue to be small and such ancient customs as cooking on three rocks with wood for fuel stubbornly persist. The only exceptions to the tlacuil were two oil stoves introduced in 1948 and four electric plates which had been in use since 1947.

The food consumed in Moctezuma is more varied than that in Atlapulco. Tortillas and beans have lost their importance as basic foods and are supplemented by wheat bread, meat, milk, and vegetables. The basis of nutrition in Atlapulco, as in most of Mexico, is corn. Beans are another indispensable item in the diet. Eggs and milk are usually regarded as articles for sale. Sample menus indicate that they are bought occasionally. Except at fiesta time, corn is consumed almost exclusively in the form of tortillas. In Moctezuma people usually eat at a table using spoons, and the tortilla merely accompanies other foods; in Atlapulco meals are not eaten at a table, and the tortilla is used to carry other foods to the mouth.

On Sundays in Atlapulco when meat is sold on the market place most families have a little. Although the village supplies a wide variety of vegetables for the Federal District, the natives are accustomed to eat only produce such as tomatoes, squash, chile, and cabbage that traditionally have been cultivated with the maize. Other products of the soil are generally thought of as "cold," indigestible foods.

Wheat bread was beginning in 1949 to come into daily use in the village. Prior to 1945, when the first bakery was established, special merchants brought wheat bread in from Milpa Alta. By 1949 there were three bakeries. The influence of the White Cross clinic, which since 1940 had provided breakfasts for 150 to 200 school children, has been important. This breakfast, which included cereal, a piece of bread, and a cup of coffee-milk, cost only ten centavos per child. Adults say, however, that they will never exchange the tortilla for bread; tortillas really give power for work. When they eat bread alone they sit down, weak and discouraged, without strength for their tasks! The reason the bread that Jesus fed to the multitude went so far is that it was actually tortillas!

The number of daily meals in Atlapulco varies according to the family from two to four. The content of the meals also varies with the resources of the particular household. A family of five with scant funds will get by on a half dollar per day; a similar family with a good economic base will spend nearly three times that. A five-person family of average resources will spend 90 cents American daily for the following menu:

Breakfast (between 6:00 and 10:00 A.M.): for each person a quarter of a liter of black coffee or coffee-milk sweetened with sugar, plus one or two pieces of bread; or a little *almuerzo* (late breakfast or lunch) of tortillas and frijoles with chile sauce.

Dinner (between 1:00 and 4:00 P.M.): a *sopa de pasta* (thickened soup), a vegetable stew, or egg, or beans, many tortillas, and pulque as a drink.

Supper (between 6:00 and 8:00 P.M.): a quarter of a liter of black coffee for each person, anything left over from dinner, pulque, and plenty of tortillas.

The ordinary meal in Atlapulco is served in the cocina. All of the family surround the mother. Some are seated on the ground; others, on diminutive benches; the father, on a small chair. In order to serve the family freshly cooked tortillas, the mother remains behind the metate. She serves father first, then the oldest son or daughter and so on successively. No one complains that he does not like the food. The plates are not heaped; they are adjusted to the capacity of the child—more likely too little than too much—but no one is denied a second helping if he wishes it. The mother is usually the last one served but should the grandmother live with the family, as among the Apangos, it is she who serves everyone before she eats.

If there are married sons or daughters, they always come to see the father and mother at the meal hour in order to bring a portion of their food and to eat something of what the parents have prepared. If there is not time to wait and eat, they leave what they have brought and receive in the same plate something which the parents have cooked. They never return with empty plates.

Whoever arrives at the house during mealtime, whether relative, neighbor, or friend, is offered something to eat and is under obligation to accept. Otherwise those offering would be deeply offended. There is among the natives of Atlapulco a profound feeling of spontaneous hospitality without thought of the possibility that the article may be scarce.

One factor in the conservatism so characteristic of the Mexican kitchen among campesinos is that the woman has few opportunities to go out of the pueblo to eat meals that are prepared in a different manner. She lacks contacts that would give her new ideas for her own cooking. The food which the people of Atlapulco now eat enables them, nevertheless, to work hard and to carry heavy loads on their backs for great distances. Although the food pattern of the Mexicans is different from that in the United States, it seems capable of providing the required nourishment at a much lower cost. "We have noted," writes R. S. Harris, "that a school lunch based on United States food habits costs approximately five times as much in Mexico City as a more nutritious school lunch based on Mexican food habits."[9]

When compared with Colonia Moctezuma, Atlapulco seems backward. The nearness to Mexico City does, however, make a difference to the five thousand people in Atlapulco. Three bakeries which provided wheat bread, a meat market, and seven nixtamal mills showed changes by 1949 in food habits and in the method of making tortillas. Public services were represented by thirty-two widely distributed water taps, a system of fifty-three 200-watt street lights, and five landing places for the produce from its island garden tracts. A doctor's office, a health clinic, a veterinarian's office, a lawyer's office, a carpenter's shop, and three barber shops were indices to specialization. Although pre-Columbian food and habitation customs persist, compared with more isolated villages, Atlapulco shows material progress.

When visited in 1961, additional changes in the village were evident. There were several new buildings. The old primary school was being conducted in two sessions, but on the northern edge of town there was a brand-new secondary school. As in Tepoztlán, students from Atlapulco now attend the National University. There has been an increase in the number of professionals. As formerly, farmers cultivate the chinampas, raising vegetables for the city, but the proportion of campesinos in the total population is declining. Following the route of the abandoned streetcar line between Atlapulco and Xochimilco, a new highway had been built. Yet many of the ancient customs persist. While less money is spent on them, fiestas continue to be held. Some brick homes have been constructed, but the majority are of adobe. Although there are still roofs of thatch to be seen, most are of tile. Nevertheless, side streets remain rough and narrow.

We parked our car on the highway and walked a short distance down a lane to the large wooden gate that is the entrance to the home of a farmer we shall call Filemón Azuela. In spite of the fact that there had been no warning of the visit, as godmother to the baby girl and *comadre* to *papá* who in turn is *compadre* to her, Sra. Pozas, our guide, was warmly greeted. In Mexico these relationships are important.

The composed dignity of the mother of the five children was impressive as she met what must have been a difficult situation —three unexpected callers, too near dinner time. She was taller than many Mexican young women, well built and strong, with clean, intelligent face, her long black hair neatly combed and braided. Of the three little girls, the oldest, who was eight and apparently not yet in school, carried the heavy baby in her rebozo as an adult might do. Part of the time the infant slept in a homemade cradle which swung from the ceiling. When eleven-year-old Ramón came home from the morning session of the third grade, he pulled silage from the stack in one corner of the yard to feed the two cows and calf, then with a heavy axe cut wood for the cooking fire. There was no unpleasantness or bickering among the children, no need for reprimand, during the four hours we spent with the family.

A jolly aunt had a real place in this household, carrying the heavier loads, making the tortillas. When she and the mother were ready to cook the meal under the long shed, they swept the cement floor with a crude broom, untied the calf which was in the way and took it to the opposite side of the enclosure, threw the swept-up straw and fodder to the mother cow to calm her, and built the fire between three rocks in the ancient way. In addition to the eight persons of the household, the small area within the walls (some 50 by 40 feet) sheltered the two cows and a calf, two litters of pigs, chickens that laid their eggs in nests close to the house, and seven rabbits in three hutches.

The midday meal (*comida*) was served at a long table near the doorway of the windowless dirt-floored home. The big tortillas freshly made from blue *maiz* were delicious. There was also the soup, a mildly spiced stew which included a sizable piece of meat, and the unfermented juice of the maguey (*agua miel*). None of the cauliflower, spinach, cabbage, coriander, or lettuce which we later saw in Sr. Azuela's chinampa were included.

There was little evidence in this peasant family of the material progress that might be found in the increasing number of middle-class homes in Atlapulco, but here under what many would consider "primitive" conditions lived a group of warm, gracious, dignified, happy human beings.

"Now You Know the Way"

Turning to the state of Oaxaca, interesting statistical items were available in 1940 and 1950, but not in 1960, for smaller units than in the Federal District.[10] These census data reveal sharp differences between the agricultural village, the small town, and the state capital. Of three agricultural villages studied, San Francisco Lachigoló seemed most representative; of four small towns, Ocotlán. Lachigoló may be recalled as a Zapotec-colonial village ten miles east of Oaxaca, and Ocotlán as the town twenty miles south where oxcarts are still the predominant form of transportation. Table 3 shows dramatic contrasts be-between these three communities.

The greatest differences may be seen in the percentages of persons eating wheat bread, sleeping on the ground, sleeping in beds or on cots, wearing shoes, and working as farmers or cattlemen. Illiteracy, the sex ratio, the percentage of persons engaged in industry, and of couples united by religious marriage only also show clear-cut gradients. All of the eighteen items evidence at least some gradient.

Physicians help more than any others to introduce one naturally to family life in smaller communities. This was true for the town and village included in Table. 3. There was Carlos Cervantes Rasura of Ocotlán, a generous guide in 1949. In his office overlooking the central plaza, where colorful buyers and sellers could be seen every Friday, he explained the health problems of the area. Then he took the author up an *arroyo* in his 1946 Ford to make a call on a family in which five members had measles. Later we visited his kindly compadre in the adjoining agricultural village of San Antonino. Sr. Aranda (not his real name) showed us his diminutive orchard with its orange and citron trees, and his "garage" which housed a two-wheeled oxcart. As a gesture of hospitality he gave the writer a set of *jícaras*. These half spheres of gourd are used in Oaxaca for everything from pouring bath water over one's person to being worn as hats by women on their way to market. Our host also insisted that we try a *poquitito* (tiny bit) of delightfully flavored *mezcal* that had been soaked in grapes. As we sipped, this pleasant gentleman disillusioned the visitor by asserting that he liked to become *borracho al suelo*, i.e., sufficiently drunk to fall to the ground. Was he joking? Probably not. Heavy drinking is traditional at fiesta times and for many individuals it is a week-end habit that seriously curtails the cycle of work.[11]

The doctor then topped off the day's hospitality by an invitation to dinner. His home is about two blocks from the plaza in Ocotlán. The electric refrigerator, the lavatory, and the flush toilet in their household were almost unique in this community of 4,800 inhabitants. They had, in fact, the only electric refrigerator in town. In the living room there was an attractive six-volume set of *El Libro de Oros de los Niños* (The Book of

TABLE 3. *Percentage of the Total Population, or of an Indicated Part, in Three Municipios of the Oaxaca Trade Area, 1940 and 1950*

Item	Oaxaca 1940	Oaxaca 1950	Ocotlán 1940	Ocotlán 1950	Lachigoló 1940	Lachigoló 1950
Born in the state of Oaxaca	92	93	99	100	100	100
Catholic	98	99	100	100	100	100
Servants	3	°	1	°	0	°
Eat wheat bread	95	91	55	69	6	41
Sleep on the ground	20	°	24	°	94	°
Sleep on *tapexcos*	4	°	35	°	0	°
Sleep in beds or on cots	76	°	41	°	6	°
Wear shoes (*zapatos*)	†	62	†	19	+	4
Population six years of age or over who cannot read or write	36	28	60	54	82	55
Males to females	82	85	94	95	109	110
Single men to single women	62	73	86	87	108	133
Widowers to widows	17	19	32	37	28	54
Farmers and cattlemen to total employed population	†	12	†	59	+	96
Persons engaged in industry to total employed population	†	31	†	21	+	1
Persons united by civil marriage only to persons living together as man and wife	13‡	15	8‡	5	1	7
Persons united by religious marriage only to persons living together as man and wife	21‡	14	38‡	31	62	66
Persons united by free union to persons living together as man and wife	32‡	26	22‡	17	15	9
Persons united by civil and religious marriage to persons living together as man and wife	35‡	45	31‡	47	22	18

° Not available for 1950.
† Data for 1940 not comparable to 1950.
‡ Because of rounding, these percentages do not add up to 100.

Gold for Children),[12] some of whose stories and pictures were by Walt Disney. At dinner a mozo acted as butler. Food came from a hidden kitchen through a porthole-like opening. The menu was partially Mexican: *tacos* (rolled tortilla sandwiches) in broth, macaroni, meatballs with vegetables, large handmade tortillas, a Mexican dulce of canned apricots, excellent limeade, and a demitasse of Nescafé. Sra. Cervantes, who was educated in Mexico City, likes the metropolis "much better" than her native Ocotlán. They bade farewell with a cordial Spanish version of: "Now you know the way."

Another day there was a picture-taking expedition with Dr. Ruperto Vera Castro. As head of the Health Department in Tlacolula, a town some twenty miles east of Oaxaca City on the Inter-American Highway, he had recently sent three blood samples from typhoid suspects to Oaxaca. Two had come back positive. We therefore drove to Lachigoló where the samples had been taken.

Lachigoló is a village of 700 people. The community is divided into two sections by a flat stretch of fertile land which is used for raising onions, garlic, beets, and alfalfa. Crops are watered from big black jars that are let down into the many wells located in the fields.

On our way to the typhoid cases we stopped at the school where one of the two nurses in the party, Sra. Variantas, showed the young "professor" how to vaccinate for smallpox. In Mexico City a teacher could rent a house or apartment for his home. Since no houses are available for rent in villages like Lachigoló or Nuxaá, a new structure must be built for the teacher. In Lachigoló this consisted of a one-room dwelling of plastered adobe. Enough blocks to build such a house may be bought for eighty pesos ($11.50). Blocks are made of mud mixed with the undigested fodder fibres of dried ox dung. This modest shelter, occupied by the director of the school, his wife, who also teaches, and their young son, was furnished with a bed, a table, and a chair. Since the 1950 census showed that in this village less than one-half of the persons over five years of age knew how to read or write (in 1940, one-fifth), the need for the four-grade school is obvious.

We visited seven homes where there were proved or suspected cases of typhoid. To combat spread of the disease, all healthy individuals in these abodes, as well as Felipe Vásquez, the comical *presidente,* were given their first shots. The big president of the community objected humorously and winced but set a good example. On the following Wednesday the entire population was to be lined up by him in the village center to receive the protective injections. As he escorted us to the different homes, carrying a German-made machete as if it were a sword and wearing huaraches with unusually wide strips of leather and double soles, his bearing fitted his station.

Lachigoló is more "primitive," more backward, more Zapotec than even the peripheral sections of Tlacolula or Ocotlán. One person out of seven over four years in age speaks Spanish only; the remainder speak Spanish and Zapotec (1950). In 1940 one in eight spoke Zapotec only. Most of the people live in the traditional reed jacales sometimes daubed with mud or replaced by adobe blocks. Within the huts sleeping on petates placed on the ground is almost universal (94 per cent). Only one *cama de tablas* (bed made of boards placed across horses) was seen in the homes visited and this was used by the man; his wife slept on a petate. Often animals share quarters with the families. At the patient's feet in the first jacal visited was a hen with little chicks. In the yards were oxen, burros, chickens, turkeys, forage, and pigs. A few iron plows were used, but most of the plows here, as in the rest of Oaxaca State, were of wood.

Both the doctor and Sra. Vera Castro (the other nurse in the party) are graduates of Oaxaca's Institute of Arts and Sciences. For the important work which he was doing, the doctor received only $55 American a month (1949). Actually, because of various deductions, his "take-home pay" was only $45. There was a small income from his wife's salary and from private practice.

We visited Dr. and Sra. Vera Castro twelve years later in their Spanish-style home in Tlacolula. They had six children ranging in age from fifteen to three. The doctor's practice was then entirely with private patients. He reported that the village of Lachigoló showed no change—same school, same work. The sanitary situation in Tlacolula was similar to what it had been in 1949. Almost all of the townsmen have wells, the majority of which are still unprotected from contamination. As a result, especially during the period of rains, there is trouble from parasites, diarrhea, dysentery, and typhoid, Although twelve years previously there were many cases of malaria, thanks to the national campaign against this disease, there are scarcely any now. Vaccination against whooping cough had been added recently. Adolfo López Mateos, President of the Republic, was scheduled to dedicate the new airfield in Oaxaca City on July 15, 1961. On the same day he would open the new, and much needed, elementary school in Tlacolula and turn on the electricity for Mitla. Electric power would then be available in Tlacolula too.

Inventions and techniques, it seems clear, arrive first in Mexico City; later but with decreasing lag, in Oaxaca City; still later, in Atlapulco; and with the exception of an occasional visiting auto, almost not at all in Lachigoló. Trains and highways are important factors. The privileged classes of the metropolis change housekeeping habits more rapidly than the underprivileged classes but, compared with campesinos, the latter have shifted to very modern ways. Furthermore, specific items in the family or community culture of Oaxaca City, Ocotlán, and Lachigoló show sharp gradients. As one moves from the provincial capital to the small town to the agricultural village, traits are less European, more Indian.

In peasant villages south of Puebla the security of marriage is enhanced by storing maize for winter in structures like this. Among skilled workmen of the metropolis family crises can be mitigated by social security.

7

Courtship and Marriage

It is encountered less frequently than in the past and in modified forms, but the old Spanish custom of "playing the bear" still persists in Mexico. First the young man is seen loitering across the street from the girl's home. Perhaps he sings or plays his guitar or hires musicians to give a *serenata* for him. He is making progress when he dares to talk with the girl through the iron bars of her window. Eventually he may hold her hand or even steal a kiss between those bars. It is then time for the ordeal of

111

a meeting with the family. If accepted as a fiancé, he is allowed to escort her to dances or the theatre, chaperoned, of course, by her relatives.

It was described thus in Guadalajara (1941) by a young American of Mexican ancestry:

> You must see the girl in church. Then you may come to her house at night and give a peculiar whistle. If she likes you, she will open the curtain just a crack. After that you must come every night, standing outside always, even in the rain. You cannot take her swimming or to a dance or to a show. "Playing the bear" still continues here, but it is breaking down.

One variation of this custom was observed in 1948 from our Mexico City apartment. The young man would drive up in a snappy brown and cream coupe, give three little toots, then wait in the car until two comely *señoritas* appeared in the yard with its ironwork fence. With one foot on the fence the boy would talk for a half hour or so while the girls fluttered around inside. One Sunday afternoon three boys came in two cars. There was much bantering. The boys leaned on the car fenders, stepped up on the cement which formed the lower part of the barrier, hung onto the ironwork with its sharp spear heads. After trying the gate unsuccessfully, one of them climbed up and sat on top of a cement pillar. The girls pushed him off. Sometimes the older girl came out alone, but only when there were two or three boys. If there was just one young man, the sister was with her.

Whether upper-class or plebeian, chaperonage is very important in the best families. It is defended by such proverbs as: "Man is fire, woman is kindling, and the devil comes and fans" or "Even between saints a strong wall" (*"Entre santa y santo, pared de calicanto"*). The Spanish-colonial arrangement of rooms around a central patio with one locked door to break the outer walls provided the strict supervision deemed necessary along with some opportunity for young women to enjoy sunshine, fresh air, and flowering shrubs.

As recently as thirty years ago in provincial Oaxaca, a young woman of good family was not permitted to walk on the street alone. She had to be accompanied by a relative or servant. She could not work outside the home. Fifty-five years ago no women were employed in the stores; today many are. Women were not hired as stenographers in public offices before 1916. In that year the revolutionary Carrancistas, who had conquered the town, employed the first woman stenographer.

In 1920 there were just twenty-five girls registered as students in the Oaxaca Institute of Arts and Sciences, now known as the Benito Juárez University of Oaxaca. They were limited to the obstetrical, bookkeeping, and secretarial courses. By 1943 there were 225 women in the Institute compared with 477 men and, as proof of their increasing emancipation, women were admitted to all courses.

Strict rules formerly governed the relations of young men and women before marriage in Oaxaca. They could talk with each other through the barred windows of the girl's home if these conversations were concealed from the parents. Although some ultra-religious, upper-class parents still hesitate to let their daughters go out with men, many young women from the better families are now free to go with men to dances, picnics, or even bars. Whereas eighteen years ago a young woman who worked was looked upon as "some strange animal," her employment is now more common. Marriage is no longer exclusively a family matter. As one *señorita* expresses it, "I can select my own *novio* (boy friend) now. If my parents want me to marry someone, I can say no. Being able to work makes me independent."

The legal age for marriage is 16 for men and 14 for women. Unions occurring at earlier years may be legalized by presidents of the municipios "for serious and justified causes." Only males 16 and over and females 14 and over are counted by the census as married, however. If the persons wishing to marry are not 21, the consent of parents is required.

In Mexico, only those persons married by civil authority are legally married. Of the four types of marriage listed by the census, two are legal. The first, marriage by civil ceremony only, included 15.9 per cent of all persons who were living as husband and wife in 1950. The second, marriage by civil and religious ceremony, made up 51.5 per cent. This is the most respectable way to be married in the Republic. Although illegal, the third group, united by religious ceremony only, comprised 12.5 per cent. The fourth type, free union, i.e., living together as husband and wife without any ceremony, made up 20 per cent. The proportion of the last is higher in rural districts than in urban, and is greater among young people, declining with age. The census explains the social phenomenon of the free union as "the result of very unfavorable economic conditions" and points out that during periods of good crops persons who have lived many years in free unions participate in the civil and religious ceremony accompanied by their "more or less large" children.

THE IDEAL MATE

To discover the attitudes of young men and women on mate selection it was arranged to have students in Oaxaca and Mexico City fill out questionnaires.[1] The questions about personality traits desired in a spouse were similar to those used by John and Mavis Biesanz in their study of *Costa Rican Life*.[2] Twenty-four traits desired in a husband were rated by 210 young women from a private and a public school in Mexico City, 98 from a private school in Oaxaca, 171 from a public school in Costa Rica, and, for comparison, 108 from a public high school in Seattle, Washington.[3] (See Table 4.) Most of these girls were sixteen or seventeen years of age. Latin-American *señoritas* are a little closer to marriage at these ages than are Anglo-American girls.

Latin-American groups agree that faithfulness and good health are essential in a husband. Importance quotients on a scale of 1 to 5 were 1.12 and 1.15. Seattle girls agree on faithfulness, it will be noted in Table 4, but put less emphasis on health. There is less need to do so. Mexican girls rate education much higher than do the Costa Rican or Seattle girls. The Revolution of 1910, we should remember, was a struggle for books as well as for land. Twenty-five older Costa Rican women, interviewed by the Biesanzes, rated education second and faithfulness fourteenth. Apparently their attitudes had been modified by the facts of life. Lamented one of these women: "A faithful husband—he would be nice, but you can't get one."

To secure the attitudes of young men, a similar method was used. Twenty-seven personality traits desired in a wife were rated by 89 young men from the Mexico University Center, 198 from the National Preparatory School, 48 from Oaxaca,[4] 103 from Costa Rica, and 89 from Seattle. (See Table 5.) The most frequent ages of these boys were seventeen and eighteen.

On traits desirable in a spouse the young men of the various groups are in closer agreement than the young women.[5] Averages for the Latin-American rankings place faithfulness at the top, good health next, followed closely by neatness, fondness for children, chastity, and liking for home life. American young

TABLE 4. *Ratings of Personality Traits Desired in a Husband by Young Women of Mexico City, Oaxaca, Costa Rica, and Seattle, Washington (1949)*

Trait	Rank; Importance quotient on scale of 1 to 5									
	MEXICO CITY				OAXACA		COSTA RICA		SEATTLE	
	Private		Public		Private		Public		Public	
Faithfulness	1	1.01	1	1.08	7	1.29	5	1.12	2	1.31
Education	2	1.13	2	1.11	1	1.07	13	1.42	14	2.21
Fondness for children	3	1.17	4	1.31	5	1.25	8	1.27	4	1.52
Temperance in use of liquor	4	1.18	16	1.99	22	3.08	6	1.16	7	1.81
Good health	5	1.18	3	1.21	2	1.13	3	1.09	8	1.88
Chastity	6	1.19	24	3.89	12	1.63	19	2.36	15	2.26
Piety	7	1.24	19	2.19	11	1.55	15	1.90	16	2.56
Liking for home life	8	1.33	6	1.41	10	1.54	4	1.11	5	1.58
Agreeable disposition	9	1.36	11	1.78	3	1.21	14	1.60	3	1.47
"Culture"	10	1.46	5	1.33	4	1.21	1	1.04	18	2.68
Poise	11	1.56	14	1.95	19	2.01	12	1.41	11	2.16
Earning capacity	12	1.69	7	1.50	6	1.26	7	1.19	6	1.76
Personality	13	1.71	18	2.04	9	1.37	2	1.08	1	1.25
At least equal social status	14	1.72	13	1.82	13	1.66	18	2.20	20	3.09
Intelligence	15	1.72	10	1.68	8	1.32	10	1.33	10	2.16
Affectionate nature	16	1.72	8	1.56	17	1.91	9	1.27	9	1.93
Vivacity	17	2.15	12	1.81	15	1.84	17	2.12	17	2.65
Sociability	18	2.19	15	1.95	14	1.79	11	1.36	12	2.17
Temperance in smoking	19	2.38	21	2.67	24	3.42	20	2.89	21	3.10
Conversational ability	20	2.41	17	2.00	18	1.97	16	1.93	13	2.19
Wealth	21	2.84	20	2.41	21	2.29	21	2.92	24	3.61
Love of sports	22	3.12	22	2.89	20	2.29	22	2.96	19	2.84
Good looks	23	3.15	23	3.31	16	1.84	24	3.59	22	3.29
Dancing ability	24	3.95	9	1.59	23	3.23	23	3.24	23	3.56

men agree in giving a high rank to faithfulness, neatness, and fondness for children; but, reflecting Anglo values, include in the top six: agreeable disposition, personality, and temperance in the use of liquor. Latin-American young women include in the highest six traits all those listed by the young men except chastity which receives an average quotient of 2.26. On this item, however, a marked difference is shown between the *señoritas* in private Catholic schools (1.41) and those in public (3.12). The high ranking of chastity by the former probably reflects both

TABLE 5. *Ratings of Personality Traits Desired in a Wife by Young Men of Mexico City, Oaxaca, Costa Rica, and Seattle, Washington* (1949)

Trait	Rank; Importance quotient on scale of 1 to 5									
	MEXICO CITY				OAXACA		COSTA RICA		SEATTLE	
	Private		Public		Private		Public		Public	
Faithfulness	1	1.03	2	1.20	6	1.26	4	1.16	1	1.28
Chastity	2	1.08	6	1.57	9	1.28	8	1.36	12	2.06
Fondness for children	3	1.23	4	1.36	7	1.27	2	1.12	5	1.70
Neatness	4	1.28	1	1.06	2	1.11	10	1.42	2	1.63
Good health	5	1.37	3	1.26	1	1.08	3	1.15	11	2.05
Liking for home life	6	1.50	5	1.40	8	1.28	1	1.12	7	1.74
Agreeable disposition	7	1.52	9	1.78	5	1.23	13	1.53	3	1.63
Temperance in use of liquor	8	1.52	16	2.31	21	2.19	14	1.61	6	1.71
Education	9	1.61	8	1.75	4	1.15	7	1.32	21	2.67
Housekeeping ability	10	1.62	7	1.61	3	1.15	5	1.24	9	1.88
Piety	11	1.97	15	2.30	12	1.51	20	2.18	23	2.80
Affectionate nature	12	1.99	11	2.06	13	1.62	11	1.51	8	1.80
"Culture"	13	2.05	10	2.01	11	1.40	6	1.26	20	2.51
Personality	14	2.13	13	2.20	17	1.98	9	1.38	4	1.67
Intelligence	15	2.14	12	2.12	14	1.81	12	1.51	15	2.25
Temperance in smoking	16	2.27	23	2.67	24	2.47	19	1.91	22	2.73
Sociability	17	2.33	14	2.20	16	1.89	15	1.70	14	2.17
Poise	18	2.37	20	2.48	23	2.24	18	1.89	17	2.27
Beauty	19	2.83	22	2.58	19	2.02	22	2.22	18	2.36
Vivacity	20	2.38	18	2.40	15	1.89	24	2.32	19	2.43
Ability to cook well	21	2.45	17	2.32	10	1.32	16	1.75	10	2.01
Conversational ability	22	2.46	21	2.53	20	2.15	23	2.22	13	2.12
Ability to be a good hostess	23	2.85	19	2.42	18	2.02	17	1.81	16	2.26
Love of sports	24	3.01	24	2.97	25	2.73	25	3.35	24	3.15
At least equal social status	25	3.03	25	3.11	22	2.23	21	2.21	26	3.37
Dancing ability	26	3.68	26	3.74	27	3.42	27	3.71	25	3.27
Wealth	27	4.11	27	4.02	26	3.04	26	3.71	27	3.92

religious training and middle-class backgrounds. American young women from a working-class area give a ranking identical with the average for the *señoritas*. Least important to boys are wealth, dancing ability, love of sports, at least equal social status, and conversational ability. On these points, except for "at least equal social status," the girls concur.[6]

The following questions were added to the Oaxaca schedules: (1) Would you prefer to marry a foreigner or a Mexican? (2) If a foreigner, of what nationality? (3) If a Mexican, even though an *indígena* (Indian)? Nine of the 98 girls indicated preference for a foreigner; two of the 48 boys. In answer to the second question, even though in most cases they did not prefer a foreigner, 43 girls and 22 boys put down nationalities. The most frequent choices by the girls were Spanish, English, American, Argentinian, and French, in that order; by the boys, American, Spanish, and French. Two young ladies commented that they would prefer marrying a Mexican to a foreigner "so that the race would not degenerate." In response to the question about marrying an Indian approximately 40 per cent of each sex said yes.

A whole book could and should be written about the ideals and problems of Latin-American young people. The changing role of the *señorita* would be especially interesting.

One handsome medical student in Oaxaca summarized the attitudes of young men as follows:

> Boys prefer girls for sweethearts (*novias*) who are very straight morally, intelligent, jolly, unreserved, natural. They also want them sweet, romantic, always provocative. The girls should not be too intimate with other boys. Education is not essential.

DOMINANCE OF THE MALE

In contrast to the Pilgrim fathers of the United States, the Spanish conquistadors came without women. Marriage with them was "a seizure, not a courtship." The inferior role played by women in Spain was matched by their almost complete submission among the Aztecs. Modesty, respect, and obedience were the primary virtues for Aztec daughters. This pattern of male dominance persists. Even today, Mexico is a man's country.

There is, it is true, a great deal of respect for women as mothers, but not for women as companions. It is woman's place to make the home. If she works outside, it is usually from necessity. Even as a mother, however, the power of the *mexicana* may be limited. When her children need punishment, she frequently waits until her husband comes home in order to let him administer it. As a result the children look to *papá* as the big boss and have less admiration for *mamá*.

In October, 1948, the writer gave a lecture at the Law School of the National University on "Success in Marriage" ("*El Exito en el Matrimonio*"). The talk summarized Anglo-American studies in that field. Entirely contrary to usual procedure for Mexican lectures, the audience was encouraged to write questions on slips of paper. One of these queries, made in Spanish of course, was very pertinent. It said: "In American social conduct there exists the 'date.' Is this considered an engagement as it is understood in Mexico?" The answer is obviously no. In fact, the Spanish language has no adequate word for "dating." For this reason (not explained to the audience) when American girls arrive in Mexico City for the University Summer School there is rejoicing among Mexican male students. The latter find a type of friendly companionship with these young women from the north that is not possible between Mexican boys and girls.

Other questions asked at this lecture were: "Are marriages between North Americans and Mexicans frequent? Are they successful?" There is no accurate way to measure the frequency, but probably the incidence is not great. When the woman is American, the marriage is less likely to be successful than when the man is American. This is true because there is a difference in expectation of the roles that should be played in marriage. The Mexican man expects to dominate; the American woman, to be independent. The prognosis for such a marriage seems to be especially unfavorable if the American wife tries to live with her husband in a peasant community. After trying life for three months in San Baltazar Altimeyaya, a village on the southeastern slope of Popocatepetl, one such couple returned to a community near Los Angeles. The wife, who knew little Spanish, had found adjustment to the backward ways of this mountain hamlet too difficult. An *americana* who did adjust to a Mexican husband was a city dweller in the border state of Nuevo León.[7]

But the Mexican male is slipping in his dominance. Increasing employment of women in paid occupations away from the home is helping them to achieve independence. In public administration and commerce the 1940 census shows a ratio of one woman to three men in Mexico City; in Oaxaca, one to three for public administration but two to three for commerce. For industry the ratios were one to five and one to seven, respectively. The proportion of women in public administration doubled in Mexico City between 1930 and 1940; it increased fourteen times in Oaxaca City.[8]

One professionally trained woman who has gone into public administration is Señorita Guillermina Llach. Srta. Llach has the title of *Licenciada* which means that she is a graduate of the Law School. Of those following a professional career at the National University in 1961 roughly 20 per cent were women. An increasing number graduate each year. Many of them have set up private offices for the practice of law. In 1948 Lic. Llach was in charge of the distribution of personnel in the Department of Social Prevention.

Another illustration. With the encouragement of her doctor husband, Mexico's pioneer woman flyer, Sra. Encenas de Gutiérrez, has turned part of her energies into organizing Mexican women for civic and political action. She noticed that women seeking jobs were "underpaid by their employers and ridiculed by their families." She became secretary-general of a Women's Federation which includes sixteen women's clubs. A major aim of this Federation is to secure for women the rights to which they are legally entitled. "We have to teach our women that they can be good wives and mothers," she comments, "and still participate in the affairs of the larger world."[9]

In an address to the Fourteenth Annual Conference of the International Federation of University Women meeting in Mexico in July, 1962, Dr. Jaime Torres Bodet, Secretary of Public Education, presented convincing evidence of these wider activities. "When more than 80,000 women participate in the teaching tasks," he said, "we can affirm with satisfaction and with gratitude that, in the great educational campaign to which Mexico is pledged, the woman, in her own right, is in a place of honor."[10]

Dr. Ignacio Chávez, Rector of the National University, speaking to the same conference, said: "The university woman shares with the man positions of responsibility. This is one of the ways that expresses the liberation of the woman."[11] By 1959 twelve of the sixty government prosecutors, thirteen federal judges, and nine members of the Mexican Congress were women.[12]

The Changing Role of Upper-Class Women

In the courtship attitudes and marriage customs of Mexico there are differences between classes. Generally speaking, the least change is occurring in the lower strata and the greatest in the middle. We have noted the development of a group of independent middle-class professionals like Licenciada Llach. Less extreme but nevertheless profound changes have been taking place in the role of upper-class women.

Among the students at the French School in Mexico City a few years ago was Carmen. Her story shows the evolution in culture, activities, and aspirations of a representative woman of the higher social classes. It is an example of adaptation to a new environment without, in this case at least, the compulsion of any immediate economic necessity.

This story is translated and adapted from a paper prepared for this book in 1949 by Sra. Ernestina Madrazo Castillot, at that time a social worker and language teacher in Mexico City. The names used are fictitious, but the people are real. Sra. Castillot is herself a member of the upper class.

Carmen M. G. was born in 1927 to an established wealthy Mexico City family. Without being beautiful she is attractive and distinguished looking: tall, slender, and well built, with brown eyes and hair; a creole of pure white race. Economic abundance is so habitual for her that it has not spoiled her natural, affable ways.

She was educated with careful attention. After the six years of *primaria* she studied five years in one of the leading private schools for *señoritas,* the Colegio Francés, where she learned to speak English, French, and German.

Later she completed the course in interior decoration at the Universidad Feminina. Without weakening her love of home— for she weaves, sews nicely, and can cook a meal—in case of necessity she is prepared to earn a living.

The monthly income of her parents is about $2,000 American. The family lives in Colonia Juárez, one of the better neighborhoods of the city, in a residence built especially for them. There is a garden. On the ground floor are the garage and the rooms for the servants; on the second, a hall, drawing room, library, dining room, office, and kitchen with gas stove, refrigerator and every type of electrical gadget; on the top floor, the bedrooms and three baths. The family has five maids and four automobiles, one car for each member. There is also a house in Cuernavaca and a recreation farm on a beautiful site in the state of Hidalgo. In these places they spend weekends and vacations. They frequently travel in foreign countries.

The men (father and son) fill their time with professional activities and the administration of family properties. They begin work very early. Everyone is up by seven. The mother manages the home, goes to market to buy flowers and fruits, and is entrusted with the maintenance of social relations.

Carmen is employed two hours daily giving free classes in a charity school. The rest of the day she divides between her favorite sports: horseback riding, swimming, and tennis. Or she may meet with feminine friends to sew and talk. Often at night she attends movies in the company of her parents. She has never been to a cabaret and is not in the habit of taking cocktails.

It is clear from this story that daughters in wealthy families may now study for careers. If, after marriage, their husbands are able to support them, however, they will not be permitted to use this training, except in their own homes. The preceding generation studied, it is true, but not for careers. The grandmothers were permitted to study very little for it was thought that in the home, separated from business, women would remain submissive to their men. However, being ignorant, women were sometimes tricked, after their husbands died, into signing away their fortunes.

Among men the evolution in activities occurred with much greater rapidity. The sons of the old landowners devoted themselves to commerce and to regional industries. The grandsons took professional courses in the universities and settled more and more in urban centers.

Although slower than with the men, the change in the life of upper-class women has been spectacular. Up to the middle of the nineteenth century their cultural preparation and their capacity to be valuable in their own right were rudimentary. Later the idea developed that, while it was desirable to keep their range of external action within the old restrictions, the education of girls could be broadened so as to enable them to sparkle in society. Still, if the daughters did not wish to be an economic burden to their fathers and brothers, the only doors open to them were matrimony or the convent.

The reform movement of Juárez and later the Revolution of 1910 broke many old molds and modified the absolute legal and habitual dependence of women both in the family and in society. When the agrarian program disorganized rural fortunes, and political-financial shocks either destroyed the majority of urban fortunes or put them in new hands, there arose the need for giving young women preparation so they could earn their own living. This situation has awakened in these women an interest in acquiring university degrees and in training to perform important labors outside the home.

Notwithstanding this growing change in the position of women, the moral standards and domestic relations of the Mexican family have not suffered important deterioration. The primary mission of every woman continues to be to make a home and educate her children. With the exception of the urban proletariat and the lower strata of the middle class, who live in crowded areas of dangerous promiscuity, the Mexican woman almost always comes to marriage a virgin. Premarital sexual relations continue to be the object of severe preventive vigilance and of the most inexorable personal and social reprobation.

Growing out of Catholic teaching as well as maternal example, the upper-class Mexican woman frowns on divorce. In order to preserve the home, she prefers to suffer the fickleness and even brazen misbehavior of her husband. There is always the possibility, she believes, that, sooner or later, out of respect for her and affection for the children whom her self-denial is protecting, he may come back.

Marriage in Atlapulco

Drawing again on the special study of Atlapulco made by Sra. Pozas for this book, it is possible to present an intimate picture of courtship and marriage customs in the village by the canals of Xochimilco.

Courtship in Atlapulco is initiated by the boy. He tries to start a conversation with the girl he is seeking to win for a novia (sweetheart). Opportunities occur at fiestas, during the thirty-minute recess periods at school, on the street when the girl goes on some errand, on the chinampas or at the embarcaderos where she may go to wash clothes, and in the early morning when she takes the nixtamal to a mill for grinding.

A girl has few opportunities for getting a novio outside the village. The watchfulness which the parents exercise is very close and the possibilities for outside journeys very limited. If a girl does go to a neighboring community, it is always in the company of an adult, usually a woman. For these reasons the girl easily adjusts to one novio.

A boy may have two or three novias at the same time. He might have a novia in each of the three barrios (districts) of Atlapulco, or in Xochimilco, or in the neighboring villages of Santa Cruz or San Luis. Some of the young campesinos like to enroll in the night classes that are offered in Xochimilco with the object of

winning one or two novias. They are said to be easier to win in
the town than in the village.

It is the custom for sweethearts to make presents to each other
of objects which have a higher sentimental than actual value. The
boy may give the girl a brooch, a bracelet, finger rings, wool
yarn in bright colors to braid into her hair. The girl, in turn, may
give her novio a handkerchief embroidered with his initials. It
is common for them to commission a small child to deliver a
message during recess. Friends also serve as intermediaries between the two.

Disputes between sweethearts and a break in the relationship
may be due fundamentally to lack of faithfulness on the part of
one or the other. The young man breaks the courtship most
readily if he learns that the girl has another novio; the young
woman, if she learns that the boy has other novias.[13] Generally
the boy has good arguments to convince the girl that the stories
told about him are pure lies.

An effort is made to keep engagements like these hidden from
the parents. Often, however, the parents simply do not refer to
the engagement until the request for the novia has been made in
an official manner. Generally the romantic relationship is kept
secret for a period of six months or more, which is regarded as
sufficient time for getting well acquainted.

When the boy decides that the girl has the qualities needed for
a good wife, he tells her that he wants to ask permission. If the
girl replies affirmatively, it means that she is willing to marry
him; but if she replies either evasively or negatively, it is understood that the engagement is ended.

The qualities which a young woman must have to be a
candidate for marriage are: (1) faithfulness, which she proves
during the engagement, and (2) virginity. A girl who has had
premarital sex relations cannot hope for a normal marriage in
this village.

The age at which girls begin to have romantic affairs varies
between thirteen and sixteen years, but the best age for marriage
is between fifteen and seventeen. When a woman becomes
twenty without marrying, they say that she is old for marriage.
Boys begin to have amorous adventures at twelve and direct
their pursuits toward matrimony between eighteen and twenty.
By twenty-five a man is considered old for marriage.

Once accepted by the girl, the young man arranges for the

priest to make a first visit to her parents. Then his parents visit them taking gifts—trays of fruit decorated with flowers, baskets of egg bread, demijohns of wine. Finally the father calls in his daughter and asks her: "Is it certain that you belong with this boy? Do you wish it? Do you want to marry him?" If the girl says yes, he tells the boy's parents to return another day for the reply. He wants to talk more fully with his daughter. When they return, the reply is generally affirmative. At that time the date for the marriage is fixed. This depends on the economic resources of the parents and godparents. Since three thousand or more pesos ($350 in 1950) are needed, the date may be one and a half to two years in the future.

During this period it is customary to flatter the novia with gifts, which are given in the presence of the parents, and with serenades in which ranch and love songs are sung. Often these *serenatas* are not pleasing to the parents, who go out crossly and disperse the musicians.

It is the function of the boy's godparent to provide all of the clothing needed for the marriage ceremony. The novio wears a black suit, white shirt, tie, black shoes and socks; the novia, a long white dress extending to the feet, a veil and crown, white underclothing of silk, fine stockings and high heels.

From the moment a girl is engaged she may not accept attentions from other boys and they usually respect the betrothal. If a novio surprises his future wife merely talking with another boy, this is sufficient reason for breaking the engagement. If a novia surprises her future husband talking with a girl, she becomes angry with her novio, but he always has an opportunity to convince her that there is nothing of importance between himself and the other girl.

In order to celebrate the matrimonial fiesta, it is necessary for the parents of the novio to have collected 1,500 pesos ($175), the parents of the novia 1,500 pesos, and the boy's godfather 500 to 1,000 pesos. For the fiesta a pig, a beef, some turkeys and chickens, and one or two loads (*cargas*) of corn are also needed. The boy's parents supply the pig and beef; those of the girl, the corn, drinks, and poultry. The music is provided by the godfather.

The religious ceremony is performed in the church. The bride leaves the house of her parents and joins the bridegroom at the church. Afterwards they go to the bridegroom's home to celebrate the wedding.

The bride wears her wedding finery the entire day of the

ceremony, but on the following day she dons one of the changes of clothing which her parents provide for her when she marries. The parents should give her the following: a dozen sets of underclothing, two dozen dresses, four rebozos, a dozen aprons, a quilt. When the bride has left the church and is walking toward the home of her in-laws, her parents send two women with the box of clothes which is delivered in the presence of those attending.

The mother-in-law has the obligation of providing the remainder of the bedclothing. For the night of the wedding she prepares the conjugal bed, either in a special bed, if she has one, or on a new *petate* placed on the ground. On this *petate* she arranges two new sheets, a clean pillow with a new slip, and the quilt from the bride's parents.

On the day following the consummation of the marriage the mother-in-law does not permit the bride to take up the bed. She carries the sheets into the sun and examines them carefully. If there are any traces of blood, the bride is accepted with pleasure into the bosom of the family; but if no traces exist, she sends the girl home. In case such a girl stays in the house of her in-laws she is mistreated and has a hard life. When there is no mother-in-law, the husband examines the sheets and makes the decision. When a girl has been repudiated by her husband for not having given clear indications of virginity, she returns to her paternal home, but must work to support herself.

The girl who marries must go immediately with her husband because his parents have the obligation to give them a site and home in which to live, land for the husband to cultivate, farm and kitchen implements. For the present the new couple will live in the home of the in-laws, but will make their expenditures separately and will solve their problems independently. When the girl lives in the same house for some time, she must help her mother-in-law with the housework.

Sons are not free to marry independent of the wishes of their elders. Neither is marriage imposed. They do not conceive that a son might arrive home married without having previously consulted his parents or without having completed everything customary. The son who marries without the consent of his parents is disinherited. He does not receive a site on which to live. His wife is not accepted in the parental home. They regard him as a bad boy.

If for some reason marriage is opposed by the parents of the girl, she may elope with her novio. The parents look for the young people, see that they marry, and allow them to live where they please.

The customary marriage fiesta lasts a week. Sunday is the day for the religious service. After that, breakfast, dinner, and supper are served to the guests at the expense of the godfather. On Monday the "visit" takes place. This consists in taking to the bride decorated baskets of bread and fruit and also dishes and domestic animals such as poultry and pigs. These gifts are a kind of dowry given by the friends of the couple to help them in their new life. The visit is associated with music, dancing, eating, and drinking. Each day has certain foods and drinks for which certain persons or groups are responsible.

The married couple always tries to solve within the home any quarrels that arise. If unsuccessful, the godparents are consulted. The next resort is to the parents. If the husband hits his wife, her father intervenes and tries to conciliate, but he does not advise his daughter to leave her man. "Forbear," he tells her, "so you chose. Now you know what you gain."

The following situations sometimes cause dissolution of the marriage: bad treatment of the woman and her children by the man; the husband's failure to support; difficulties occasioned by the mother-in-law. A man may feel that he has sufficient basis for abandoning his wife if she fails to perform her household duties, especially the preparation of food, or if there is verified adultery on her part.

When the breakup of a home is imminent and the pair has been united by the church alone (not recognized as a legal marriage), the woman does not have the right to remain in the house with the things which the two bought after the marriage. If they were married by the officially sanctioned civil ceremony, then she has the right to stay with her children and the possessions, and the husband must go. If he is to blame and the separation is made legal, he must pay something to the family to help them with food.

Although there are obvious advantages to the man in being united by the religious rite only, reference to Table 2 in Chapter VI reveals that in the delegation of Xochimilco, which includes Atlapulco, only 21 per cent of the marriages were of this type. In contrast, 65 per cent were either by civil ceremony alone (13 per cent) or by civil ceremony combined with religious rites (52 per cent). Thirteen per cent were living together in free unions. This was less than half the percentage of free unions in Ward I of the metropolis.

There are alleged to be seven prostitutes in Atlapulco whom no man would think of marrying. They are well known as such and always live on the margin of the community.

Among the wedded the action which people most condemn is the abandonment of wife and children by the man. The Atlapulcans have great respect for the family and the home.

DIVORCE AND ABANDONMENT

Emma-Lindsay Squier declared in *Gringa* that when she arrived in Yucatán, a happily married American woman traveling alone, she was approached by no less than three enterprising lawyers, all eager to free her "from undesirable matrimonial bonds in the short space of three weeks." In the interest of understanding our Latin-American neighbors better, it should be clear that this Reno-like situation was designed for foreigners and not for Mexicans. Although the Revolution brought legal divorce, until recent years few Mexican women have had either the courage or the economic independence to take advantage of it.

"Up to the year 1917 full divorce, as distinguished from legal separation, was unknown in Mexico," wrote Ernesto Santos Calindo, a competent Mexico City lawyer, in a letter. In that year the triumphant revolutionary government issued a Law of Domestic Relations which provided for complete divorce. The majority of Mexican states either adopted this law or so amended their civil codes that absolute divorce was made possible throughout the Republic. In the Federal District there are twelve grounds for divorce—more than in most of our states. We should remember, however, that although the law of the statute books on domestic relations is liberal, in practice the man still wields the power. A wife cannot move freely outside the home without her husband's consent. It is not surprising, then, that comparatively few Mexicans have obtained divorces. The proportion of marriages dissolved by a judgment of decree is still small, but is increasing. Important is the fact that almost all Mexicans are at least nominal Roman Catholics and, as such, are not permitted to get divorces. Furthermore, from pre-Columbian times the Mexican family has been considered to have a stability that may be destroyed, when there are children, only for the gravest causes.

After the enactment of the Law of Domestic Relations in the Federal District, some of the Mexican states—beginning with Yucatán and followed by Morelos, Tlaxcala, Chihuahua, Sonora and Guerrero—issued special divorce laws. These special laws provided for more rapid proceedings and additional grounds such as incompatibility of temperament. Five hundred divorces were reported, wrote Lawyer Santos, from the small town of Apizaco in the state of Tlaxcala, but at least 95 per cent of the parties so divorced were foreigners, principally persons from the United States and Argentina. The laws of Argentina did not authorize divorce and numerous residents of that country applied to Mexican courts and, on obtaining a divorce, married again in Mexico. Yucatán included in its divorce law not only mutual consent but also "the will of only one of the parties to the marriage made known to the court." The Mexican Supreme Court has declared judgments obtained on this last ground to be null and void.

For the year 1958 the only Mexican state with an abnormally high incidence of divorce was Chihuahua, which had granted more than half of the divorces for the entire Republic. Obviously Chihuahua is a major mecca for dissatisfied *norteamericanos*. It had two divorces for every three marriages as compared with one for every 32 in the rest of the country. Other border states ranged from one in ten for Tamaulipas, one in eleven for Chiapas, one in twelve for Yucatán, to one in 21 for Sonora. As would be expected, the state of Oaxaca, strongly Catholic and not on a border, had a low incidence of divorce—one in 98 marriages. By way of contrast with Oaxaca, the Federal District had one divorce in 24 marriages and a high incidence of abandonment.[14]

Among the wealthy, it is common for a man to have a conventional wife and family in a *casa grande* (big house), and a mistress with perhaps another family in a *casa chiquita* (little house). A man may marry one woman legally and have several children by her. When they have all the children they want in their immediate family, he takes a separate bedroom and has no further sexual contact with her, but starts raising another family by a concubine. Usually the legal wife knows about the mistress.

The concubine has an almost legal status. The statistics of Social Security (Seguro Social), for example, include one column headed *esposas y concubinas* (wives and concubines). If a man is legally married, benefits in case of sickness or death go to his wife. If he is not legally married but has children by her, benefits go to the concubine. In any case, both legitimate and illegitimate children receive benefits.

A Mexico City physician, most of whose work is gynecological, asserted that contraceptives are sold in all drug stores. Mexican law permits the dissemination of contraceptive information. "The Mexicans know them," said the doctor, "but do not like them." Under questioning he admitted that not all persons of the lower class know about them and that some Mexicans like them. The druggist in a small town of the state of San Luis Potosí, for example, reports that he sells contraceptives to the campesinos of the region. He estimates that 50 per cent of the farmers in his locality are using birth control techniques.

It is significant in this connection that there was in 1950 little difference between the average size of family in privileged, underprivileged, and hinterland areas of the Federal District. Exclusive of persons living alone and families of "10 or more," the average size for Ward VIII was 4.8; for Ward I, 4.7; and for the delegation of Xochimilco, 4.6. The slightness of variation between these districts seems to be accounted for by a balance between the extent to which contraceptives are used, on the one hand, and the survival rate for the children who are born on the other. The use of contraceptives probably increases with economic and social status; but with a rise in economic position, due to improvement in health conditions, the survival rate tends to go up.

The roles of wife and mistress in the upper class are well illustrated by the following statement of a hotel man:

> The American girl who left this morning is a good example of the mistress problem in Mexico. The man who has been with her here is a general. He has five children, the oldest of whom is married. The youngest was having a party yesterday in celebration of her fifteenth birthday. This is quite an event in the best circles. The American girl wanted the general to stay last night, but he had promised his daughter that he would attend her party and went back to his home in the city. The American girl wanted him to divorce his wife, but he explained that he had never compromised his marriage. She was always the perfect wife. He had nothing to hold against her. From Saturday noon until Sunday noon, he always spends with his family. There have, however, been no marital relations with his wife for ten years. He is crazy about the *americana*—madly in love with her.

This story has a sequel. Not long afterward, the general's wife died. He then wrote to the States and asked his mistress to marry him. In a short time she was his legal wife. Later the general became very important in the government of his country.

Mexican mothers often devote themselves to their children, taking them to the parks and movies. This frequently leads to a mother fixation. The mother dotes on her son and pours on him her starved affection. The boy grows up to feel that the mother is his ideal of goodness and love. He looks for a substitute mother in his wife and acts toward her with certain inhibitions. With this attitude he develops the belief, so thinks one Mexican psychologist, that there are two sorts of women—good and bad. The good woman is like his mother, proper for a wife and to be the mother of his children, but one with whom he must curb his sexual ardor. The bad woman is unlike his mother. With one of this type he can be "natural" and have a good time. This establishes a vicious circle.

Mexico has a strong tradition favoring sex expression—for the male. The Mexican prides himself in being *muy macho,* i.e., very much a he-man. It is no doubt this philosophy of sex expression, together with the conviction that the custom keeps couples together, which permits well-behaved male prisoners to have conjugal visits.

Among the "better class" of people in Oaxaca City, if divorced persons marry it is necessary for them to go to Mexico City to escape social ostracism. If, however, a divorced man takes a mistress, he is accepted in the best circles, while she is not. An attractive "señorita" in the office of a professional man in Oaxaca was actually a *divorciada* with two children. Her husband had gone to the States as a bracero, met an American girl, divorced his wife, married the *americana,* and become a citizen of the United States. When it was suggested that things were getting better for women in Mexico, she replied quickly: "They will be better when I am a *viejita* (little old woman)." At present it is not considered proper for a Mexican woman to travel alone. Divorce is looked askance at in Oaxaca and she feels the prejudice. Because of unfavorable sex ratios, remarriage is more difficult for town widows than for village widows and more difficult for city widows than for town widows;[15] but it is most difficult of all for the divorciada. Even for this good-looking young woman remarriage is a real problem.

It is obvious that the quadrupling of population in Mexico

City's metropolitan area during the past thirty years has been largely a product of migration from the hinterland rather than of natural increase. The transition from village to city has commonly been associated with changes in behavior. Robert J. Weitlaner spoke bitterly, it will be remembered, about what happens to his Indians after contact with civilization. Two years in that modern Babylon "ruins them completely," he said.

Many a man on coming to the city breaks away from the code of his native village and becomes a violent individualist. The length of time such a man stays with a woman is based on his own personal desires. The chief problem in helping cases at the Asistencia Infantil (Child Welfare) is the irresponsibility of fathers who abandon their wives and small children.[16] After a child is born it is common for the man to look for another woman. Sometimes one man will start several families without giving any support. This antisocial conduct is rarely noticed or criticized by friends and companions. Jesus Sánchez, described so interestingly by Oscar Lewis, had children by four women, but "Jesus is unusual among lower-class Mexican men because of his strong sense of responsibility to his various wives or children, none of whom he has abandoned."[17] Legal marriage on the part of wife deserters is more the exception than the rule. Not only are the abandoned mothers unprepared to earn their living, they also need to learn how to care for their children. Mexican women pride themselves on being good mothers, but this often means affection without adequate knowledge.

In rural communities and small towns, as we have seen in Atlapulco, parents are strict with their unmarried girls. When these daughters come to the city, however, control becomes difficult if not impossible. They talk with other housemaids, go to the movies, have sweethearts. It is not long before they may find themselves *embarazada* (pregnant). Servants with children of uncertain origin are widespread phenomena in the city.

Although there is considerable evidence of family maladjustment, especially among the lower classes of the metropolis, old courtship customs, like chaperonage, tend to persist in modified form. Young people show high standards in their rating of personality traits desired in a mate. Both boys and girls consider good health, faithfulness, fondness for children, and liking for home life "very important." Mexico is, however, a man's country and the double standard of morals is strongly entrenched. Family life in all classes is marked by the dominance of the male.

Handicrafts carried on in the homes are the most important source of household equipment in Oaxaca State. For twenty-five years Rosa of Coyotepec has been making beautiful black ollas without benefit of a potter's wheel.

8

Handicraft to Factory

The Industrial Revolution that started in England around 1760 was just getting under way in Mexico by 1950. Here manufacturing runs the gamut from handicrafts carried on in homes to modern factories. Many of the needs of its predominantly rural people are still met without benefit of machinery.

Covarrubias asserted that the state of Oaxaca "produces perhaps the finest assortment of objects of popular art in all Mexico."[1] Assuredly its handicrafts show great diversity and a

132

high degree of artistic skill. Some crafts, such as the making of certain types of pottery and textiles, have survived since pre-Spanish times, while others, like leather work and the forging of steel knives and machetes, were introduced by the Spaniards. The Zapotecs of the Sierra and of the valleys centering in Oaxaca City produce interesting wares, but the more advanced techniques are usually to be found in the city itself. Most of the industries of Oaxaca City are still small. With the exception of a plywood factory employing 150, a flour mill, three soft-drink bottling plants and one for castor oil, they are to a large extent handicraft shops of the enlarged kin-group variety.

In a manner similar to that in other parts of the world, medieval London for example, the handicrafts of Oaxaca City tended in the past to concentrate in certain localities. With improvements in transportation and communication, however, the weaving of textiles and the making of leather huaraches have scattered through the town. Pottery making still concentrates in the area south and west of the Zócalo and about seven tanneries employing an average of fifteen workers each continue to operate in the northeastern barrio of Jalatlaco. Some of the tanneries find a stream that runs through this barrio convenient for soaking hides. Furthermore, because of the odors from leather making, the moving of a tannery into another neighborhood would probably meet with resistance. To grind the bark needed for the tanning process, one place (Casa Navarro) used in 1949 a device rarely seen today, a huge millstone turned by an old nag. The same establishment boasted a fancy cutting machine (from a factory in Frankfurt, Germany) for slicing the better outside layer of the hide (*flor*) from the fleshy part (*carnaza*). The flor, which may be dyed various shades from light red to dark brown, is sold to leather shops in Mexico City where it is utilized for such items as traveling bags and briefcases. The carnaza is fashioned into huaraches in Oaxaca itself.

The trend during the last twelve years has been toward a decline in the number and relative importance of these handicraft shops and an increase in factories such as those mentioned above and in establishments devoted to the repair of automotive equipment and machinery. Fifteen years ago there were more than a hundred textile shops in Oaxaca; the 1956 Industrial Census reported only 17, employing 146 persons in the city and its immediate environs (*Ex-Distrito del Centro*).[2] The failure by all but two shops to use fixed colors in the making of the distinctive tablecloths and aprons of the region was one factor in this decrease. Huarache shops had declined to seven with 48 employees. The custom mentioned above of using the inferior fleshy part of the hides for this purpose helped Guadalajara to take the lead in the industry.

In contrast to the diversified handicrafts within Oaxaca City, many of the surrounding villages specialize in particular products. San Bartolo Coyotepec makes large black Zapotec jars widely used in this region for storing beans. Atzompa manufactures Mixtec green-glaze ware that withstands fire. Teotitlán del Valle weaves wool serapes that are famous throughout Mexico. The women of Santo Tomás Jalieza, a Zapotec hamlet near Ocotlán, use saddleback looms to weave stiff belts of intricate red or blue designs on white or gold backgrounds. The men in two mountain villages cut five- by six-inch wooden beams about seventeen feet long which oxen drag down to the city. Other villages make attractive maguey-fibre bags adorned with colored bands of purple, blue, cerise, and yellow, or twist rope, or form hammocks of the same material. Villages tributary to Ejutla and Miahuatlán weave fine palm petates, some of which are decorated with geometrical designs in color. Near the ruins at Mitla, women sell long woolen rebozos. Very popular with tourists, these hand-woven and hand-dyed stoles are one-toned, of natural, yellow, shocking pink, emerald green, or aqua.

The more primitive methods of craftsmen in the villages may be illustrated by Rosa Nieto of Coyotepec. For twenty-five years, without aid of a potter's wheel, she has been making the distinctive deep-gray ollas of this Zapotec village. The people in the next village are Mixtecs but as Rosa says, "We don't have anything to do with them." She sits on the ground outside her one-room adobe home to shape up a jar. She twirls the soft clay expertly, using only her hands, two saucers and a stick. When we observed her, she worked so fast that her large jar was completed long before the tiny one which was being fashioned by her charming six-year-old granddaughter. The orphaned child cuddled her pet, a small black kid, while Rosa finished the toy olla. The pride that these peasants have in their skill is reflected in Rosa's dignity and graciousness. As much as anyone, she helps one to understand Anita Brenner's penetrating statement that "only as artists can Mexicans be intelligible."[3]

Since among the common people dishes and cooking utensils are still predominantly of pottery, it is interesting to see how and under what conditions these are usually made. The late Sr. Bellon, pioneer French merchant of Oaxaca, owned a pottery factory in 1949. After the clay was washed, strained through a sieve, purified, and kneaded, it was ready for his workers. There were twenty-three regular employees in this "pottery house," which was one of the three largest of fifty in the town.[4] Each painter or pottery maker had an apprentice whom he paid six to nine pesos a week. An apprentice labors from one to four years before he is able to work by himself as a regular maestro. Until this time he is not counted as an employee. The maestros made from $10 to $16 American weekly depending on how industrious they were. A painter does not earn quite as much as a pottery maker, but one record showed about $13 a week. These two groups of employees were paid by the piece. Workers in the mill which ground up the paints received 50 cents a day including Sundays and holidays. Actually they worked a 48-hour week. At that time the only confederation of pottery workers in Oaxaca was organized under the Catholic-sponsored Centro Obrero. By 1961 workers in factories had to a large extent allied themselves with labor unions.

Most of the skilled workers in the Bellon factory did not appear on Mondays. Some did not arrive by Tuesday. Heavy drinking on Saturdays, Sundays, and fiesta days is almost a folkway among the male workers of Oaxaca. It takes time to recover. Since the pieces molded on Friday and Saturday determined the week's pay, these skilled employees usually worked Friday evening. Tuesday, Wednesday, and Thursday were used for finishing.

The state of Oaxaca is famous, too, for a special type of steel. It is like the Toledo steel of Spain and is guaranteed, when shaped into a knife and dropped point first, to penetrate a centavo piece without blunting. During World War II as many as 10,000 knives a week were made in Oaxaca. In 1944 it is alleged that one thousand persons were engaged in this industry. Unfortunately, during this period of high production, the quality of steel was not maintained.

Both Ocotlán and Ejutla have been centers for the manufacture of machetes and knives. José Cruz in Ocotlán proved to be a pleasant knifemaker who worked with five brothers and a nephew. When the demand was greater he employed other workers, but not in 1949. In a shop across the street from his home there was a forge for heating iron blades of various sizes.

After heating, the knives were pounded with hammers and tempered in a narrow water container. The metal part of the handle—aluminum for the four-inch knives, bronze for the larger ones—was cast in a mold. Later this part needs clever finishing by a craftsman. The etching on the blades of fancy machetes or knives was done by Sr. Cruz in his home, using a chemical process. A thirty-inch machete bought by the writer has a humorous etching of a hunting scene on one side and the following boast on the other: "José Cruz Ortega is my name. Though you may not care to believe it, I am a lover of the truth and I am strong and never give way. If you wish to put me to the test, you will discover the keenness of my blade."[5]

About fifteen miles east of Oaxaca is the above-mentioned village of Teotitlán del Valle which specializes in serapes. There are approximately four hundred weavers in the community. They have no organization—they are *hombres libres* (free men). The first step in making a serape or rug (*tapete*) is to buy wool from the Mixtecos in the Oaxaca market. This is washed, dried, and carded. It is next spun on a wheel and then colored with aniline dyes or left in its natural white, black, or red-brown state. The natural or bright yarns thus prepared are wound onto spools in readiness for weaving on a hand loom. Beautiful rugs in natural colors with simple designs may be purchased in this village.[6]

For fine cotton tablecloths, bedspreads, aprons, skirts, and woolen scarves, colored with carefully prepared dyes and woven by hand on upright Spanish-style looms, the outstanding establishment in Oaxaca is that of Guillermo Brena. Men from curio stores along the Border have told Sr. Brena that they do not care about quality. "I see the tourist once," said one. "I am not interested in satisfying him. Just give me a price, not quality." The poorest grade of textiles would mean cheap yarn, colors that fade, shoddy workmanship. This does not interest Brena. To keep his 112 employees busy (there were 35 in 1949), he is selling directly to Mexican homes. A down payment is made to the salesman at the house, and the merchandise is mailed C.O.D. His business, therefore, does not depend on tourism. This method of marketing is unusual in Mexico where many merchants fail to realize the importance of good quality or a reputation for honesty. Their attitudes are in general like those of pioneer lumbermen in the United States: "Cut and get out."[7]

In the Oaxaca region it seems clear that, although people in villages and on the margins of small towns may show great skill, the more advanced techniques are to be found in the town centers or in Oaxaca City. For example, the late Ignacio Jiménez made lovely cream-colored pottery with small Mitla designs in brown; and Austreberto Aragón, still living in Oaxaca City, is famous for his method of tempering steel. Village shops tend to be family affairs, like Cruz y Hermanos, the knifemakers of Ocotlán, or at least situations in which the relation between worker and employer is intimate and personal. In town or small city there is more likely to be a Bellon or Brena type of establishment where the owner is upper class and the workers are lower. Even in the latter, workers are not, as a rule, organized into *sindicatos* (unions) and wages, as compared with those in the large factories of the metropolis, are relatively meager. With the introduction of larger factories and shops in recent years, unions have tended to come in and wages to rise. The workers in Brena's impressive establishment, however, voted to stay out of the union, preferring the wages and generous fringe benefits he provides.

Progress in a Mountain Hamlet

About two-thirds of the way from Oaxaca to Mexico City the motorist passes through the old colonial town of Atlixco. In this region during 1948 and 1949 Wilbert E. Moore, Princeton sociologist, was directing a study of the impact on the agricultural peasant of work in a modern factory. The field work for this research was being done by the Mexican anthropologist, Sr. Ricardo Pozas A. The plan called for detailed questioning, with a 29-page schedule, of each man between 13 and 60 in two representative villages: San Juan Huiluco, strictly agricultural, and San Baltazar Altimeyaya where about one-third of the men either were or had been employed as obreros in factories. The existence of a strong sindicato in this region added interest to the project.[8]

In December of 1948 the author visited San Juan Huiluco and two other agricultural villages with Sr. Pozas. All were located near the highway in the valley south of Atlixco. In Huiluco, the largest of the three, there were 180 heads of families. Food crops, notably peanuts and tomatoes, were being raised by these peasants for shipment to Mexico City. Each of the villages presented an Indian-colonial picture: jacales with carrizo sides, thatched roofs, and, with few exceptions, dirt floors; beds usually consisted of boards raised above the ground; the *temascal*, or sweat bath, was in common use; women went barefoot, men wore huaraches. One day in fifteen was given as a service to the village; malaria was prevalent; herbs were used to combat fever. The only evidence of material progress was the presence of power mills for grinding nixtamal. Social control was strong enough to force a woman who had been raped by an outsider to leave the village and live in Atlixco.

In a home where a man was shelling the red pods of a local tree, the woman was making tortillas. As we ate of the delicious cornmeal cakes she told about the four children she had lost. Their deaths were due to wizards in the village, she said. Animal spirits (*naguales*) went out from these wizards and destroyed the children. This belief that certain men possess the power to release these invisible naguales that enter into victims to cause sickness or slow death is common among the Indians of Middle America.[9]

Next day we traveled by car six miles northeast from Atlixco to Metepec. There were around 1,700 workers in the Metepec cotton factory, about half of whom lived in Metepec itself in company houses provided free. The other half lived either in Atlixco or in nearby villages. The sindicato (Regional Confederation of Mexican Workers—C.R.O.M.) owns buses that transport workers to and from Atlixco for a fare of twenty centavos each. Of the seven textile mills in the region this is the largest. A Mr. Robinson, who had been the general manager for eleven years, was a textile engineer trained in Manchester, England. Toweling, seersucker, handkerchief, and many other types of cotton cloth are woven in this mill.

The C.R.O.M. has provided a cooperative store, a sport field, a band that plays Thursdays and Sundays, an orchestra, a group of *mariachi* singers, a $150,000 sanitorium, and, in cooperation with state and national governments, a beautiful school. This sindicato takes the place of government in Metepec. It has a police force and sometimes uses a small jail (*calabozo*).

From Metepec we drove three miles northwest over a rough road toward Popocatepetl to reach San Baltazar Altimeyaya with its three hundred heads of families. The Indian part of this name means "spring of water." Here is located one of the sources for the water power that provides electricity to run the mills.

The houses of Altimeyaya were on the whole better constructed than those in San Juan Huiluco. They were predominantly of stone with tile floors and roofs. Only an occasional house had a grass roof. Often the rooms had plastered walls. And the homes of the considerable number who worked in the factories seemed to be better than those who lacked this source of income. They had, for example, money to buy sewing machines and radios.

Two of the three small mills for grinding nixtamal were purchased with money earned in the States by two braceros. In addition to their mills, one of them had acquired a radio and a sewing machine; the other had a radio, four double beds (all in one room), but no sewing machine. In general, then, the level of life was higher in Altimeyaya than in Huiluco, and the standard of living of those who had worked in the United States was the highest of all. Probably the very site of Altimeyaya on a less productive mountainside had encouraged participation in factory life with subsequent material progress. On the other hand, the people of Huiluco and the other villages located on the fertile valley land of an expropriated hacienda seemed for this very reason to be more conservative.

Labor Problems in the Metropolis

The struggle between labor and management becomes an increasingly important aspect of the industrial scene in Mexico City and its environs. There are, of course, small industries in the capital; but, since a group with less than twenty members—unless they are in the same occupation—cannot organize a sindicato and bargain for better terms, conditions of work and pay in these small shops are usually less satisfactory than in the large establishments. At least half of the workers in the Federal District, however, are members of sindicatos. There are industrial unions and craft unions and those limited to a single enterprise. In this last type, all of the members are employed by one factory. Trusted employees, such as the manager, secretary, chiefs of departments, and the private policemen who check workers at the gate, are not included. Industrial unions cover more than one factory. The ice-cream and textile industries, for example, have hundreds of factories but only four or five unions. Craft unions organize those in the same occupation—window makers, blacksmiths, carpenters, solderers, or electricians. The three strongest unions are industrial: Petroleos (oil workers), Minas (mine workers), and Ferrocariles (railroad workers).

In Mexico, pickets are called "strike guards." After putting up the red and black flag to signify a strike, they camp on the site twenty-four hours a day. Unions sometimes contribute money for athletic teams, but they rarely sponsor recreation programs or education as in Metepec. Unions and their leaders have no official connection with the Church. Since most of the workers are Catholics, however, unions request that religious days be holidays. Important new enterprises are usually inaugurated by the President of the Republic and blessed by the Archbishop of Mexico. It is also the *costumbre* in many factories to put up the picture of a revered saint such as Our Lady of Guadalupe. Since 1940 unions have been active participants in politics. The leader of the Railroad Workers is, in fact, a communist, as are the labor leaders in the telephone and communications field.

Since the labor movement in Mexico has not only brought benefits to workers but has also suffered from abuses, for better understanding it seemed wise to consult a specialist in labor law. Both in 1948 and in 1961 Licenciado Salvador Laborde, who is such a person, spent many hours answering questions.

When a worker joins a union, he usually pays nothing. Each week thereafter his wages are docked a peso or so for the union. Contracts may be renewed or revised every two years. Eight or ten months before the date for the new contract the union may decide to collect *cuotas extraordinarias* so as to have money with which to buy food during a possible strike. This may amount to five pesos or more a week.

The total membership of the union (*asemblea*) is the final authority according to the Federal Labor Law. A large union has a general secretary and other functionaries; a small one, a secretary who continues to work but may miss work to meet his union obligations. So reads the law, but one must always ask in Mexico, as in the United States: How does the law work out in actuality?

Lawyer Laborde thinks that both syndicalism, i.e., direct action to get control of the means of production, and communism have some influence in Mexican worker ideology. A corruption similar to our Anglo-American gangsterism used to be found among construction workers. Now the usual practice is for a construction engineer to have a labor leader friend who controls a union for construction workers. A contract is drawn up with the friend for the particular project and signed by the entrepreneur. The friend is given $160 to $240 for an enterprise like building a house and is paid, in addition, $16 to $32 each month. With these payments there is no trouble.

In sindicatos which organize employees of big factories, Laborde distinguished three types of labor leaders: (1) honest men, (2) leaders who must be paid to avoid trouble, and (3) "absolute gangsters." The honest leader makes a deal and keeps to it. He defends the union members without trying to break the factory. He might ask for an increase from fourteen to twenty-one pesos a day. The manager might show him the books and say: "Look at last year. We didn't do so well. If we give you 50 per cent, we will go broke." He settles for 15 per cent.

The second type does the same thing but must be paid not to make trouble. One cannot say to a worker in Mexico: "You are fired." He has the right to work. He may have been drunk, late, and a thief, but the employer must prove to a tribunal that there was cause to put him on the street. The factory manager might come to the plant and find that a worker is not at his post. There are witnesses, but they are members of the union. This second type of labor leader will tell the owner: "The man absent from his post was fired and well fired, but I will say to the asemblea: 'These witnesses are traitors to the cause of labor. They should be fired from the sindicato.'" There is a clause of exclusion in the contract which means that only members of the union may be employed. If the owner makes an arrangement with the leader about the absent worker, everything is all right.

When a contract is being revised, this second type tells the workers that the owner is a thief. He should double the wages. He tells the owner that the men are angry and want a 100 per cent increase. He can persuade them to be content with 25 per cent, but this will take much work. There must be renumeration for this service. After a month of talking, the owner and leader arrive at a deal. Eight hundred dollars is paid to the leader. In a small factory $80 to $160 may be enough.

Some leaders are "not even half good." They make problem after problem. To pull out of these problems takes money. During the past twelve years the number of dishonest leaders has been decreasing.

One must distinguish clearly, Laborde pointed out, between the contract reached by collective bargaining and the statutory contract. The former is an agreement between the sindicato and the factory such as described above. The Federal Labor Law guarantees double pay for extra work, one day rest in seven (but pay for seven, not six), that those under twelve cannot work, six work days of vacation after one year of employment, eight days after two, ten after three, twelve days after four or more. This Federal Labor Law merely sets minimum standards. In the biennial bargaining sessions the tendency of the union, as in the United States, is to ask for "the sea and its little fishes" ("*el mar y sus pescaditos*"). This not only includes higher pay and more vacation days but many other fringe benefits. The results vary with the strength of the union. After thirty years of bargaining a chauffeur belonging to a weak union might be paid 30 pesos a day; a chauffeur in a stronger sindicato, 60 pesos; a chauffeur for Petroleos Mexicanos, whose employees are regarded as the aristocracy among workers, 90 pesos.

"Our people defend workers' rights but don't always understand workers' obligations," Laborde explained. "Usually they work very badly. Often they cannot work Mondays. With 150 workers there may be twenty that do not work. In one plant when a worker was found sleeping at his post, in order to be able to fire him he had to be found sleeping more than eleven times!" In this admittedly unusual case the contract was referred to a court which appointed a committee of three experts to study the factory. The experts turned in a 23-page typewritten document reporting on the physical equipment and techniques, the financial condition, and the costs and marketing outlook for the product being made. The most important part of the report was the four-page *dictamen* (recommendation), later approved by the court, which cut down the number of workers 50 per cent and modified some of the unreasonable provisions of the contract such as the one cited. Being caught asleep at his post only once was now cause for a worker's suspension.

When two-thirds of the factories in a specific industry and region are under collective agreements with sindicatos, a statutory contract for the whole industry is declared.[10] It is revised biennially. This law specifies wages and conditions for all factories in the industry and prevents unfair advantage by any branch.

The manufacture of tires is an industry where the contract is decreed as a law. For example, sweepers in the Compañía Hulera Euzkadi, S.A. (S.A. is equivalent to our Inc.) received in 1961 $2 daily. This was the minimum established by the strong sindicato. In contrast, a few of the skilled workers in this Goodrich Euzkadi factory, by working very hard, earned $14 a day. The average was around $4. Assistants received $3. Men who tended the ovens or molds that formed the tires earned better than $4. Mechanics, in a separate department, also received the same but on a daily rather than a piecework basis.

A distinction is made in Mexico City factories, as indicated earlier, between *empleados* and *obreros*. Those working in the office and those who are *jefes* (foremen) in the factory are empleados. At the Goodrich Euzkadi they have a separate dining room. The obreros are those who do the physical labor of the factory. About three-fourths of the employees at the Euzkadi plant are obreros.

The plant is approximately thirty-three years old. Its tires are alleged to be identical in quality with those produced by Goodrich in the States. In certain respects, such as the predominance of six-ply over four-ply casings, the Mexican tires are better adapted to rough roads. Tire production in Mexico tripled between 1950 and 1959.[11] This strong demand for tires is an index to the spread of modern highways and the increasing use of both private cars and "the noisy and democratic truck (*camión*)."[12]

The manager of personnel and public relations in the nearby Compañía Hulera El Popo, S.A., estimated that 30 per cent of the workers used their wages for vices, mostly drinking and women. Some workers, whose wages have increased twenty times, continue to live in the same jacales. Another problem common to both Oaxaca and Mexico City is the decrease in attendance with increase in pay. At the "General Popo" plant—cleverly advertised by means of a jolly, corpulent, old-fashioned general—about 12 per cent attend poorly. As in Oaxaca, Monday is the off day. "If they can cover expenses with what they earn in four days, they work only four," commented the personnel manager. "This is a problem throughout Mexico."

Both of these tire factories are located in the west side industrial belt which is probably the largest in the city. Most of the obreros live in the poor colonias north of this narrow east-west belt. The impression is that these people—many of them recent migrants from the countryside—are gradually advancing. Most of the school children wear shoes. Many families live in jacales, it is true, but many also are living in, or are building, houses. Clothing has definitely improved. Young girls are attractively dressed. Many of the empleados in these factories live in the better colonias to the southwest—areas like Polanco, Anzures, and Cuauhtemoc which make a vivid contrast in level of life with Tacuba and Anáhuac.

In the same narrow industrial zone between Tacuba and Polanco there is also a glass factory, Vidriera México, S.A. The manager reported a problem in the use of money similar to that in the rubber factories. Four years ago, he said, when his plant was in the habit of settling with the men on Saturday, many women would come on Monday to ask if their husbands had been paid. A receipt could be shown but the husband had already spent his money drinking or gambling. A system was therefore instituted whereby each man was required to buy at cost, early in the week, basic commodities for his family, the amount being deducted from his Saturday pay. The number of persons in each man's family had already been recorded. This served as a check on the adequacy of his purchases. A man with four children, for example, was required to buy a certain amount. Some individuals interested in the welfare of workers are skeptical of this plan. It reminds them of the plantation store (*tienda de raya*), on the pre-Revolutionary hacienda, where the peons were forced to buy their food and clothing. The hacienda store was managed in such a way as to keep the peon continually in debt. The wages paid by the glass factory are at least twenty times as high as those received on the typical hacienda, however, and commodities are sold at cost. The possibility of debt bondage arising from this plan seems remote.

"Industrial City"

The industry which the people of the Federal District praised most in 1948 was the D. M. Nacional, S.A. This company was founded in 1929 and was still, twenty years later, directed by Antonio Ruiz Galindo. The enterprise was manufacturing steel furniture. Its new plant was inaugurated by President Avila Camacho in November, 1946. As part of a so-called "Industrial City," it is located on an old rancho about a mile and a half east of the Basilica of Guadalupe.

In October, 1948, the minimum wage in this ultra-modern factory was $1 daily; the average, $3; the top, $7. (These wages had increased to about $2, $6, and $14 daily in 1961.) As a production-boosting device, a prize, such as a new bicycle, was given each month to the individual with the highest output.

Materials moved through the plant in assembly-line order. New machines imported from the United States were used for making the furniture. In addition to wages, free transportation from the city center was provided for the workers. At noon a balanced meal, cooked in a sanitary kitchen, was served to eight hundred employees. During the forty-minute lunch period, classical music was played in the attractive dining room. A library nearby was patronized by only fifteen to twenty employees daily. There was also a medical clinic equipped with X-ray machine, operating room, sterilizer, and four hospital beds.

A new apartment building which would house twenty-five families free, except for electricity and gas, had just been completed in this "Industrial City." The master plan called for a total of six such buildings. To educate the children in these families a kindergarten and primary school had already been constructed. A spacious gym (basketball is the favorite indoor game) accommodated eighty to one hundred daily—more on Sunday. The most popular recreation of all, however, was provided by the swimming pool. This is available at different times for men and women.

It was said that between 1945 and 1947 the new plant and program cut by two-thirds the hours lost by sickness and unjustifiable absences. During the same period the number of minutes of effective work in each hour was reported to have increased from 23 to 56.

In a letter dated July 30, 1963, Antonio Ruiz Galindo, Jr., Executive Sub-Director of D.M. Nacional, S.A., wrote as follows: "We have now 2,300 workers in our three plants of Industrial City and our incentive wage system has been very successful and copied by many other industries in Mexico." The second plant, located nearby, makes wood furniture and the third, truck bodies.

"Industrial City" was intended as a model for other industrialists to follow. The project suggests that in Mexico today paternalism can be a desirable development. As the Republic continues to industrialize, "the relations between employer and employee will be reduced progressively to an economic plane," wrote the late Professor Sanford A. Mosk. "Paternalism along the lines of Ruiz Galindo's program can be very useful in easing this process of readjustment."[13]

From the above discussion it is evident that the role played by unions in the large factories of Mexico City and its environs is greater than in the handicraft shops of Oaxaca. The custom of renewing contracts every two years, whether by collective agreement or by law, has gradually improved the lot of the workers. Differences between the conservative life of an agricultural village and the comparative progress of a mountain hamlet with factory workers' homes have been illustrated by Huiluco and Altimeyaya, just twelve miles apart. Difficulties in the wise use of money are common in both Oaxaca and Mexico City. Education, not merely in school but especially in the family as the child is growing, may be the basic answer. Attendance and personal efficiency problems seem to have been at least partially solved, however, by the unusual program at "Industrial City."

Catholic saints underwent considerable change when they were adopted by Mexicans. This process of Mexicanization is illustrated by the Virgin of the Petate, a lovely Indian Mary Magdalene in Oaxaca's Santo Domingo Church.

9

Resurgence of the Catholic Church

The most difficult and yet the most interesting institution to study in Mexico is the church. Four months elapsed in 1948 before it was possible to locate an assistant to help in this field. The candidates leaned toward two extremes: cynical rejection of the church as a reactionary organization or fanatical support of the church.

One extreme emphasizes the traditional interest of the Spanish Catholic church in power and politics as evidenced by the role it has played in Spain; the deterioration from a missionary zeal for souls in the first one hundred years after the Conquest to a selfish accumulation of property; the corruption of some priests as revealed by solicitation in the confessional[1] and open recognition of their natural children; the failure during four hundred years of opportunity to educate and raise the standard of living of the Mexican masses. The other extreme stresses the many beautiful churches erected by the people under the direction of the priests; the role of the church in the education of the elite; the movement of the early apostolic spirit to the frontiers as manifested by the building of the California missions during the eighteenth century; and the increasing efforts, especially by the Salesian fathers, to improve the economic condition of industrial workers.[2]

There is, of course, a small but powerful anti-clerical group in Mexico. For the rest of the population Dr. Manuel Gamio classified the religions of his country into four categories: (1) pre-Columbian or pagan, (2) Catholic mixed with pagan elements, (3) Roman Catholic, and (4) Protestant.

Paganism is more likely to be prevalent in isolated areas and in the southern or southeastern sections of the country where the majority of the truly primitive groups are to be found. The religion of the Mayas of east-central Quintana Roo, for example, shows a high proportion of pre-Cortesian traits. Twenty years ago this was true also for the Tzeltales in Chiapas,[3] but by 1962 the New Testament had been translated into the Tzeltal language and about 70 per cent of the group had become Protestants. In his chapter on "The Mountain Spirits" Ralph Beals cites numerous instances of pagan rituals among the Western Mixe.[4] Although located in the north, the Tarahumaras of Chihuahua are reported by Filiberto Gómez Gonzáles to be also "basically non-Catholic":

> In all their religious manifestations the Tarahumaras are pagan: when God appears to them in dreams at night and orders them to kill a hen or a goat "because He is hungry"; when they show respect to the sun which they call "Our Father"; when they celebrate the fiesta of some saint "who wishes to see them dance"; and, finally, when they bid farewell to their dead and give fiestas "to help them ascend into heaven," the Tarahumaras are as pagan today as when Padre Font found them four hundred years ago.[5]

It is in the villages more than in the metropolis that one finds Catholicism mixed with pagan elements. In the village of San Juan Cópala, District of Juxtlajican in the Mixteca Alta of Oaxaca, there is a *santo* (image of a saint) famous for its miracles. At a special time each year a fair is celebrated in this town which brings money to the authorities. Thousands of natives from the surrounding region, many of whom are not on friendly terms with the people of San Juan, attend the fair and kiss the saint. At the conclusion of the fair the parishioners, indignant with the santo because it has permitted undesirable visitors to kiss it, carry it to the Cuchara River, wash and punish it with a rod of thorns.

To the average villager the local santo is more important than any of the greater saints, including even Our Lady of Guadalupe. It is the physical image of the santo that seems to be worshiped rather than the person it represents. Any disrespect to the santo, real or imagined, is vigorously resented. The late Federico Holm, genial tourist guide and amateur anthropologist, once took two American boys and an American girl, dressed in trousers, into the mountains of the Costa Chica (Pacific Coast region) in Oaxaca. When the party arrived at one isolated village "he" went into a church with "his" hat on. The villagers wanted to kill "him." Holm had to explain carefully that the "he" was really a she. It was a difficult idea to get across. To settle matters, a fine had to be paid.

When the Spaniards came to Mexico it was their policy to destroy native pyramids and erect churches in their places. The impressive cathedral facing the Zócalo in Mexico City was built on the very site of the Aztec teocalli. The church in Mitla goes further and includes walls and a foundation from a Zapotec temple. The church of Our Lady of the Remedies in Cholula, Holy City of Anáhuac, stands on top of a great Aztec pyramid. In spite of this effort, pagan symbols often appear among the decorations of Catholic churches; witness, for example, the stars, sun, and moon of the Aztecs above the church door in Tepoztlán, and the face of Tlaloc, the rain god, which shares with Biblical figures a church column in the city of Guanajuato.[6]

The saints themselves take on new character under Indian influence. The so-called "Virgin of the Petate" in the church of Santo Domingo in Oaxaca City is a lovely Indian Mary Magdalene with bare feet and skirt of matting. Brown Virgins and Black Christs are common. It is usual for the blood, thorns, wounds, and agony of Jesus to be greatly accentuated. The first bishop of Mexico showed genius in his work of conversion when he substituted the cult of the Virgin of Guadalupe for the worship of the Aztec Goddess, Tonantzin, on the same hill of Tepeyac.

Four characteristics of the old pagan ritual persisted with little change: the offerings, human sacrifice excepted; the lavish use of flowers; dancing; eating and drinking. Idols went out of style and saints took their places. Sometimes an idol was placed under or behind a cross. Similarities in the religions helped the Indians to accept Christianity and make it their own.

In the following story Anita Brenner pictures vividly the kind of saint that is revered by Mexican peasants today:

> A pious lady, owner of a great estate, long after the colonial period, visited a native chapel and was so shocked by the "ghastliness of their St. Anthony," that she substituted it with a new and prettier image. But the Indians refused to have anything to do with it. They brought no candles or flowers, and would not pray at the once popular shrine. They said that the new Anthony was "pink and white and richly clothed, therefore a snob, a Spaniard, who wouldn't listen to our prayers, while the other was poor and dark and humble, like ourselves, and will take our part in Heaven."[7]

The magical nature of certain church activities and their popularity with the lower classes is illustrated by an annual ceremony known as "the benediction of the animals." On the afternoon of the ceremony in Oaxaca, processions of people can be seen moving toward the patio of the Merced Church from all directions. Our houseboy carries the macaw; the maid brings the canaries in a cage decorated with ribbons. Most of the animals are dressed up in some way: a white sheep has been dipped in pink paint, white cows are daubed with red spots, chickens have pink and yellow ribbons around their necks, small dogs wear hats and trousers. When the padre finally comes into the courtyard, bird cages and chickens are raised high and the crowd surges forward. After a sprinkle of holy water, the suppliants depart with their birds, bulls, and burros to make way for others. The ceremony has the quality of a lark, for there is much fun, but the padre's blessing is deemed important for animal health and fertility.

No matter how much the humbler folk of Mexico may mix idolatry with their worship, the accessibility and use of the church for meditation at all hours is, from the standpoint of a religious person, "commendable." It is market day in Oaxaca. Dressed in their best, a mustachioed father from a remote village, his patient wife, and their two small sons reverently enter the vaulted building. They burn candles before a favorite santo, cross themselves, kneel, whisper a prayer. With a love of beauty evidenced in the artistic touches they add to the products they make, and in the use of flowering plants no matter how poor, the magnificent interiors of many of these churches must have meaning for them. While participation in traditional acts of worship may carry little weight in the realm of ethics, it does strengthen the loyalty of worshipers to the church as an institution.

Although Mexico City may not be as ardently Catholic as either Puebla or Guadalajara, it too has devout Catholics and pilgrimages to sacred shrines. The suburb to the north, Villa Guadalupe,[8] contains the most important Catholic shrine in all Latin America, the Basilica of Guadalupe. Because it was Friday rather than Sunday when we visited the basilica, we were able to work our way toward the front. It was impressive to watch the devout attitudes of the worshipers—many of them in family groups—as they knelt and looked toward the shrine. Some were dressed in the Indian-colonial way. One peasant woman added a touch of color with a bright red blouse. Children were being baptized on the steps of the altar, the number of adults in each group suggesting the presence of godparents. One of the priests with a very friendly face met the people pleasantly. At intervals there was chanting by choirs of men and boys.

Sacred relics in the east transept of the basilica received special attention. A certain glass case held a cross that had been bent by the explosion of a bomb intended for "Our Lady" who remained unharmed. The devout put 20-centavo pieces in this case and rubbed their hands over the glass that protected the image, then over their heads and necks.

On December 12 especially, all good Catholics, wherever they are, honor this Virgin of Guadalupe, "Mother of the Mexicans." Once in Valles on the eve of Guadalupe Day, we joined a procession of men, women, and children led by a man playing a homemade flute. Up in front men and boys danced to the music. In a few blocks we came to a cathedral that was in process of construction. It had two walls, one tower, two temporary altars, no roof. Its unfinished aspect (beautifully completed now) combined with the enthusiasm of the thousand or more worshipers seemed to symbolize the resurgence of the Catholic Church in Mexico.

Near the main altar there was a chanting group of girls and women. At one side men played an accompaniment on tiny guitars and a harp. The only modern device in this setting was the loud-speaker used by a priest. Flickering light from candles reflected on the men's black hair and on the women's dark faces enveloped in their blue rebozos. A bell tolled. Mass was intoned from a high platform at the front of the church. All this was punctuated by occasional rockets. Stands selling native foods lined the adjacent street. With something exciting happening all the time the fiesta was greatly enjoyed by men, women, and children. And throughout the long night at intervals could be heard the explosion of rockets, the shouting, and chanting.

"THE PARISH PRIEST IS THE VOICE OF GOD"

Priests still have power in Mexico. They control the conscience of the humbler people. If the priest says, "Cooperate with Aftosa" (the campaign against hoof-and-mouth disease), the people cooperate; if he even hints casually a negative attitude, they don't—they hide their stock. As an aid to nutrition surveys, which the Rockefeller Foundation was sponsoring among the Otomí Indians of the Mezquital Valley, the priest made a brief explanation to his people at the time of mass on Sunday. With this help these uneducated, almost idolatrous natives responded surprisingly well.

On his expeditions over the state of Oaxaca, with a servant and two mules, the American mining engineer, Claude B. Finney, found that even in rather recent times a letter from the governor received no attention from the old men who are usually the leaders in an Indian village. A letter from the archbishop, however, made it possible to buy forage for his mules, and eggs, chicken, meat, and tortillas for himself and his mozo.

"The parish priest is the voice of God,"[9] commented Dr. Herculano Espinosa G., who in 1949 was head of the health department in the town of Miahuatlán, sixty miles south of Oaxaca. In Mexico, prenuptial physical examinations are required by law. Dr. Espinosa sent in a blood sample for a young man. The report came back positive. The doctor refused to certify the man, which meant that a civil marriage—the only official ceremony—would be impossible. The priest performed the marriage anyway. Legally he could be fined for this, but the fine is never imposed. The doctor talked with him about the matter, but it did no good.[10]

These are, however, examples of economic and social rather than political power. In times of crisis such as those during the struggle between the government of the Republic and the Catholic Church beginning in 1926 and continuing until 1940, the majority of the people, even though at least nominal Catholics, did not follow the political leadership of the priests. Except in limited areas such as Los Altos in Jalisco, hotbed of the *Cristero* insurrection, the summons of the clergy was not heeded. The political power of the priest today has been overstressed. In 1935, after an interesting discussion of "the present situation" in their book on *Religion in the Republic of Mexico*, G. Báez-Camargo and Kenneth G. Grubb prophetically concluded: "There will not be a revival of the temporal and political power of the clergy."[11]

The sharp decline in the number of priests in Mexico during the past two centuries suggests that their power, whether used constructively or otherwise, cannot be as great as formerly. In 1767, prior to the expulsion of the Jesuits, there were 8,500 *sacerdotes* (priests) for a total population of 4,400,000. By 1946 this number had declined to 3,863 for a total estimated population of 22,000,000. In 1767 there was one padre for each 515 inhabitants; in 1946, one for 5,695. Although most Mexicans are listed in the census as Catholics, probably not more than one in seven is a Catholic in the sense accepted in the United States.[12] The ratio of priests to practicing Catholics would be about one to 800. In the Roman Catholic Church throughout the world there was in 1946 one priest for each 724 members; in the United States, one for each 623; in Canada, one for each 493.[13]

The distribution of priests among the 33 dioceses is highly differential, varying from one priest for every 1,918 inhabitants in the archdiocese of Guadalajara to one for 77,226 in Tabasco. The archdioceses of México and Oaxaca are close to the national average with one priest for every 4,870 and 5,990 inhabitants respectively.[14] As for Tabasco, about thirty-five years ago an extreme revolutionist, Governor Tomás Garrido, not only killed many priests but even tried, unsuccessfully, to abolish the greeting, "Adiós" (literally, "to God"). Garrido had no use for God in anything!

In Oaxaca City there is a Roman Catholic seminary where priests are trained. Although founded in 1531, regular instruction did not begin until sometime between 1785 and 1796. Its courses in philosophy, medicine, and law were later transferred to what was for many years called the Institute of Arts and Sciences. Almost all of the 150 priests in the archdiocese of Oaxaca[15] received their training in this seminary. Some great personages were once students there, among them Porfirio Díaz and Benito Juárez.

Between 1926 and 1940 was a difficult time for seminaries in Mexico. The Oaxaca Seminary changed its location from the Guadalupe church to Carmen Alto, to a private house at Independencia 24 (1934), to its present site (1940) in the block north of Carmen Alto. The years 1934 to 1940 especially comprised a period of crises and persecution by the governors. A usual attendance of 25 to 30 dropped during this period to as low as two to four. Since 1940, however, there has been in Oaxaca as in the rest of Mexico a resurgence of the Catholic Church. In 1955 it was reported that there were 34 seminaries in the country preparing about 2,000 young priests.[16]

Six of the eight teachers in the Oaxaca Seminary have studied in Rome. It is the policy in Mexican seminaries to send the best students either to the Montezuma Seminary at Las Vegas, New Mexico (about sixty miles east of Santa Fe), or to the Latin-American College in Rome where priests are trained for Spanish America and the Philippines. Padre Hermenegildo Pérez, director of the Oaxaca Seminary, went to Rome in 1938, was caught in the war, and stayed until 1946. He was also a student in the United States and in Mexico City. The four hundred students (1961) in the Montezuma Seminary "come from all the dioceses of Mexico." It was located in New Mexico to help students avoid persecution.

In March, 1949, there were 106 youths in the Oaxaca Seminary. All of them were boarding students who lived in the seminary. Only two or three knew indigenous languages, but nearly all were from the "humble class." A few from families in comfortable circumstances paid two dollars monthly of the seven-dollar actual cost, but most families pay nothing. The students are ordinarily expected to have completed the sixth grade before they enter. At present it takes twelve years (eleven in 1949) to complete the seminary course of study.[17] After graduation they are likely to be sent to isolated villages. Like other educated persons, a padre deteriorates without contacts. To prevent this the hierarchy shifts priests from one location to another, circulates a weekly journal giving news of the church, and gives examinations in certain subjects, suspending those who do not pass.

When they are not playing games, the students (*seminaristas*) wear black robes buttoned down the front. These are set off attractively by light blue woven belts about four inches wide. White collars have been abandoned because they are too hard to keep clean.

The daily program both in 1949 and 1961 was approximately as follows:

A.M.		P.M.	
5:15	rise	12:30	dinner followed by recreation
5:45	chapel, including meditation and mass	2:00	siesta *en camas*, i.e., on the beds
7:00	study (all study periods are in silence)	2:45	study
		4:00	classes
7:45	breakfast	5:00	classes
8:15	study	6:00	recreation
9:00	classes	6:30	study
10:00	classes	8:00	supper
11:00	recreation	9:15	chapel and bed
11:30	study		

The nuns who prepare the meals are completely separated from the students. "Even between saints, a strong wall," says the Spanish proverb. While the boys eat in silence, one of them reads to his mates on a topic such as the history of the church. Occasionally the seminaristas are permitted to talk at meals.

The seminary has three basketball courts and one for volleyball. In the latter game the boys exhibited a good quality of playing. They knew how to pass and "spike." In the States we call the player who jumps high to strike a passed ball hard toward the ground on the opposite side a "spiker." In Mexico they use a comparable term, *clavadero* (nailer). The importance of sports in this training program is suggested by the fact that the boys are not allowed to go anywhere outside the seminary except to the playing field.

The twelve-year course of study is grouped into three divisions: (1) five years of Latin together with subjects similar to those in secondary and preparatory schools outside; (2) three years of philosophy supplemented by other courses including

Christian sociology, psychology, and the history of Mexico; (3) four years of theology associated with such courses as church history and Catholic action. The emphasis on Latin is due to the fact that many books are obtainable in that language. By using Latin the Church is able to make books available for priests no matter what their native tongues. The seminaristas also study French two years and, since 1961, two years of English.

Many of the classes are held in the open air under an immense India laurel. On opposite sides of a path are two concrete benches for the students. The professor uses a table and chair.

The boys appeared to be healthy and of a character suitable for priesthood. The story is told that when one archbishop came into office several years ago, he lined up the lads and asked those with a real calling to the priesthood to step out. Many did not move. The archbishop promised these boys, who were merely using the school as a means for getting an education, that he would help them, but affirmed that he wanted only good priests from this seminary.

Although churches in the state of Oaxaca have been renovated (like the one in Ejutla which has a new 50,000-peso front and neon lighting for the paintings of the more important Virgins) and some, as in Cuixtla near Miahuatlán, are in process of reconstruction, no entirely new Catholic church came to our attention. In Mexico City, however, as many as twenty new churches (*templos*) have been constructed in one year. For the Republic as a whole, the increasing number of churches, the growing importance of private schools under Catholic supervision, the new hospitals under Catholic sponsorship, as in Zitácuaro,[18] do provide evidence of a resurgence. Since the inauguration of ex-President Avila Camacho in 1940, with his statement, "I am a believer," persecution has lessened and hostility between church and state has quieted.

Now that the Catholic Church is less opposed to the state, even occasionally expressing support, its prestige has risen. This growing esteem was symbolized on September 28, 1948, when the Rotary Club of Mexico City devoted its regular Tuesday meeting to giving homage to the late Archbishop of Mexico, Doctor Don Luis María Martínez, in honor of his twenty-fifth anniversary as bishop. Rose petals were scattered in his path as he entered. A Rotarian eulogized his work and personality, referring to him as a lighthouse of happiness and fountain of welfare. "If perhaps

I am," the bishop modestly replied, "it is because I have in me something divine and as a priest am a representative of God. . . . I pray God to fill me with celestial grace in order that this poor representative may be a true lighthouse and a true fountain." After the meeting several of the members, among them an ex-president of the organization, expressed the opinion that Rotary should not have held a meeting with such definite homage to the church. Liberals in the club and members of the government interpreted the session as a slap in the face. Some of them, in fact, stayed away as a protest. But one member, impressed by the adoration from the visiting ladies, facetiously remarked that he wished he too could fix it up with God to be His representative.

PROTESTANT STRUGGLES IN A CATHOLIC LAND

In 1947 and 1948 the Mexican Congregationalists, Presbyterians, and Methodists celebrated their diamond anniversaries. During the 1850's the political liberalism of Benito Juárez proclaimed freedom of worship and of conscience. The first actual break in the religious monopoly of Rome occurred in 1861 when a priest, Ramón Lozano, proclaimed in Santa Barbara, Tamaulipas, the deviate statute of the Mexican Apostolic Catholic Church. In August, 1873, the Methodists acquired part of what had been the oldest Franciscan convent in the Americas (1531) where Fray Pedro de Gante,[19] renowned for introducing primary schools into Mexico, had occupied a cell. This completely renovated and attractive edifice on Calle Gante, Mexico City, is in the same block as the new forty-four-story Latino Americana Tower. By August, 1948, the Methodists had thirty-five churches in the Republic with about 18,000 members. The total 1940 Protestant constituency was estimated by G. Báez-Camargo as 240,000 and for 1960, prior to release of census figures (578,515), as 500,000[20]—only 1.4 per cent of the entire population, but a number equal to perhaps 10 per cent of practicing Roman Catholics.

During recent years, at least, there is evidence that the leaders of the Presbyterians and the Methodists have become very conservative—almost as *fanático*, i.e., aggressively reactionary, as their Catholic rivals. They are fundamentalist in philosophy, and their church emphasis is almost purely evangelistic in the narrowest sense of that word. Apparently, militant fundamentalism is a natural reaction to the fighting role in which the

Evangelicals find themselves. Whether they will abandon this role for a more constructive approach will depend in large part on the attitude of Catholics.

In spite of conservatism at the top, some of the missionary work in the field has much which progressive-minded Christians would commend. Two Presbyterian missionaries, the Reverend Hugh Nelson and his wife, Beth, came to Oaxaca in 1944. Hugh is a graduate in sociology from Whittier College in Southern California and has his B.D. from San Francisco Seminary. Beth is a graduate nurse from Stanford University. Their primary interest was in a social gospel that would make tangible contributions to the life of the people.

The real test of a missionary enterprise is what happens after the missionaries have left. Has conversion to evangelical Christianity brought about changes in the behavior of those converted? Have the people in communities with a substantial proportion of Evangelicals taken on a different way of life? The changes described by Hugh Nelson in his case study of Inés de Zaragosa (near Nuxáa) answer these questions in the affirmative. Although he had active professional contact with this village, Nelson prepared the following statement as a student of sociology rather than as a missionary.[21]

In the area known as La Montaña, in the district of Nochixtlán, is the village of Santa Inés del Rio. [Under the influence of the Evangelicals who prefer to omit the saints, it is increasingly called Inés de Zaragosa.] Santa Inés is divided religiously, with the evangelical group assuming leadership in municipal affairs. There was the usual course of persecution in the first years of establishing the Protestant church, but peace was achieved when the fanatics saw that the new faith did not endanger the village and that on the contrary it seemed to bring benefits to the community. Being but one of six congregations of Presbyterians in the Montaña, Santa Inés has never had the systematic care of an ordained minister. What leadership they have enjoyed from the organized church has consisted of occasional visits from minister or missionary and sometimes the services of an unordained native leader.

There are two influences for social progress in this poor, isolated little village: the public school and the evangelical church.

The school is taught by Froilan Hernández Ruiz, a native of Santa Inés, son of Evangelicals and an active member of the congregation. In the six years that he has been working as "Maestro" in the school (four grades, about 165 students, one assistant teacher) he has accomplished many changes. The village square was a dry, open, desolate piece of ground. Hernández brought in eucalyptus trees and planted them. The green and shade of these trees has changed the aspect of the Zócalo. There was no place but the plaza square for the market. Hernández has succeeded in moving the village fathers to construct a building for the market. He has taken an interest in the higher education of village youth, has sought scholarships for gifted students and now has several young people studying toward a more adequate education in Oaxaca City. His sister has successfully finished nursing studies in a missionary hospital and it is hoped she will return to give her people the benefit of her learning. This year, largely due to the influence of this evangelical teacher, a road has been constructed to connect the village with the International Highway.

Israel Cruz, a young man from the neighboring Santo Domingo Nuxaá, came to Oaxaca for two years of study in the Oaxaca Bible School. The Bible course also included hygiene, and Israel was an apt pupil. After his graduation he was sent to Santa Inés to serve as the unordained spiritual leader of the congregation. While he was resident in the village, typhus developed in epidemic proportions. The disease strikes every winter in the Montaña because the people have always believed that during the cold weather it is harmful to bathe. Such an unsanitary custom naturally leads to the multiplication of lice— and typhus. In the winter of 1948-49 while Israel was in Santa Inés the plague struck hard. A visit was made by the health department of the federal government, but the disease could not be checked, and with the death of one of the doctors the health authorities would not send more aid. During the winter more than two hundred people died. Whole families were wiped out and rancherías were left deserted. Israel Cruz had learned in his hygiene course about the cause and control of typhus, so he began to preach cleanliness to his flock. He exhorted them to bathe themselves daily, to clean their homes and kill the lice. He visited his parishioners daily to inquire if they had followed his directive. As the death toll continued to mount, the villagers began to make a superstitious observation— the Protestants were not losing any of their group to typhus. Even many of the Evangelicals considered that their religion had protected them, for of all those who died of typhus in Santa Inés del Río, not one was a practicing Protestant. And perhaps it did, for their religion by means of the Bible School worker had taught them that cleanliness was next to godliness and had delivered them from the hands of the enemy, typhus.

Other varieties of missionary enterprise are to be found. By the end of 1948, eight hundred American college students had given service to Mexico under the auspices of the Society of Friends. This work had been distributed in twenty-two communities located in eight states. During six weeks of each summer the Society has six or seven projects in as many different villages. For seven of the ten years prior to 1949 there had been one or two year-round programs.

In October, 1948, the Quakers had been working continuously for two and a half years in Yautepec, Morelos. Here under the direction of Mexican government officials young American men and women do unskilled, non-competitive physical labor. The students use cooking utensils similar to the natives and sleep on beds without mattresses. They pay fifty dollars a month for the privilege of serving. The girls keep house, take turns in preparing meals, help in the Salubridad (health department) clinic and in the public school; the boys work on a municipal hospital, build sanitary toilets, supervise games on the playfield. For the hospital they have carried heavy stones, chipped and painted walls, knocked out a very thick section of wall for a doorway and put on a new roof.

Ed Duckles, who manages these assignments, states very clearly in a letter dated May 27, 1950, the objectives and philosophy of the Friends Service Committee in Mexico:

> One of our main methods and philosophies is to do the things which the people of Mexico themselves consider are important rather than come to the country with the attitude of telling them what we think the good life for them should be. In order to carry this out we have always had a policy of working under the direction of Mexican supervisors, either a public health doctor, a rural school teacher, a village president, a committee of village people charged with the responsibility of securing good drinking water for their village, etc. Our role in all of these situations is to provide a fund of volunteer unskilled labor to serve as an encouragement to any of these people to get the job done which they have set for themselves.

In his annual report for 1958, Duckles points out that, as compared with previous years, a larger number of Latin-American volunteers had served with the Committee; that a new project will provide a team of five men to drill water wells for villages by means of a motor-driven rig furnished by CARE; and that the municipal president of Salamanca, Guanajuato, has asked the Committee to help rebuild some of the two thousand homes destroyed in his community by the disastrous flood of October, 1958. By 1961 work camps were being held also under the auspices of the Evangelical Council of Mexico, the Committee on Cooperation in Latin America, and World Youth Projects.

The most welcome Protestant missionaries, at least from the government point of view, are the Wycliffe Bible translators. When Lázaro Cárdenas was president, he was favorably impressed by their work and encouraged these linguistic missionaries. They go into peasant or, in some instances, isolated Indian communities and spend many years translating the New Testament into the native languages. They believe that the Bible can best be understood in the mother tongue. Miss Velma Pickett and Mrs. William Nyman, Jr., for example, spent five years getting a thorough grasp of the Zapotec language in Juchitán on the Isthmus of Tehuantepec. Walter Miller, another *linguistico,* who lives in Mitla with his wife and four children, has spent at least six weeks of each year since 1936 in San Lucas Camotlán, a conservative village of 750 in the Mixe region, four days by horseback or walking, east of Mitla.

Walter Miller has come to admire the work of the old Dominican fathers. Even today the women of Juquila Mixes, a village where Dominican activities centered, know the Catholic doctrine by heart and in Mixe. There was no science of linguistics in the sixteenth century. In Camotlán, which is about a day's journey from Juquila Mixes, the church was constructed before 1600. Miller found a 400-page Latin manuscript in this old church, dated April 12, 1609. Staffs for music had been ruled by hand. Square notes were used. It was bound in cedar boards. Probably months were required to copy it.

It has been difficult for Miller to get the natives of Camotlán to help him. People who came to talk with the linguist in 1938 were put in jail. At a later date neighbors would put their heads in the window and abuse the person who was assisting. As a result, informants will not sit in a house and work on the language. Miller has found that he can learn more Mixe in the fields and on the trail.

Walter Miller is liked by the people of Oaxaca City. As one old-timer with no love for Protestants put it: "He does not monkey around much with religion. He is a linguist. Unfortunately he has chosen the Bible to translate."

The affectionate attitude shown toward linguistic missionaries in southern Mexico is not taken toward the Mexico City Y.M.C.A. Ninety-five per cent of its members are Catholics, it is true, and the Association tries to remain aloof from the Catholic-Protestant issue. It has succeeded, however, in gaining the enmity of the Catholics and the distrust of the fundamentalist Evangelicals. In order to serve workers who are free on that day, its greatest activity is on Sunday. This alienates the conservative Protestants, who feel that the Christian message is diluted. Religious services, worship, or Bible classes would, of course, make the "Y" a religious institution and subject to expropriation by the government. The Catholic hierarchy is officially against the "Y". A 1948 strike of employees was alleged to have been inspired by Catholics.

Liberal Protestants, however, feel that the "Y" is serving a valid secular purpose. The first organized camp with an educational program in Mexico was an outgrowth of a Y.M.C.A. campsite. It is the Camohmila Rural Center just east of Tepoztlán. A pioneer director of this center was Dr. D. Spencer Hatch, whose background included twenty years of rural reconstruction work in India. Near Tepoztlán in villages with elevations varying as much as 3,500 feet he tried to grow seventy different food plants. Twelve or fifteen of these proved to be adaptable. He also built a model house "which the *campesino* can easily copy."

Because most of these examples of constructive Protestant activity happen to have been at least partially Anglo-American in sponsorship, it is important to emphasize the fact that there are also liberal-thinking and liberal-acting Mexican Protestants. Professor Gonzalo Báez-Camargo is one. In the *Christian Century* for January 7, 1953, he told Americans about the defeat in Mexico's Congress of a bill to include Catholic "indoctrination" in the public schools, and the killing of a lay evangelist by Catholic "fanatics," but also of a priest who gave a fair estimate of Mexican Protestantism in a lecture series.

In 1961 Báez-Camargo told the author more about this priest. He is a Basque who has served in Belgium and knows the European situation well. The Catholicism of Belgium, France, and the United States is more tolerant, Báez-Camargo explained, than that of Spain which has been the model for Mexico. Under the influence of the Maryknoll priests of New York, the Catholics of Chile and Peru are more liberal also, but American Catholicism has had little influence in Mexico. The Basque priest in his lectures raised the question: "Why do Protestants win converts?" "Let's face the facts squarely," he urged. "It is not true that they win converts by paying out money." He gave three reasons. (1) Because of the importance given to the Holy Scriptures. (2) Because they put Jesus Christ in the center. "Everyone knows that I love Mary," he affirmed, "but Christ who is really the center of our church has been pushed aside by her." (3) Every member has something to do in a Protestant church. "You come to mass, walk away, and nothing happens." After this lecture Báez-Camargo had a long talk with the Basque priest. They became good friends and often eat lunch together. The priest said that he had cleared the outline for his lectures with his bishop before they were delivered. Later he remodeled his church and put away many of the images. "They are sheer idolatry," he said. He kept only two images, the crucifix on the altar and a painting of a saint on the wall.

Báez-Camargo has been employed by the American Bible Society to make a new translation for use in Latin America. He wants to put the Bible into words "the man on the street" will understand.

In the final paragraph of his second book on Mexican Protestants, and under the influence of what he had learned about them, Pedro Rivera R., S.J., makes the following affirmation: "The Protestant invasion in Mexico is permitted by divine providence in order to serve as a stimulant to the Catholic Church. The noise molests, but awakens; the cauterization hurts, but regenerates."[22]

THE BEGINNINGS OF SOCIALIZED RELIGION

Catholic persecution of Protestants ranges all the way from signs on house doorways objecting to the "Protestant invasion" to brutal killings. Strange attitudes and beliefs are current. Catholics on seeing a Protestant infant have been heard to exclaim: "There is no tail!" (*"No está la cola!"*)[23] Some of the propaganda is very effective. A pamphlet available in the central cathedral of Mexico City for seven cents American (1948) is entitled, "Why Protestantism is False." It quotes on the outside cover, in Spanish of course, a statement attributed to Theodore Roosevelt: "The absorption of these Latin countries by the United States is long and difficult while these countries are Catholic." In Guadalajara's main cathedral the mummy of an eight-year-old child is displayed as a martyr. The Protestant father is alleged to have killed her because she wanted to become a Catholic. The glass case that holds this gruesome relic is one of the most popular shrines in the cathedral. Twenty-centavo pieces drop into the box and hands rub over the glass.

Forty Protestants from Oaxaca City were holding a meeting in El Cerezo, a village of the Sierra Juárez. Late in the meeting there was heavy pounding on the door. The Protestants were arrested. Enrique Pérez, a stonemason, who was a member of the Oaxaca group, could hear the elders discussing the case. Some urged that the Evangelicals be killed and buried. No one would know. A friend, however, hiked the eleven miles to Oaxaca and got an official demand for their release. The village authorities were removed from power and a stiff fine was imposed on the community.

The following excerpts from the anti-clerical *Tiempo* for March 26, 1948, document the fact that death is sometimes the penalty for being a Protestant in Mexico:

> The residents of the Ranchería de Tixacoto [a village not far from Nuxaá, composed of hard-working, non-drinking Protestants] suffered an attack Sunday, February the twenty-ninth. A mob of fanatics stirred up by the parish priest from Yodocono threw themselves on the village and looted all the houses. The *Cristeros* [an organized group of Catholic "fanatics"] of Yodocono went to the house of the mayor where they found the chief of police, Don Juan Cruz. Enraged, and excited by alcohol, the crowd urged J. C. to abandon the pueblo. When he was not disposed to go they shot and stabbed him. His daughter, eight years of age, who tried to defend her father, was also shot down. . . .

Fortunately, as Padre Pedro Rivera suggests, the conflict between Catholics and Protestants has its more constructive side. When the late Cardinal Villeneuve of Canada visited Mexico in 1945 for the coronation of the Virgin of Guadalupe, the cardinal said that the most effective way to defeat the Protestants was to put in clinics and do other good works. Due to this competition from the Protestants and the increasing number of genuinely Christian priests, the Mexican Catholic church may gradually shift from its traditional emphasis on power to a new stress on the socioeconomic welfare of the people.

One superficial evidence of a trend in this direction was the

1948 "Exhortation of the National Episcopacy to the Clergy and to Catholics to Alleviate the Situation of Mexican *Campesinos*."[24] This seven-page document was prepared under the leadership of Luis María Martínez, the liberal archbishop of México, but was signed by nine archbishops, twenty-four bishops, six titular bishops, and the apostolic administrator of Lower California. The document states in part:

> We declare: . . . It is indispensable to explain and propagate among the *campesinos* the cooperative idea which the Catholic sociologists are teaching. . . .
> It is indispensable to continue with great intensity the campaign against illiteracy. Technical agricultural education is also necessary. . . .
> Constant and well-organized campaigns against alcoholism are an urgent necessity. . . .
> Give the *campesinos*, as the Pope orders, not only religious and moral assistance, but also social and economic assistance. . . .

One method used by Acción Católica Mexicana to carry out the exhortation of the bishops was to hold three-day institutes for campesinos. The program included instruction in modern farm methods: personal and household hygiene, management of agricultural machinery, better methods of cultivation, improvement of the soil, fertilizers adapted to the region. The writer was shown photographs of such an institute held at Tejupilco in the state of Mexico. Students trained by experts in a project jointly supported by the Rockefeller Foundation and the Mexican Department of Agriculture[25] were used in such church-sponsored institutes. Beginning in January, 1949, a national rural week was started by the Catholics. Eight hundred campesinos attended the first rural-week session held in Toluca. Unfortunately, these institutes and rural weeks were not long continued.

To assist in the solution of socioeconomic problems, Acción Católica developed a number of helpful booklets. *Higiene Rural,* for example, gives rules for the care of the hair, head, mouth, and hands. The values of milk, meat, eggs, vegetables, water, and balanced diets, as against "false foods," such as alcoholic drinks, are illustrated and discussed in simple language. Data are included on the sleep, bathing, clothing, feeding, and sickness of the small child and on elementary housing standards. Wise community policies for the prevention of pneumonia, tuberculosis, malaria, smallpox, and other diseases are presented. Another

Acción Católica booklet, *Para Aprender a Leer* (Learning to Read), shows the growing interest of the Church in combating illiteracy. How widely these were used is uncertain.

In addition, the bishops have encouraged the clergy to alleviate the situation of the workers in handicraft shops and factories. The Archbishop of Oaxaca, for example, assigned Padre Bulmaro Ramírez to social work and particularly to the administration, in Oaxaca City, of the Centro Obrero which claimed a membership of 2,000 men and 500 women. The padre conceives the basic social problems of the campesino and the worker to be nutrition, housing, and clothing. Malnutrition, he says, is due to low income. While the range was from 40 to 90 cents, the average daily wage in 1949 for the workers at his center was just 50 cents American. Mothers did not work outside the home. The 500 women members were probably either unmarried or widowed. Some mothers did laundry at home, but most did not. This means that many families had to live on $15 a month.

By the payment of 3 cents American a week an individual member of the Centro Obrero was entitled to medical attention and medicines, and for 10 cents weekly the entire family was covered. If hospitalization was needed, members were sent to the Charity Hospital, a Catholic institution, where patients pay according to ability. When a member died, each man in the Centro paid 14 cents (one peso). A good burial cost $44. The Centro put 10 per cent of the pesos collected into its savings fund. The remainder went to the family.

Padre Bulmaro was an active promoter of athletic sports—baseball, boxing, basketball, soccer football, volleyball. Space was provided also for indoor games such as dominoes and ping-pong. Sunday was, of course, the important day for all of these activities. This priest gave money from his own monthly salary of $88 to buy balls and other sport equipment.

The workers in the Centro were divided into five groups. Each of these met in the old church of St. Augustine at 8:00 P.M. on a special night of the week. Carpenters, construction workers, weavers, and mechanics met on Monday. Potters, butchers, barbers, saddlers, and makers of rebozos met Tuesday. Wednesday was the night for the curers of hides and the makers of shoes and huaraches.

By eight o'clock on a certain Wednesday only one or two members had arrived. Through the entrance to the large church came a little girl of about eight years leading her brother who was not more than three. Just inside the doorway the two kneeled facing the main altar. She crossed herself and turned to make the sign of the cross for him. This appealing ceremony took no more than two minutes. Then they left. About two out of every three of the workers kneeled and crossed themselves as they passed one of the side altars on their way to the seats. When the meeting began at 8:30 there were perhaps sixty in attendance; by 9:00 there were eighty.

With professional courtesy Padre Bulmaro had the visitor sit by his side in front of the group. There was a reading of the minutes of the previous meeting followed by a religious ceremony lasting approximately thirty seconds. Then the padre talked about cooperation. His language was clear and simple. He discussed producers' cooperation. One man doesn't have sufficient capital to do things, but twenty-five do. He talked in more detail about consumers' cooperation. By buying directly from the manufacturer, the resale price is avoided. Shoes that are retailed at $5.60 can be bought direct for $2.80. If the barber is assured of a large trade, a 14-cent haircut can be had for 7 cents. This argument was used also for the *médico*. Here were points that fitted in with the episcopal exhortation.

After the talk and short discussion, a voluntary collection was taken. The $3.50 contributed were given to a sick member's wife who was present with baby in rebozo. To pay their weekly dues, the men then crowded around the padre. Some paid more because they had skipped from two to four weeks. About ten new members paid one peso each.

One of the men approached the padre with his back scrunched up. He said something and the priest took a card and brushed an object from the man's head to the floor. Another worker stepped on it deliberately with his big huarache. It was a five-inch scorpion! The cool of the evening had loosened its grip on the high ceiling. "*Pican muy fuerte*" ("they have a powerful sting"), a man explained. In the hot country the sting is fatal to infants.

Perhaps the most significant feature of this center was not its membership but the fact that its leader also taught philosophy four hours a day at the seminary for training priests. Mixed with Aristotelian principles the seminary students must learn something of the doctrine that expresses itself in "good works."

By 1961 the Centro Obrero had been discontinued. Sindicatos had come in, helping to raise wages; Social Security had built a new structure on the International Highway, ten blocks north of the Zócalo, and was serving the more skilled workers; the Department of Health and Welfare had improved its assistance to the poor. Welfare services by the Catholic Church were still needed but less urgently. The bishops had set a high mark for the parish priests, but actual results have fallen far short of the stated goals. Similar pronouncements have been proffered since but still with little effect.

Legally the Church is not supposed to administer schools or hospitals or do social work. Strict interpretation of these laws is, however, increasingly a thing of the past. The government realizes that it cannot carry the entire burden of education and has permitted many private schools, mostly under Catholic auspices, to share the load. The same situation is true in the field of health and in social welfare. If Church leaders would become more socially minded so that they could work smoothly with anti-clerical officials, and if government leaders continue to permit religious people to apply their Christianity in practical fields, progress in combating illiteracy and in teaching hygiene and farm techniques should accelerate.

It is interesting, however, that certain "weaknesses" of the Catholic Church in Mexico from the Protestant point of view and certain "weaknesses" of the Protestants from the Catholic standpoint actually coincide with specific Mexican social values. In the field of moral behavior the Catholic approach, say the Protestants, is superficial with concern over length of skirt or depth of neckline. There is much talk about the importance of the family and divorce is opposed, but there is no campaign against illicit unions or prostitution. This traditional attitude of the Catholics fits in with admiration for manliness (*machismo*), a value that is firmly established in Latin America.

The Protestants, on the other hand, are criticized by the Catholics for their "dangerous" emphasis on Bible study and books. It is felt by many *católicos* that the stability of the social order is threatened by encouraging the common people to read.[26] These educational activities of the Evangelicals are close to the more recent values that were strengthened by the Revolution, namely, personal freedom and education.

The Catholic Church in Mexico customarily places an emphasis on ritual, on the splendor of its ceremonies, on pilgrimages, on formal congresses and on fiestas. Although these expressions may have little positive effect on behavior, they are popular with the people. They probably are suited best, however, to an authoritarian rather than to an increasingly democratic society.

It is significant that late in 1961 a group of Mexico City Catholics took the position that they had a common Christian mission with Protestants to the world at large. During a "Missions Week" the Catholics organized a round-table dialogue, with three Protestant pastors and a Protestant layman joining in conversation with three priests before an audience of over 200 Catholic priests, seminary students, and laymen. The dialogue was cordial, but it was agreed that it would be kept unofficial. Both Evangelicals and Catholics will increase in numbers. It is probable that gradually they will cooperate more.

Country boys have useful work to do under the watchful eyes of relatives. In the large city almost any job a boy can get brings him in contact with patterns of delinquency.

10

Delinquency, a City Problem

Among peoples who are chiefly agricultural, juvenile delinquency seldom occurs outside the larger cities. Where family and community controls are effective, formal agencies such as the courts are not needed. So it is in much of Mexico. During the year ending August 31, 1945, only two cases of juvenile offenses were reported to the Court of Second Instance from the entire state of Oaxaca. The new law providing separate hearings for juveniles is rarely activated. Parents are strict and family discipline strong in all classes. The situation is similar to that in pre-Communist China where, in the more isolated interior villages, juvenile delinquency simply did not exist.[1]

On the outskirts of the Mexican capital, near Xochimilco, is the village of Santiago Tepaloatlalpam. The long second name of the village, meaning "place where the dishes are broken," refers to the Aztec custom of smashing the pottery at the end of each fifty-one-year cycle. This peasant community sent its first case to the Juvenile Court of the Federal District in 1945. Sra. Adelina Zendejas, a social worker from the court, took the writer with her on the investigation. It was a boy-girl problem brought to public attention by the pregnancy of the girl. As we have seen from the details on courtship and marriage in San Gregorio Atlapulco, attitudes are so strong in villages like this that an unmarried mother might easily be forced into prostitution. In this instance the boy, who lived only a block from the girl's home, had been taken into custody. His mother bitterly opposed marriage as a solution. As is customary in such circumstances, it was decided to send him into the army. The girl was placed with her godparents in Mexico City who were to care for the baby while the young mother continued in school.

From the metropolitan court[2] for which Sra. Zendejas worked, three statistical series of Federal District juvenile delinquents were secured. The great bulk of these cases came, of course, from Mexico City. Details are given in Table 6. It will be noted that with the one exception of Ward III boundaries of police delegations are identical with the wards as shown on Map V on page 76. The extensive size of these wards does give in some instances erroneous impressions. Ward XI, for example, includes both the Lomas de Chapultepec, the best residential area in the city, and the one-time separate town of Tacubaya, some of whose neighborhoods were at the time of Series 3 mere aggregations of poverty-stricken squatters.

North American studies of the geographical distribution of delinquents usually separate the sexes, but Mexican studies do not. It is interesting, however, that although there are five or six times as many males as females in the various series of delinquents, the pattern of offenses is roughly similar for the two sexes. Series 2 in Table 6, for example, showed a percentage of stealing and offenses against property that is substantial for each sex: 64 for boys, 41 for girls. Reflecting the double standard, the

TABLE 6.   *Rates for Juvenile Delinquents in the
Federal District, by Delegations*

Delegation	Series 1 °	Series 2 †	Series 3 ‡
I	1.6	2.5	0.68
II	3.2	4.3	1.1
III §	2.2	3.8	0.74
IV	2.5	4.7	1.7
V	2.1	2.9	0.70
VI	2.4	3.4	1.3
VII	0.9	2.5	0.75
VIII	1.7	2.3	0.67
IX	1.9	1.6	0.48
X	1.8	1.0	0.36
XI		2.3	0.52
XII		1.0	0.38
XIII		2.2	1.0
All other delegations		0.7	0.17
Arithmetical mean	1.94	2.4	0.68

° Percentage of boy and girl delinquents received by the Juvenile Court of the Federal District from ten police delegations, 1927 to 1931 inclusive, using as a base the 1930 population 10 to 19 inclusive by wards. The series includes 3,578 cases.

† Percentage of boy and girl delinquents received by the Juvenile Court of the Federal District from the police delegations, 1932 to 1938 inclusive, using as a base a special compilation of the 1940 population 7 to 18 inclusive provided by the Dirección General de Estadistica. (Comparable population data for 1930 are not available. When the 1930 and 1940 populations 10 to 19 inclusive are averaged for 10 delegations and used as a base, the resulting percentages are higher but the pattern of rates remains the same.) The series includes 11,428 cases.

‡ Percentage of boy and girl delinquents received by the Juvenile Court of the Federal District from the police delegations 1942 using the same base as for Series 2. The series includes 3,189 cases.

§ Part of Ward III as used by the census is included in Delegation XIII as used by the police. This difference has been corrected in Series 2 and 3, but not in Series 1.

biggest difference was for insubordination in the home: 8 per cent for boys, 28 per cent for girls.

Another characteristic of these data is that the delegation in a specific case is determined by the place of arrest rather than the place of residence. A substantial proportion of Mexico City delinquents have no homes. In general, however, there seems to be a closer geographical proximity in Mexico between arrest and home (if there is one) than in the United States. As is true north of the Rio Grande, youthful crimes against the person usually involve people from the same neighborhood—acquaintances, friends or relatives. Some juvenile thieves, notably those who steal from markets, also live in the same locality in which they commit their offenses; other thieves, however, including many who break into cars or into houses, live at some distance from the scene of their crimes.

With the growth of the city, areas of highest delinquency have tended to move westward. In 1927-31 Ward II was highest and IV was next. By 1932-38 this situation had been reversed. The 1942 series shows IV still highest but VI next. Ward VII has become relatively more delinquent (tenth, seventh, and fifth from the highest) as it has been increasingly invaded by the apartment houses and commercial establishments that mark the westward expansion of the city. Delegation XIII, which includes La Villa and the part of Ward III north of Peralvillo, is an exception to this westward trend. It rose from tenth place in 1932-38 to fourth in 1942. A comparable 1962 study would show a continuation of this increase. In fact, the area of high delinquency would be larger now with the greatest extensions to the west and north.

Ward IV, with the highest rate, was the only entire *cuartel* that decreased in population between 1930 and 1940. By 1960 Wards VI, VII, and V were also declining. Decrease in population has been found, in the cities of the United States, to be correlated with various forms of personal and social disorganization including juvenile delinquency.[3]

Another phenomenon often associated with recorded delinquency is deteriorated housing.[4] It has already been pointed out that there are numerous ancient *vecindades* unfit for human habitation in Mexico City's central "horseshoe" of slums. In recent years the mere widening of streets has destroyed some. The broadening of San Juan de Letrán north of the center of highest land values, for instance, put 15,000 families out of sub-standard dwellings. More than a few vecindades remain, however, and many of these tenements, like quite a few of their counterparts in the United States, are owned by wealthy individuals who live in the best residential neighborhoods. Some vecindades, it is true, have been replaced by modestly priced apartment buildings and, on the northern edge of the inner "horseshoe," by the largest housing project in Latin America.[5] The following example of a *casa de vecindad* in Colonia Balbuena of Ward II is perhaps a little worse than average but certainly not the worst.

A narrow door in the street wall, the only entrance, led through a long, open corridor into two patios around which were 50 one-room dwelling units. The stucco construction had deteriorated and the old wooden doors had no locks. The dirt-floored patios were still muddy from the previous night's rain. There was one water faucet before which many girls and some men waited to draw water. Eight dirty toilets were quite open to view in the center of the rear patio. Several toddlers wore short dresses with no panties. The place was swarming with children of school age who were not in school.

Even under these conditions the Mexican love for flowers was shown by many potted plants, arranged on crude tables to protect them from the children, chickens, cats and dogs. We saw two units where coated peanuts were being sacked in small cellophane bags for distribution in the better shops of the city. In the first of these rooms, with no light or ventilation except from the open doorway, fourteen children were busy around nine big bowls. The boy of nine who had been accused of stealing some money was found here.

Then we looked at this boy's "home." It was one room, about six feet by twelve. There were a few dirty quilts on the double bed, a charcoal brazier near the door with a small table beside it to hold the pottery. Here lived a man, his wife, and four children.

The center of the city not only presents a picture of deteriorated housing, it also seemed in 1948 to have the greatest concentration of begging[6] and prostitution. The geographical distribution of the latter has been shown in Chicago studies to correlate positively with girl delinquency.[7]

Thirty-five years ago there were two "zones of tolerance," or red-light districts, in Mexico City, one about a half mile north and the other about three-quarters of a mile south of the center of highest land values (intersection of Avenida Madero and San Juan de Letrán). These have since been abolished, but it was a matter of common knowledge in 1948 that prostitutes, with the unofficial protection of the police, solicited customers in the Alameda and on major arterials like San Juan de Letrán, Cinco de Mayo and Avenida Madero. If the charge to a patron was six pesos, the policeman expected two pesos from the prostitute as his "bite." At night the Zócalo was notorious as a place where the poorer prostitutes solicited workingmen. In March, 1943, long after the abolition of "zones of tolerance," a field study of the southern part of Ward III, with its dense child population, was made by investigators from the Department of Social Prevention. They found twenty-one hotels, three houses of assignation, two boarding houses, one tavern selling beer, one private house, and one entire block used for purposes of prostitution. It is a curious fact that of the twenty-one hotels most of the proprietors were either alien Spanish men or Mexican women.

Prostitution, like the city's juvenile delinquency, seemed in 1948 to be moving westward. There were alleged to be about 600 clandestine houses of prostitution in Colonia Roma. Although other colonias of high economic and social status contained houses of this type, Roma had more. Many women who were not registered as prostitutes practiced here. It was the custom in a house to exhibit an album of photographs. When a choice was made, the girl was called. One and a half to three dollars were paid to the house and an additional seven dollars to the woman. On the Calle del Organo[8] in Ward III, however, the price was 70 cents American.

Toward the city center from Roma on Calle Tolsa was the office for medical inspection of registered prostitutes. How thorough this was may be gathered from the fact that one prostitute might take with her to this office cards for two or three of her girl friends. For a *mordida* (literally, a "bite") the cards were stamped as if the girls had been examined. If found to be venereally diseased, a prostitute was supposed to go for treatment to the Hospital Morelos which is located in an old monastery just north of the Alameda; but again, by paying a mordida, she might avoid this. It should be added that, although soliciting clients for a prostitute is a crime in Mexico, being a prostitute is not.

LACK OF PROTECTION FOR CHILDREN

Mexico City shows a basic difference between reported adult and juvenile delinquency. The registered delinquency of adults is primarily against the person; the delinquency of minors predominantly against property. A study of 82,008 cases of adult crime (1927-35) showed 65 per cent against the person, 26 per cent against property, and 9 per cent other crimes.[9] In contrast, 13,409 cases of juvenile crime (1932-38) showed only 34 per cent against the person, 57 per cent against property, and 9 per cent other offenses.

An American linguistic missionary who has lived in Mexico a long time advises his friends who come down from the States:

"We hate to say things about the Mexicans because we like them, but lock up your car, take the windshield wipers off and do not leave anything of value visible in it when you park. Keep your pen and pencil in an inside pocket; button your coat; hang onto your purse. For after all, it's necessary."

This stealing is not done by juveniles only. It is more frequently done by adults using considerable skill. Handsome young fellows, aptly called "coyotes," sometimes give American women students a good time in order to steal their purses later. Not long ago a geologist and his wife parked their car while attending a movie in the capital. On returning they found the car still locked but $200 worth of irreplaceable camping equipment missing. Stealing is the big crime problem in Mexico City.

One factor accounting for the relatively low percentage of registered crimes against property for adults is the lack of confidence in, or even fear of, the police. Citizens hesitate to report a burglary because of the two to four hours it takes to do this; they hesitate also lest the investigating detectives make additional thefts. Policemen who serve as night watchmen are especially feared because of a tendency to connive with thieves. The extent to which thieves are known to the police is unusual for such a large city.[10] As soon as a theft is reported the thieves may be warned by a dishonest policeman and thus have an opportunity to move to an unknown location. Even if caught, professionals, such as pickpockets, are too frequently released after paying a fine.

Allowing for this failure to report instances of stealing, *lesiones*, or physical injuries to the person, are still very important. In the 1927-35 series cited above they made up 59 per cent of the cases for men and 75 per cent of the cases for women. One of every five offenders was known to have been drunk at the time the "injury" was inflicted. The number of *pulquerías* (taverns selling pulque) was greatest in proportion to population where "injuries" were most frequent and smallest where the rate for "injuries" was lowest. When a transparent spot map for *pulquerías* is superimposed on a spot map for lesiones, a close correlation can be seen.

The large proportion of offenses against property in the juvenile group is probably accentuated by a relative lack of protection for children in Mexico as compared with the United States. Public education has made great strides since the Revolution, but in 1945 only 14 per cent of the delinquents coming to the Juvenile Court were in school. They usually leave school because they are very poor and come from large families. Even if five children have died in the family, there may still be five living. If the mother was a laundry woman, she made in U.S. currency 30 to 60 cents a day (1945). The father might make 70 to 90 cents. When one egg cost 6 cents and a pound of meat 70 cents, how could one to one and a half dollars a day support a family of seven? There was no money for books, paper and writing materials. As a result, progress in school slowed down. Finally the child dropped school. Mother insisted that he must help. The easiest and poorest occupation is that of basket carrier in a market. Boys got two to two and a half cents for carrying a basket and made 20 to 30 cents a day.

Another occupation for a child who drops out of school early is selling on the streets—newspapers, lottery tickets, candy, or fruit. Shining shoes is more difficult. The child must buy a box and other equipment. Somewhat higher in status is work with the *artesanos* who run small shops—cobblers, plumbers, tailors. The boy is an apprentice in such a shop only by word of mouth. Actually he is a servant. He does all sorts of jobs. He may be sent to buy pulque. His pay is 30 to 60 cents a week. If he learns the craft, he has to pick it up by himself using the trial and error method.

Much work, such as the making of boxes for shoes or for matches, the fabrication of paper flowers, the sewing of men's shirts or women's underwear, the sacking of candy as in the *vecindad* described above, is done at home in Mexico. Children are employed in this work, usually receiving no wages. The mother makes from $3 to $7 a week.

Generally speaking, street occupations are more fraught with danger for children than inside occupations.[11] The great Merced market, which covers many blocks in Ward II, has in the past exhibited the city's highest frequency of juvenile offenses. Recent construction by the Federal District government of new buildings to house the various sections of this immense market has not only improved sanitary conditions greatly but has made stealing more difficult for juvenile shoplifters, or more precisely, stall-lifters.

That the worlds of mature criminals and of minor offenders are closely related is suggested by the variety of ways in which adults facilitate criminal behavior in juveniles. Children exploited as vendors of sundry commodities have numerous opportunities to filch articles of food from the market or automobile accessories from the streets. Frequently adults have been picked up by the Protective Police (Policía Tutelar) of the Department of Social Prevention for using children as beggars. Twelve per cent of 500 cases treated for venereal disease at Morelos Hospital were minors. With the control of the family weakened in 70 per cent of the cases (Series 1) by the absence of one or both parents, it is surprising that more children in the disorganized neighborhoods were not delinquent.

In working toward a degree in social work at the National University, Sra. Esther Juárez, a supervising social worker in the Juvenile Court, made a 1948 study of 300 juvenile delinquents, 80 of whom were recidivists. Although 48 of these minors were not employed at the time of committing their offenses and 20 were pupils in school, the remainder were working in the following occupations: apprentices for various positions (42), bakery workers (32), newsboys (27), basket carriers (23), ambulatory salesmen (22), mozos (male servants) (19), construction workers (18), shoe shiners (17), machete wielders (10), workers (9), workers on trucks (6), prostitutes (4),[12] campesinos (2), seamstress (1).

Sra. Juárez gives a vivid picture of the problem presented to poor mothers who must raise their sons in the central areas of the metropolis. Since she herself reared two boys[13] in this part of the city, she speaks not only from observation as a social worker, but also from personal experience. Young boys find few opportunities for wholesome recreation in these central slums. Mothers fear that their sons will come under the evil influence of *pandillas* (gangs). As long as possible they keep the boys in the patios of the vecindades, crowded unsatisfactory places to play. If they live within twenty or thirty blocks of a public sport field today, in spite of heavy traffic, the older boys can make it to the field.

Thus juvenile delinquency, which in the rural areas of Mexico remains a minor problem, has long been recognized as a challenge in the metropolis. This seems to grow out of the social disorganization and lack of protection for children to be found in both the central and peripheral areas of the capital. Street occupations are especially hazardous. The poverty of the masses in Mexico City is reflected in the high incidence of stealing by both girls and boys. Still, the problem is not as serious as in the larger metropolitan areas north of the Border. Industrialization and delinquency tend to increase together.

Tossing roof tiles for a new unit in a Mexico City motel, with rounds of laughter when they missed. Bars on the window and a high wire fence are to protect against thieves.

11

Homicide to Thievery

Crimes against property are more frequent in the United States than crimes against the person. Except for urban juveniles, the reverse is true in Mexico. A study of 2,237 offenses committed by adults in Oaxaca State shows a preponderance of crimes of personal violence. When the thirty-seven different types of offenses reported to the Court of Second Instance in the capital of the state during a twelve-month period ending August 31, 1945, are tallied for each district, the three leading ones are: physical injuries to the person (27 per cent), homicide (18 per cent), and stealing (12 per cent). The ratio of injuries to homicide is three to two; that of homicide to stealing, three to two. In no district is stealing more prevalent than injuries and homicide combined. Since most of the cases involved campesinos or, in the towns, manual workers, these figures reflect the passionate, often inebriate nature of lower-class crime.

For persons detained in the Oaxaca State Penitentiary (Cárcel de Santa Catarina), the ratio of violent crimes to stealing was ten to one. On March 25, 1949, there were among 212 prisoners, 98 cases of homicide, 18 of injuries, and 12 of stealing (*robo*). For 57 the crime was not specified. Of the 25 serious crimes (*delitos*) coming to the attention of the Oaxaca City police during January of that year, there was only one case of *robo*, and that also involved an injury. Police have noted a slight increase in stealing since the completion of the Inter-American Highway from Mexico City, but few local residents are involved. Thieves come in from the metropolis on trucks, steal a few items, and are gone again. In recent years there has been some increase in bicycle theft in Oaxaca City, but as yet (1961) no auto thief has been sent to prison.

In 1949 the Inspector General of Police for the state of Oaxaca, José González Alvarez, emphasized the bloody character of Mexican crimes. Although on the Isthmus of Tehuantepec guns are used, murder in most of Oaxaca is by machete, knife, or dagger.

Criminal behavior in Oaxaca City exhibits daily and weekly cycles. Few serious crimes are committed in the daytime when men are working. Trouble for the police begins in the evening. From 6:00 P.M. to 6:00 A.M. there is an average of fifteen cases. To handle these problems the police force is tripled at night. On a weekly basis, police are busiest on Saturdays and Sundays. Fiesta times are also troublesome. Monday is a bit worse than any other work day, reflecting shop attendance problems. From Tuesday through Friday during daylight hours, it is almost quiet on the Oaxaca front.

When Lieutenant Haro, the Inspector General's able assistant, was asked if there were more homicides in the Sierra than in the valleys he said, "No. In the Sierra if a man murders or rapes, the punishment is death, and the same penalty is used for stealing."

Claude B. Finney, who had fifty years of experience as a min-

ing engineer in all parts of the state, told how a pack train loaded
with pesos to pay a group of miners in the Sierra was robbed by
five men. Three of the robbers were captured in the highland.
They were mountain people who had gone away and gotten "new
ideas." One was a cousin of the general in charge of that zone.
When told of his relative's arrest, the general replied: "*Si rató,
mata*" ("If he stole, kill him"). The three were shot against the
wall of a church. The two others were apprehended in the valley
town of Tlacolula, twenty miles east of Oaxaca City. They were
free after one year in jail.

In the delegation of Xochimilco near Mexico City a study of
123 individuals indicted for serious offenses during the four-year
period ending June 1, 1949, showed an interesting difference between the criminal behavior of lower and middle classes. The
lower-class group, composed of 73 campesinos, 23 unskilled
laborers and artisans, and 10 domestic servants and housewives,
had four times as many crimes against the person as crimes
against property. The middle-class group, made up of 12 merchants and 5 professional people, had the same number of crimes
against the person as crimes against property, except for one
individual who presented a combination of both.

Why are homicides and injuries relatively more frequent than
stealing in states like Oaxaca and among the lower classes of the
Federal District? Most Mexican scholars think that socioeconomic
factors are significant. It is true that there is a larger number of
individuals with Indian ancestry in Oaxaca or Xochimilco, but
race is not regarded as of major importance. "If the Indian is
inferior," say the Mexicans, "it is because he is poor and not because he is Indian."[1]

A biological explanation for the relatively high incidence of
blood crimes is, indeed, not needed. Differences in criminal behavior between Oaxaca and Mexico City or between privileged
and underprivileged classes in the Federal District can more
convincingly be accounted for by differences in social situation.
Some pertinent factors in the Oaxacan social setting are: (1)
family feuds similar to those in the mountains of Kentucky or
Tennessee; (2) private disputes over land limits, water, cattle, or
women; (3) disputes between villages over boundaries, religion,
or other matters; (4) drunken fights. A man who knows well the
isolated Mixe country described a cacique who was in the habit
of killing and taking the property. People were afraid for their

lives if they testified against him. Such a man would not remain long among the living, it was predicted. Someday he would go out for his oxen and not return.

In Mexico City, stealing, as compared with injuries to the person, is relatively more important. Especially on holidays or at night when no *cuidadores* are available to watch the car, it is common to return and find a rear view mirror or the hub caps gone. It is a widespread practice to fasten hub caps on with chains, which at least prolongs the time it takes a thief to remove them.

It pays to count your change in Mexico City. At the central post office, for example, there is a sign above the windows which reads: "If the money and stamps go out, no complaint is permitted."[2] Without moving from the window, count your money. If you have been short-changed and say so quietly, the clerk without even checking may flip the stolen peso from the machine. Or when you are buying gasoline at a service station and indicate that the change is 5 pesos short, the boy without hesitation may go back to the manager for the bill that has purposely been withheld.

If one resides in a Mexico City apartment, a large number of keys must be carried. For the entrance door to the building at least one key is needed, sometimes two. The apartment door itself calls for a minimum of two keys, occasionally three. In addition, there is a special key for the wire cage on the roof where clothes are dried and another to guard the gas tank which supplies the kitchen stove. If the car is housed in another apartment building, two more keys are required for entering the outer door there and the garage door. Key cases with snaps for eight keys are popular.

A careful statistical study of the trends and seasonal fluctuations of criminality in Mexico City[3] reports that men presumed to be guilty of offenses against the person (1932-37) made up 55 per cent of the offenders studied; those presumed to be guilty of offenses against property, 35 per cent; others, 10 per cent. The corresponding percentages for women were 64, 28, and 7. It is interesting, however, that the number of sentenced homicides in the Federal District per 100,000 population decreased from 18.0 in 1905 to an average of 8.4 in the period 1927-35. During practically the same interval injuries which resulted in sentences decreased from 1,376 per 100,000 to 161. In 1936 the ratio of presumed injuries to homicides was six to one and to stealing two to one, but the injuries were decreasing and the cases of stealing were increasing. Comparison of a series of men and women who were "presumed delinquents" in the Federal District during the years 1927-36 with a similar series for 1937-47 showed that injuries decreased from 56 to 39 per cent while thievery increased from 19 to 30 per cent.[4]

The total incidence of criminality in the state of Oaxaca is, of course, much less than in the Federal District. Francisco Valencia y Rangel in a study of the "principles of criminal geography for the Republic of Mexico"[5] includes a table and map showing the average annual number of individuals brought to the offices of the police ("presumed delinquents") in each major entity of the country during the period 1932-36. Comparing these figures with the 1930 census of population, the average annual rate per 100,000 for the Federal District was more than four times as high as that for Oaxaca (635 and 154). The rates for murders per 100,000 were, however, exactly even (33); for injuries, five times as great in the Federal District (277 and 55); for thieveries, almost six times as great (145 and 26); for suicides, 22 times (11.0 and .5).

In his 1958 study of criminality in the Mexican Republic, Dr. Alfonso Quiroz Cuarón gives rates for sentenced homicides per 100,000 population for Oaxaca and the Federal District that are equal (6.5). For "presumed homicides," however, his rates are higher by three times for Oaxaca (73.1 as against 26.9). These differences are interpreted as evidence for less effective justice in Oaxaca State than in the Federal District.[6] Explanation of the increase in homicide rate for Oaxaca from 33 in 1934 to 73 in 1958 would make an interesting problem for sociological research.

THE PROFESSIONAL THIEF

A man and a woman who appeared different from most patrons entered the fashionable dress shop on the Reforma where Sra. Z. was manager. The woman said they wished to buy something expensive for their daughter; they could spend as much as 300 pesos. Unnoticed by the manager or her employees, the two were stealing articles all the time the clerk was waiting on them. During a five-minute interval when the *señora* was out of the room they took 225 pesos from her purse. Foolishly she had said something in their presence about having cashed a check. The man certainly did not look like a fond papa nor the woman like his wife. Although it was a warm day, he carried a heavy over-coat. These things the *señora* remembered after the money and goods were gone.

The owner of the shop warned against an immediate report to the police. Instead he employed as detective a police sergeant. Sra. Z. then reported the theft, giving, on the advice of the detective, a false address and name. This was to prevent the thieves from being tipped off. As it was, the detective found them with little trouble. He took pains to have Sra. Z. enter by the back way at police headquarters, when she came to identify them. Although the couple appeared in different clothes, the *señora* recognized them easily. She agreed not to prosecute if they would return certain items—a partial list. These things they brought back. Since this was tantamount to admission of guilt, she then gave a complete statement of losses and they returned everything.

The woman in this instance used her real name. If they had been warned, they surely would have changed at least their addresses. Here again a close relation is suggested between professional thieves and the so-called "preventive" police.

In 1949 a gold mine of information about the professional thief was discovered in the group of special investigators for the Bank of Mexico. The group is comparable to the special police of the Treasury Department in the United States. To answer the writer's questions, Dr. Quiroz Cuarón, Chief of the Special Investigators, suggested a round-table conference with his staff of fifteen.[7]

Promptly at 1:00 P.M. on the following Saturday the men gathered around a spacious table on the top floor of the Bank of Mexico's Guardiola Building. One investigator kept detailed notes. The lively question-and-answer session proceeded as follows:

In the Federal District what type of professional thief is most common and what methods does he employ?

The theft most frequently committed is house burglary. This crime is committed by individuals who have great skill in opening door locks. They are known in the underworld as breakers of padlocks (*chicharreros*) or makers of false keys (*espaderos*). Some break the lock completely, while others scarcely leave a trace of violation. Ordinarily at least two persons operate together in house burglaries. These techniques have been known in Mexico City for more than two hundred years.

How does the pickpocket work? Does he operate alone or with others?

In Mexico City the professional pickpocket begins his career very early, usually working alone in the markets or crowds, snatching purses from the *señoras*. Later he associates with some pickpocket of greater experience who uses him as a "stall" or partner, to distract the victim while the professional pulls out ("hooks") the wallet. They work on trains, streetcars, buses, in recreation centers, churches, and the crowds that attend public ceremonies. In Mexico City there were two female pickpockets, commonly called "Las Charras," an expression referring to feminine horseback riders who do cowboy tricks. These two girls dressed elegantly and operated at grand ceremonies attended by persons of high social and economic position. They were regarded as the most skillful of their kind. They were so bold they went to a wedding, embraced the bridegroom, and "lifted" his wallet! These women also devoted themselves to improving neophyte purse snatchers, providing for and keeping them as lovers until the apprentices acquired sufficient dexterity to work as partners.[8]

Another facet of criminal behavior, not discussed at the round table, is the way Mexico City is used as a home base from which thieves go out and to which they return. When there is a big fair at Aguascalientes, for example, or a fiesta at Tampico, pickpockets and shoplifters stream out from the center. Or again if the situation becomes too "hot" in the capital, they may temporarily seek "employment" elsewhere.

What is the relative social position of various types of thieves in the underworld?

The swindler or confidence man enjoys a better social and economic status than other delinquents. Although he usually has several assistants, he is admired by other thieves because he must have intelligence, skill, boldness, patience, good manners, and knowledge of practical psychology. Whether it is selling to a simple newcomer a guitar that is supposed to be full of gold but actually holds lead, or soliciting financial aid from a gullible American to get from a U.S. customhouse a mythical trunk containing $450,000 in bank notes, the con man is the aristocrat of the Mexican underworld.

The pickpocket occupies middle status between the house burglar and the confidence man. Since his task is also difficult, the falsifier of paper money rates high. In the lowest position of all Federal District delinquents are the counterfeiters of metallic money. Mexico is both the number-one nation in the world in silver output and a country of handicraftsmen. Combine these two and rather frequently spurious silver pesos result.

How do fences operate?

As a rule the buyer of stolen goods owns an establishment to which burglars may come. Usually it has a secret door through which the thief may bring his loot without being seen by the police. To justify the purchase of a stolen article, the fence has connections with a pawn shop from which he secures a counterfeit bill of sale. Between fences in the different states there is an interchange. If a fence in Mexico City is unable to buy some object in the Federal District, he then orders it from an outside salesman. Certain buyers of stolen goods ("*chueco*") operate in automobiles. They make an appointment with the thief to meet at a specified place, buy the stolen articles, and withdraw hastily in the car. If the police succeed in grabbing the thief, he says that he sold the objects to some persons in an automobile and he does not know who they are. In this instance it is very difficult to recover the loot or arrest the fence.

When a thief is apprehended, what methods are used by the so-called "coyotes" to free him?

There is in this city a well-organized band of "coyotes" directed by J. Guadalupe Tostado.[9] This band has a representative in every police delegation. He waits for the arrival of a person who wants quick release. Tostado's "coyote" sees to it that this person is assigned promptly to a judge and takes immediate steps to obtain a bail bond from some company with which he is in contact. If the bail is to be $430, the company will charge 10 per cent plus a 5 per cent federal tax on the transaction, making a total of $45. To arrange things, the "coyote" gouges his client from $70 to $85, but with the exception of a few small mordidas to smooth matters, all he usually arranges is the bail bond. In a case involving physical injuries he may pay the examining doctor 3 dollars for a report more favorable to the client. He does not defend the man, however; his legal training is not sufficient. The substantial balance from what the offender pays him is kept by the "coyote" as his "commission."

If the judge feels that the delinquent will not actually present himself for trial, he may require an additional security in cash, which is deposited in a bank, with the "coyote" as beneficiary. When the client is at liberty, and before the trial, the "coyote" withdraws this security and has that together with his "commission." His victim is free, it is true, but technically is a refugee from justice.[10]

What methods are used by the police to help thieves?

There is widespread public discontent with the ordinary police. The career policeman does not exist in Mexico. A carpenter or other craftsman out of work gets appointed as a policeman, on the recommendation of some politico. He is paid $30 American per month. If he has an opportunity to make $30 or $40 illegitimately, he is likely to do so. Thieves pay tribute in order to work without interference. [This does not answer the question specifically, but it does give the setting for cooperation between ordinary policemen and thieves.]

In 1961 Dr. Quiroz Cuarón reported some improvement in the "preventive police." Each new recruit must now take a four-month course in a police school. During this period he is *internado*, i.e., he lives in special quarters. He receives some pay and gets practical experience in the city center. When he starts as a policeman, his salary is 80 dollars a month.

Three days after the 1949 conference the writer was guided on a criminological tour of the central part of the city by one of the special investigators. There was some hesitation when the latter was asked which was the best branch of the police department. Finally, however, he singled out the Secret Service as better than the others. "Some years ago it was a magnificent body," he said. "It knew well both the general social setting and the underworld. It had spirit. The Secret Service may not be quite as good now, but it is better than the regular police."

After a chat with the head of the Secret Service at Police Headquarters, we visited the central office for a small, carefully selected, federal police force which handles violations involving federal communications. Cutting telegraph wires would be an example. It also fights bogus check writers (federal offenders), helps to prevent the smuggling of contraband on the frontiers (whiskey, cigarettes, and American clothes are most frequently smuggled in), and has jurisdiction over dishonest government functionaries.

Colonel Lameli, subdirector of the Federal Judicial Police, said that a United Nations group had pointed to Mexico as the source for a large share of the world's opium. Sinaloa, Chihuahua, Durango, and the southern part of Sonora are the important states in this production. Poppy plantings are located at the bottom of great canyons in the mountains. When found the plantings are cut down. Two thousand photos show fields before and after cutting. Sometimes an agent has to climb up 7,000 feet and then down 3,000 to reach a pueblo. Three Beechcraft planes had been used, but they were too large to manage well in the narrow barrancas. Small planes can fly in more easily. The bigger planes are good for spotting ground parties and for dropping food and shoes. Shoes are worn out in fifteen days in this rough country.[11]

We then looked at a crowded store on a street corner four blocks south of the Zócalo. On the north side of this location there is an archway into the patio. Thieves enter through this archway to sell their goods out of sight from the police. The shop itself looked like an old-fashioned second-hand store in the States. The show windows contained guns, watches, and furs. Inside there were chairs, radios, pictures, a saddle, religious paintings.

Finally we drove ten blocks north of the Zócalo and parked on the Calle del Organo. Across Calle Argentina to the east is the market called De Granaditas after the street "of the little great ones" on which it is located. It is really a wing of the larger Tepito market. "See all these men moving toward the market?" observed the guide. "They are all thieves. All the goods in this market have been stolen." Three young men were even lugging an old mattress to sell. And as we walked past the numerous displays, he said, "Thieves sell these things; poor people buy them." A blue-uniformed ordinary policeman stood in the middle of the block maintaining order. No doubt he took something from each thief.

It is clear from our discussion that the incidence of criminality is less in the state of Oaxaca than in the Federal District. The rates for physical injuries to the person and for all kinds of stealing are notably lower. The rate for presumed homicides in the hinterland state is higher, however, and homicides are relatively more important there than other crimes. Bloody feuds between families and villages seem to be characteristic of Oaxaca. Drunken fights are found in both areas, but are more frequent among the lower classes of the metropolitan region. In Mexico City stealing is the big problem. Important in the explanation of these contrasts is the basic difference in social setting.

Although this potter in Oaxaca City was a free man, there was a small pottery factory operated by inmates in the old Santa Catarina prison. The social values and life outside are reflected inside.

12

Mexican Prisons and
Conjugal Visits

The more prisons a person visits in foreign lands[1] the clearer it becomes that any place of correction is intimately tied up with the culture of the country in which it is located. English prisons provide food cooked in an English way, bathing facilities of an English type, and a democratic stress on the value of education. On the Continent in German prisons, there are different foods, different bathing customs, and, during the Nazi regime, an

189

emphasis on punishment.[2] Likewise in Mexico the prisons are bound up with Mexican traditions. Nowhere was this better illustrated than in the old Santa Catarina prison of Oaxaca City.

A PROVINCIAL PRISON AND THE "BLACK PALACE"

This chapter will be presented in two sections. The first compares the provincial prison in Oaxaca with the so-called "Black Palace of Lecumberri"[3] as they were prior to 1950. The second tries to explain why Mexican prisoners are permitted to have conjugal visits and their attitudes toward them. The conclusions of this latter section are based largely on 1961 interviews with 42 inmates: 21 in the new Federal District Penitentiary and 21 in Oaxaca.

Legally in 1949 Oaxaca's Cárcel de Santa Catarina was not yet a state prison; it did, however, take long-term prisoners from the various districts of the state. It was located in what was once the Santa Catarina convent. To a remarkable degree this "public jail" reflected the government, occupations, folkways, educational problems, and almost complete absence of professional criminality in the outside community.

On the author's third and most profitable visit to Santa Catarina the warden introduced him to the president of the prisoner group, and he was on his own. "Headquarters" occupied one of the rooms facing the big first patio. At the side there was a Mexican flag as in any *municipio* headquarters outside the prison. Just what is the prisoner government like? There is a president elected by the prisoners for a term of six months or a year. Assisting him there is a secretary and a small group of *bastoneros*, i.e., men who carry the *bastón*, a stick which is still used as a symbol of authority in isolated communities of the state. The bastoneros act as prisoner police. Individuals who cause trouble can be put in isolation for twenty-four hours. All of these officials serve with the president and go out of office when he does.

With no warden or guard near, about twenty interesting-looking prisoners, some with pirate-like whiskers, gathered in the room. They gave close attention to a list of underworld terms that are commonly used in the Federal District's "Black Palace." *Conejo* (rabbit) is, for example, used for prisoner at the "Black Palace"; *ratón* (mouse) for "fish" or new prisoner; *chacal* (jackal) either for a guard or for a prisoner who has committed a "blood crime." These expressions were not used at Santa Catarina. In the

Oaxaca prison "politico" is used for the inmate who plays a role in the prison community similar to that of the politician on the outside; but *barbero* is more common, the implication being that the politician bows and scrapes in servile fashion like a Mexican barber. The term *gente buena* ("right guy") is less common in Oaxaca than *gente de confianza* (reliable person). In short, the underworld slang of Mexico City was practically absent here.[4]

The conclusion is obvious. These were not professional criminals. They were for the most part a group of peasants, some of them with only a rudimentary knowledge of Spanish. As pointed out in Chapter XI, the ratio of crimes of violence to stealing among them was ten to one. Compared with the inmates of the Black Palace they had little knowledge of criminal techniques or organization.

Then there was a tour of the prison, guided by the convict president and an inmate teacher. One room facing the second patio housed a carpentry shop; another, the beginning of a weaving set-up. In still other rooms were a tiny pottery factory and a *huacachería* where the distinctive Oaxacan huaraches were being made. Several men were making hats of palm leaves as they do in the Mixteca region of the state.

Dormitory rooms are usually divided into cubicles separated by walls of newspaper, or cement sack paper, strengthened with stalks of the bamboo-like carrizo. These give a minimum of privacy for the Thursday and Sunday sex visits in which 70 per cent of the 238 inmates in this section of the jail participate. Only when a woman is known as a prostitute is a physical examination required.

The school struggles along in an upper corridor of the thick-walled ex-convent with a couple of big tables, two blackboards, and a number of benches. Matching the general situation in the state, 70 per cent of the prisoners are illiterate. Special instruction is provided for this group, and attendance is compulsory. Books are available for three years of elementary schooling, the average for rural schools outside. The civilian teacher in charge of this work is aided by volunteer inmate teachers.

Prisoners receive 75 centavos (11 cents) a day with which to buy food. They may use this for food already prepared, but many prefer to cook their own. The women who come on visits bring additional food for their men.

There is a separate "Department of Distinction" in Santa Catarina. Each inmate in this division receives one-third more for food. In Mexico, as in certain parts of Europe (the central jail in Vienna is an example), members of privileged classes on the outside enjoy certain privileges when they find themselves inside. "In this department we are people of intelligence," explained the inmate president, and the percentage of illiterates was in fact somewhat lower. "The guards are our friends. They purchase items for us. We tip them—nothing more. They may have to go to the Zócalo [the central plaza six blocks away] to get what we want. The cell-block mayors in Mexico City [counterparts of the presidents here] take many *mordidas*. Here, no."

In the women's section at Santa Catarina there were ten women and one four-year-old child. It is common practice to allow imprisoned mothers to have their small children with them. However, reflecting the double standard, conjugal visits are not permitted for women. Brothers and fathers may visit on Sundays. The kitchen with its little wood fires had a certain charm. Chickens and cats roamed freely. A peach tree grew in the patio and pigeons perched on the roof.

Although the physical plant that in 1949 housed the Federal District Penitentiary in Mexico City is now legally a "preventive jail," it is still known as the "Black Palace of Lecumberri" or simply as "Lecumberri." It has cell blocks on either side of the main entrance and seven additional cell-lined corridors that radiate from a central tower.[5] There are, besides, two circular buildings some of whose thirty-four private cells with their high-walled patios were used by privileged prisoners; and others, with barred ceilings over the patios, by inmates kept in isolation. With a separate cell block for women the prison had a capacity of 2,000 but in 1950 actually housed more than 4,000. Cells originally planned for two inmates were occupied by four—two having to sleep on the floor.

In contrast to Anglo-American prisons, the cell-block corridors are open to the sky. Looking down a corridor from the center of the penitentiary, one can see signs over some of the tall cell doorways reading *peluquería* (barber shop) or *sastrería* (tailor shop). One tailor here was so skillful that a former warden of the penitentiary still brought his tailoring work to him. As in Oaxaca, the world outside is reflected inside.

On a visit to this penitentiary in 1945, with Dr. Núñez, Assistant Director of the Department of Social Prevention,[6] we entered one of these long cell-block corridors just as dinner was being served. The food was ladled out of four large containers into the crude pottery or cans belonging to convicts.[7] It consisted of meat broth, a chunk of meat, rice, lentils, and beans. Two rolls of wheat bread from the prison bakery were allotted to each man who was working; those not working received only one. Breakfast, it was said, consisted of a corn and milk gruel, bread, and beans; supper, coffee with milk, bread, and beans. This is better food than most of the people were getting in the Merced, Morelos, and Moctezuma slum areas which are located within a radius of one mile from the penitentiary.

In a shop equipped with machines owned by the prison, inmates were weaving upholstery cloth for cars or homes. A Spanish contractor said that 86 convicts, including eight women, were employed by him on a piece basis. The average daily wage was 70 cents American. The contract, including a rental, is an arrangement with the warden. The contractor must provide tools and keep the machines in repair. Thirty per cent is deducted from wages for savings and is available when the prisoner goes out or in case of an emergency. A shoe shop was also on a contract basis, but other industries were working under the prison administration. Fifty-five inmates employed in the bakery, for example, were receiving from 70 cents to $3.00 per week. Only three earned the top amount, the chief baker included. This *jefe* had trained in bakery techniques many "boys" who previously had known nothing about the work. They made plain rolls for the convicts, sweetened breads for the guards.

The count on this day, August 21, 1945, was 2,246, including the 203 women. Between 400 and 500 were working in the various shops, the number varying with the amount of work available. Twelve hundred dollars a week were being paid out to convicts for the work done. Some 200 additional prisoners were busy in their cells on such activities as shoe-shining, barbering, tailoring, and curio-making.

Inspection of one of the "circulars" which had been set aside for conjugal visits produced the following information: A physical examination showing the absence of any contagious disease was required of both man and woman. The man must have a good conduct record. Sometimes conjugal visits were denied when the woman already had nine children whom she had to support. In other words, there were social as well as medical bases for denial. Only about fifty-five visits were taking place each week. These were "contact" visits and were limited to two hours. The man provided blankets; the woman might, and usually did, bring food. Sometimes a tip was given the assistant in the circular who cared for the rooms and loaned mattresses.[8] By 1950 prisoners were permitted to have sex visits in their own cells. A similar policy was followed in the state prison in Guadalajara, where 20 per cent of the men were granted the privilege. The Guadalajara institution permitted wives to spend Saturday or Sunday night with their men.

This unique feature of Mexican prisons is a realistic method of meeting the sex problem. In 1925 it was "firmly established" at the Federal Penitentiary in Mexico City.[9] Not only does it combat homosexuality; it often changes the entire behavior of a convict.[10] It should be remembered that Mexico has a very strong family tradition. Anything that tends to destroy the family meets with opposition; anything that strengthens it is supported. It is believed that the conjugal visit keeps couples together. When the manager of a Mexican hotel gave his assistant cook her free day on Thursday so that she could visit her husband in the local bastille on that day, he was acting in harmony with Mexican mores.

Due primarily to the inclusion of material on the conjugal visit, a 1941 San Francisco address to the Wardens' Association on "Recent Observations of Mexican Prisons"[11] was given nationwide publicity. The ensuing discussion revealed that in at least one correctional institution in our country conjugal visits for prisoners were semi-officially permitted. Austin H. MacCormick in a letter dated April, 1947, said he was there when marital visits were taking place in the Mississippi Penitentiary at Parchman. "They permit them for both white and Negro prisoners, but not many of the white men have visits." At the Biloxi Congress of Correction in 1951 M. E. Wiggins, Superintendent, Mississippi State Penitentiary, admitted conjugal visits.[12]

It is clear, however, that Anglo-American mores would not at present permit the general introduction of this policy in our institutions. It is significant that it was primarily the Negro prisoners in Mississippi who availed themselves of the privilege. Like many Mexicans, the rural Negroes of the Old South are non-literate folk.[13] It is probably for this reason that 70 per cent of the prisoners in the Cárcel de Santa Catarina of provincial, Indian-colonial Oaxaca were permitted sex visits whereas in the Federal District Penitentiary the more urbanized prisoners of the metropolitan area were allowed a much smaller percentage. Although this percentage was less than 5 in 1945, by 1950, under a new administration, it had increased substantially.

There had been a riot at the "Black Palace" in 1948 and a new warden, Colonel Francisco Linares, had been appointed. To tighten discipline, this police chief from Veracruz and friend of President Alemán had replaced many of the guards with ex-soldiers and had organized the convicts into a military corps. Even in the Women's Department the prisoners were drilling. Anarchy had been characteristic of this section. With the introduction of military drill and discipline, however, there was better order. The 260 women were assigned in the worst possible way—two to a cell. They were also grouped by offense. All murderers, thieves, drug addicts, and so on, as in the rest of the prison, were placed in cells adjacent to each other. As a means of improving techniques there could hardly be a better way to help a professional thief than to put him in a cell block where all inmates were thieves.

Children were born in the penitentiary. In fact, there were twenty-three children sharing their mothers' prison life at the time of this November, 1948, inspection. A doctor supervised births and babies. Infants and mothers usually got more milk and better food here than their poverty would provide on the outside. Children could stay in the penitentiary until they were three years of age.

Although 14 per cent of the total inmate population (43 per cent of the women) were illiterate when they entered, only 6 per cent of the inmates were illiterate as of November, 1948. In ten months 375 had learned to read and write. Two civilian teachers of classes for illiterates were very effective. One was technical director for the literacy campaign in the Federal District; the other was an inspector in the same program. All other teachers were inmates who received no monetary compensation but were allowed two visits a week, better food, and better lodging.

Ten convicts were housed in a separate circular because they were regarded as too dangerous to be in contact with other inmates. One of the ten was Jaques Mornard, the man who murdered Trotsky.[14]

An article in *Life* magazine[15] featuring twenty-three excellent photographs of the "Black Palace" quoted Colonel Linares as saying: "We can't run an Alcatraz, a Leavenworth, or a Sing Sing here. We have to run this place *a la Mexicana*." Which means, among other things, that a privileged prisoner may have a large private cell in a circular and employ a fellow inmate as servant. Running the prison in a Mexican way applies also to the marital visits permitted the men and the custom of letting children share prison life with their mothers. It is, in fact, a recognition of the main idea in this discussion, namely, that prisons reflect the general culture of which they are a part.

Mexico has an advanced penal law which emphasizes rehabilitation. The practice of the law, however, leaves much to be desired. As Dr. Mendieta y Núñez, Director of the Institute for Social Research of the National University, said in 1943: "Prisons in Mexico are bad. They are not administered by scientists but by politicians and military men as a way to make money." Penologist Luis Garrido, President of the National University, described specifically the methods used in exploiting the prisoner:

> Our jails are theatres of the greatest immorality. In them the prisoner is systematically exploited by employees or by persons in league with the employees. So-called "coyotes" swarm in the environs of these jails and offer the inmate his liberty for money, which, once obtained, only helps them forget the prisoner.
>
> The prisoner or his friends are exploited by employees who offer comforts, better food, a hygienic cell, or exemption from specified work for a specified sum. The visit of relatives or friends is frequently achieved by means of a certain remuneration.[16]

In short, Mexican prisons reflect both the national and regional cultures with which they are identified. The customs in the Santa Catarina jail clearly mirror those of the provincial, Indian-colonial state surrounding it. The food, industries, educational achievements, and types of inmates in Mexico City's "Black Palace" reflect the social and economic life and the specialized skills in thievery of that burgeoning metropolis. The higher incidence of mordidas in the federal penitentiary is associated with a greater general frequency in the Federal District. The 70 per cent participation in conjugal visits by Oaxacan inmates seems to be sanctioned by the predominance of a folk culture. The decline to about 20 per cent in the larger cities suggests that this practice weakens under the conditions of urban life.

It is difficult for us to see our own correctional institutions as a foreigner might see them. The degree of detachment necessary is hard to come by. The distinctive characteristics of prison communities in the United States no doubt mirror, as in Mexico, the unique national and regional customs of our country.

WHY CONJUGAL VISITS FOR MEXICAN PRISONERS?

The second United Nations Congress on the Prevention of Crime and the Treatment of Offenders (London, August, 1960) recommended that "the advisability of permitting conjugal visits for prisoners should be carefully studied."[17] Since in Mexico, with some variations in administrative policy, all prisons allow this, it seemed opportune during the writer's 1961 sojourn in the Republic to learn the attitudes of various types of prisoners toward the custom, to examine the influence of these visits on inmate behavior, and to reflect on the reasons for permitting them. For this exploratory study it was decided to use a sample of inmates from the new Federal prison for sentenced men— located outside Mexico City, nine miles east of Ixtapalapa—and another sample from Santa Catarina in Oaxaca.

In addition to the usual background questions the schedule employed for the study contained a few on the work system and twenty-six designed to determine the prisoner's knowledge about, experience with, and attitude toward conjugal visits. Other questions were included to help the writer make a judgment as to the role played by the convict in the inmate society. Data from 42 of the 45 prisoners interviewed were adequate to conclude that they were playing one of the following inmate roles: (1) "outlaw," the social rebel; (2) "right guy," pro-convict and anti-administration; (3) "politician," manipulates staff and prisoners to his own advantage; (4) "square John," anti-convict and pro-administration; (5) "ding," the queer or outcast. As Clarence Schrag of the University of Washington sees these types, the "outlaw" is asocial; the "right guy," antisocial; the "politician," pseudosocial; the "square John," prosocial; the "ding," unpredictable.[18] Would we find any relationship between such roles and participation in conjugal visits?

Interviews in the Federal Penitentiary at Ixtapalapa were conducted by the author. Twenty of the prisoners interviewed were a representative sample of the "better behaved" inmates housed in Cell Blocks One and Two (one from every tenth cell), but not of the "less well-behaved" repeated offenders in Cell Block Three or of the disciplinary and administrative segregation cases in Cell Block Four. Four English-speaking inmates with experience in American prisons, two of them citizens of the United States, were added, making a total of 24. Six women who had participated in conjugal visits with six of these inmates were interviewed by Sra. Pozas. Her interviews were designed to get at the effect of the incarceration of the husband and father and of the conjugal and Sunday visits on the wife and children.

Eight of the 21 interviews in Oaxaca were made by the writer and 13 by a rebellious and yet intelligent prisoner raised in Mexico but with a background that included seven years of active duty and thirteen years as an officer in the reserves of a United States military service. The characteristics of this prisoner assistant were such and the "cell" distribution in the corridors of the old convent were so unnumbered and hodgepodge that the sample was biased in the direction of the more rebellious and criminally-minded prisoners. The "Captain's" intimate acquaintance with each prisoner interviewed, however, and with the colorful inmate community, were judged by the author to be definite advantages in this research. Taken together, the two samples give an approximately balanced picture.

Conjugal Visits and Prisoner Roles

When the data on roles played and participation in conventional conjugal visits (those with legal or common-law wives) are combined for Oaxaca and Ixtapalapa, as in Table 7, none of the "outlaws," two of the "right guys," and only one of the "dings" had such visits. Five of the "outlaws," five of the "right guys," and two of the "dings" had contacts with prostitutes. In contrast, all of the politicians and 12 out of 15 "square Johns" had conventional conjugal visits and none of them had contacts with prostitutes. It can be concluded, therefore, as an hypothesis for further testing with a larger sample, that inmates playing asocial, antisocial, or outcast roles in Mexican prisoner communities are likely to have contacts with prostitutes if such are permitted. If prostitutes are not permitted, it is logical to surmise that inmates playing these roles are under strong pressure to participate in homosexual relations. The converse conclusion also seems to hold that inmates playing pseudosocial and prosocial roles are not likely to have, while in prison, either contacts with prostitutes or homosexual relations.

The "square John" is more likely than other inmate types to

TABLE 7. *Roles Played in Prison and Participation in Conventional Conjugal Visits or in Contacts with Prostitutes by 21 Federal District° and 21 Oaxaca State Prisoners*

Role played in prison	Conventional conjugal visits (N = 42)		Contacts with prostitutes (N = 42)		Number of prisoners
	Yes	No	Yes	No	
"Outlaw" (social rebel)	0	6	5	1	6
"Right guy" (pro-convict, anti-administration)	2	9	5	6	11
"Ding" (outcast)	1	2	2	1	3
Politician (cons both inmates and staff)	7	0	0	7	7
"Square John" (pro-administration, anti-convict)	12	3	0	15	15
Total	22	20	12	30	42

° Includes conventional conjugal visits or contacts with prostitutes while at "preventive jail" on Lecumberri Street.

have committed homicide rather than thievery. Ordinarily, he has no connections with the underworld. He seems to choose other *homicidios* for friends and avoids prisoners with such "vices" as smoking marijuana or injecting drugs. It is obvious that he would prefer to have conjugal visits from his wife and would have no use for prostitutes. The "right guy," in contrast, is likely to be a repeated thief. Some of these thieves in the Federal District, supported in prison by the criminal activities of gang members who are still at large, expect on release to return to the gang. They tend to look with disdain on the *homocidios,* calling them novices (*primerizos*). One thief specifically expressed a preference for friends who were "out-and-out criminals" ("*puros delincuentes*"). For repeaters, like many of the "right guys," prostitutes are a convenience. In fact, a petty thief may find it impossible to support a wife.

The "outlaw" with his tendency to exhibit such antisocial traits as lack of conscience and being always in trouble, profiting neither from experience nor punishment, seems to be the least likely among the prisoners to have conventional conjugal visits and the most likely to patronize prostitutes if available. The "ding," whose behavior makes him an outcast in the "society of captives," has difficulty also in arranging normal contacts with women. The politician, on the other hand, with his facility in manipulating people, is even more likely than the "square John" ·to participate in the much-desired conventional conjugal visit.

Conjugal Visits and Mexican Values

Possession of a strong family tradition, as suggested above, is important for explaining Mexican conjugal visits but is not adequate by itself. Mexico has a much lower divorce rate than the United States, it is true, but it also has a high incidence, especially among urban laborers, of both free unions and abandonment. There is in addition toleration for the maintenance of mistresses. No puritanical tradition exists here. Sex is not suspect. In contrast to most Anglo-Americans, lower-class Mexicans who predominate among incarcerated offenders do not seem to be worried by arrangements for visiting that place emphasis on the physical aspects of marriage.

There were, no doubt, historical influences favoring such a custom. Although Spain itself does not permit these visits for prisoners, centuries of Moorish occupation seem to have implanted in that country the harem idea. Spaniards, too, wanted to keep their women away from the rest of the world. Their patio-centered dwellings with only one entrance were ideal for such a purpose. This protective philosophy was transplanted to New Spain. As a result, the Mexican husband does not easily trust his woman out of his sight. He wants to possess her. If he is in prison and has conjugal visits, he feels certain that his wife is still his. It is not only the carnal knowledge that is important but also the spiritual understanding that comes with it. Actually the custom may have originated in Mexico when some high official, placed in prison, was granted either a home visit or a visit from his wife. It is interesting that in Mexico City's military prison inmates with the rank of captain or above are permitted to go out to see their women. Lieutenants and men of lower ranks, however, have visits from their wives in prison. Once established, the practice spread to ordinary prisoners and they have from time to time fought to retain it. It is now regarded as a right, not a privilege. A couple to whom it is denied, without good reason, can get support for its retention by court action.

Then there is this closely related aspect of the Mexican ethos, admiration for the type of person who is *macho* (literally, "male"). The macho exhibits sexual prowess not only in marriage but also in the maintenance of mistresses or the patronage of prostitutes. He is a person of action. "Not all *machos* are leaders, but all leaders must be *macho*."[19] Cuba, for example, shares with Mexico a strong family tradition and a belief in machismo, i.e., the importance of being macho. It also permits conjugal visits for prisoners—or did prior to Castro—and by the payment of a *tajada*, or "cut," "a woman every day." Such visits are available at least to "gentlemen criminals" in most Latin American countries.

In February of 1962 a Mexican national with a long sentence in an American correctional institution gave approximately the following statement in Spanish to the author. His words reveal the high valuation placed by Latin-American prisoners on conjugal visits and their disdain for the homosexual:

> In the prisons of the United States there is better sanitation, better food, better clothing, and more opportunity for education, but we Spanish Americans don't feel human here. We have lost our human sense. A man has a left and a right hand. Without his left hand, his woman, he is not a human being. These conjugal visits are very important for the poor *hombre* with much time. *Latinos* are proud to be men. A leader among them in prison must be a man and must prove this. I saw a guy in a Los Angeles jail who looked like a man when he first came in. Then later he looked like a woman. If a man acts like a girl, we refer to him as "she" and treat him like a girl. I would rather serve double the time in Mexico.

If a Mexican has sex contacts with another male, he is regarded as abnormal. Concerning homosexuality, attitudes are probably more negative than among the working classes of the United States. Although in Mexico City, with its five million people, young men are known to be available to homosexuals, Mexicans hold that this type of behavior should be corrected by any means or, better still, prevented. Although no empirical data are readily accessible, it may be that this prejudice is directed more against the passive homosexual than against the active. In their thinking, it is possible that machismo could be maintained while "treating boys like women," but it would surely be more difficult.[20]

Inmate Attitudes toward Conjugal Visits

Compared with American prisons those in Mexico are definitely more permissive. Guards watch the walls and gates, it is true, but control of the cell block is in the hands of inmates. Two convicts interviewed in the United States before making this specific study—inmates who had served time earlier in Mexico—and four prisoners in the Penitentiary of the Mexican Federal District who had had substantial experience in a variety of American prisons, agree that it is easier to do time in Mexico. It is the greater permissiveness that appeals. A guard in Mexico can force a prisoner to open a letter so that he can check for contraband, but it is against the law for him to read it. With a little money a prisoner may start up a business inside the institution. He can use the phone to order supplies. He may have freedom to work on his own account.

This permissiveness, which men who have served time in both Mexican and American prisons value so highly, does not necessarily reflect a humanitarian regard for the welfare of prisoners. Recently the author used twelve empirical criteria to determine location of a given correctional system on a theoretical punishment-treatment continuum. The lowest possible score was 20 and the highest 140. Comparing correctional systems of five different countries, or parts thereof, by means of careful field studies, gave the following results: England, 107; Western United States, 92; West Germany, 85; Spain, 73; Mexico, 59.[21] Considered separately, the score for Mexico's Federal District was 73; for Oaxaca, 48; and for Tamaulipas in northern Mexico, 56. Even in the best of these three Mexican jurisdictions supervision is lacking for probationers or parolees (true also in Spain); personnel are politically appointed; classification is developed only in a crude way; and in the new penitentiary for men half of the inmates are unemployed. In brief, then, using the widely accepted standards of modern penology, Mexico ranks low.

Formerly the "president" of the inmate group in Oaxaca was elected by the prisoners themselves, but now he is appointed by the director of the prison. Control of the inside is almost entirely in the hands of this president, the inmate secretary, and the prisoner police. It is like a big kangaroo court. The president has the power to put a prisoner in the "*toro*" or "bull," as isolation is called, to have him beaten with a club (one was killed this way), or to have him whipped with lashes that leave permanent scars.

Public welfare grants are not available to help the wives of prisoners, in Mexico. In Ixtapalapa case number 9 (Ixta. 9), for example, the prisoner's former boss had paid most of the defense lawyer's substantial fee, and the wife and children were living in a tenement (*vecindad*) owned by his cellmate.

In the new Oaxaca State Penitentiary, special cells have been constructed for connubial visits. In Santa Catarina, however, only the cubicles (*cantones*) used by inmates in lieu of cells were available for the intimate visits. These flimsy cantones, located on the inside corridors of the *exconvento*, varied somewhat in size but averaged about six feet square. They usually housed three prisoners. Ordinarily there was in the cantón a small cook stove contrived out of a 10-liter can and burning kerosene, or simply three rocks for cooking as in the villages from which many of the men came.

The writer watched the women coming into one of the passageways between cantones on a Thursday visit. Many brought their small children with them. This is not permitted at Ixtapalapa. When the little Mexicana with her three-year-old child entered the huarache-maker's cantón, it was a happy occasion for all of them.

Oax. 3, the "president," commented that "those who do not get visits are the most troublesome men in the prison." Without visits there were more fights and mutinies. Oax. 18, a "right guy," said: "If we don't have sex visits, it could be real tough in here because there will be a lot of people looking for fights and other things like using boys as women." Oax. 17, the inmate secretary, remarked that the prisoners behave better with sex visits—"the desperation goes away from them." Oax. 8, a "right guy" who smokes marijuana and is vicious when drunk, with two homicides on his record, stated that the director permits prostitutes to enter "so there won't be any homosexuals."

At Ixtapalapa conjugal visits were permitted for well-behaved prisoners only and were limited to one woman. Prostitutes were not admitted, but mistresses were. The one-woman rule was enforced by the use of identification cards showing a photograph of the woman, her thumb print, her home address, and her signature. Forty-eight rooms, each equipped with couch, chair, clothes rack, partitioned toilet and lavatory, are provided for conjugal visits. In contrast with Lecumberri only one conjugal visit a week per man was permitted. The number of women participating in conjugal visits from Monday, April 17, 1961, to Saturday, April 22, was 118. Counting women who visit less frequently than once a week, who did not appear during this particular week, it is probable that more than 20 per cent of the 813 prisoners participated in such visits.

On Sundays between 800 and 1,000 relatives and friends visit the prisoners socially. For this purpose, the penitentiary theater is made available between 9:00 A.M. and 5:00 P.M. Since there is no time limit, the family will often bring food and eat dinner with the prisoner. Frequently the wife will come alone for a conjugal visit during the week and then bring the children for a *visita dominical* on Sunday. Sra. Pozas had several interviews with one wife who followed this practice. From these interviews it appears that the family organization had been strengthened by the husband's correctional experience. The regular Thursday visits were a strong bond between them. She thought even more of him than before his incarceration. The relatively non-criminal offense, a second fatal accident with the streetcar of which he was motorman, helped him to maintain his position as head of the family. He checked up on the school work and other activities of the children during the regular Sunday visits and was respected by them. Relatives were helping his family by providing food and lodging. At the time of his offense this inmate was in his second year at the National University. His wife also is an intelligent person.

About one-third of the 22 inmates participating in conventional conjugal visits were legally married. The "square John" described above was one. Two-thirds were either married by religious ceremony only or were living in free unions—neither one legal in Mexico. The accepted method for arranging visits at Ixtapalapa on a free-union basis is to answer personal ads from women listed in a magazine called *Confidencias*. Some of the men who have work in the prison will give all that they earn—the average amount was $3 and the highest $10 per month—to the women who visit them. Visits last from one and a half to three hours at Ixtapalapa. Mistresses sometimes bring food, wives always.

Inmates and staff agree that conjugal visits "keep homosexuality down." In Block Four at Ixtapalapa there were, however, about 15 homosexuals. It is probable that these were exclusive rather than incidental homosexuals. Inmates affirm that five more were at large in the population. One prisoner with experience in American prisons referred to both the segregated and unsegregated "homos" as "queens." Judging from its policies, the administration concurs, but not completely, with the popular Mexican belief, supported by women as well as men, that sexual intercourse is "a necessity for the man." It is convinced, however, that conjugal visits provide the most effective stimulus for obtaining good inmate behavior. Thus prisoners in Cell Block Four are not granted this "privilege" (exclusive "homos" wouldn't want it), and other prisoners have to earn it. The administration may realize also that the more relationships between inmates and their families are strengthened, the less likely it is that these inmates will join subversive groups within the prison society. With the semi-military control over inmate interaction exercised by the staff of most close-custody correctional institutions in the United States, supplemented by the rich program of activities and services provided in many Anglo penitentiaries, conjugal visits are not needed to keep prisoners from rebelling. Even in a new Mexican institution like the Federal District penitentiary, however, most of the control over prisoners is delegated to the inmate mayors in the various cell blocks and to their assistants. Conjugal visits help to offset the injustices that are likely to develop with this delegation of authority to inmates. The prisoners interviewed were surprised to learn that conjugal visits are not permitted in most foreign countries.[22]

The president of the Oaxaca prisoner community at the time of this study estimated that 250 out of the 350 prisoners were having conjugal visits—150 every week, the rest occasionally. Independently and using a different method, the prisoner assistant for this project came up with practically the same percentage, 70. The fact that the estimate given to the author in 1949 was also 70 per cent suggests a consistent policy over a considerable period. That most of the prisoners in the Oaxaca State Penitentiary are "folk" in the sense in which Dr. Redfield used that term has already been advanced as a partial explanation for the difference between 70 per cent and the 20 per cent participation in sex visits at Ixtapalapa. There is also the permission in Oaxaca and in Lecumberri (where about 40 per cent receive sex visits) for prostitutes to visit the prison. It may be that this latter policy which has been in effect at the Oaxaca prison for at least twenty years grew out of an effort to maintain discipline among the "right guy" and "outlaw" elements of a prisoner-dominated society. With sex visits there is less desire either to fight or to escape.

It should be stated, however, that in both the Oaxaca and Ixtapalapa institutions there has been a struggle for control of the drug traffic. At the new Federal District Penitentiary during its first three years (1958-1961) there were seven killings by inmates, several of which were linked with an effort to dominate the traffic in marijuana and heroin.

In our own country, the earlier semi-official practice of permitting conjugal visits at the Mississippi State Penitentiary, mentioned above, has become official. The custom is now strongly defended by both prisoners and staff. One inmate who had served a total of seven years in various institutions commented that he had "seen less rioting, less homosexuality" at Parchman. A staff member declared, "I wouldn't want to be around this place if the conjugal visit were taken away."[23] However, much of the guarding at Parchman is done by trusties, referred to as "shooters" since they are armed with rifles, shotguns, or submachine guns. Such a policy places prisoners in positions with even more power over fellow inmates than is held by the presidents and mayors in Mexican penitentiaries. For this reason alone the Mississippi institution would be given a low rating by most present-day penologists. Here again the conjugal visit seems to be used as a means for maintaining inmate morale in a situation that would otherwise be intolerable.

Loaded with hot rolls he leaves a Mexico City bakery to weave his way through hectic traffic. Perhaps he doesn't pay mordidas but his employer, the baker, does.

13

The Custom that 'Bites'

Any discussion of government should distinguish between law and reality. This is important for Mexico too. Individual leaders have more weight than any body of doctrine, and the actual functioning of a law, whether in labor, farming, penology, or education, is of more consequence than the law itself.

Take, for instance, honesty, an important test for any government. The most revealing of the older statistical studies of crime by Mexicans includes a differentiation between criminality that is known to the authorities and criminality which is either not known or not recorded. The former is largely proletarian because members of the lower class have "scant economic resources" with which to pay fines or bail and much less than enough to hire competent lawyers or bribe fraudulent officials.[1]

There is an old Spanish saying: "Each town has the government it deserves." This is true of Mexico City. In 1949 the ordinary policeman received only $30 a month. Since it took $43 to support a family of four at a minimum subsistence level under the inflated conditions in the metropolis,[2] it is not surprising that the mordida had become more of a custom than a crime. This is illustrated by the practice on the part of the police of supplementing their incomes by extracting petty fines for minor infractions of the law, these "fines" being paid directly to themselves. For example, the owner of a grocery store accidentally closes at 8:30 P.M. rather than eight o'clock as required by law. He gives a peso (20 cents in early 1948) to the policeman, who notices the open store, and the policeman in turn slips 50 centavos to his superior who happens to pass by. Unless the grocer wishes regularly to keep open late, with this mordida the incident is forgotten.

Before red and green lights were installed at the two traffic crossings nearest the Caballito on the Paseo de la Reforma, these corners reputedly called for payments of 20 to 30 pesos a day to superiors in the police department. This meant that a traffic officer on one of these corners had to "bite" at least ten drivers at two pesos each before he could begin to make money for himself. In 1957 the Associated Press reported from Mexico City: "Traffic violators complain that city police are now demanding five pesos (40 cents in 1957) to let them off instead of the two pesos they used to ask."

Three American young women from the University Summer School were out on a date in an automobile with three Mexican men students. At a street intersection they were stopped by a traffic officer for violating a rule. He said the fine would be 25 pesos. The Mexicans protested that they were only poor college students. The officer finally agreed to settle for 5 pesos to himself. The boys suggested tossing a coin for "double or nothing." The policeman was in a sporting mood; the coin was tossed and he lost.

It may be that the incidence of mordida-taking by the police declined a little between 1949 and 1961. This is the conclusion of several Mexican criminologists who are in a position to know the trends. As pointed out in Chapter XI, each new recruit for the "preventive police" (blue uniforms) now receives four months of training before he starts to work as a policeman. The traffic police for the Federal District (brown uniforms) attend school for three months at the beginning of their careers. An increase in courtesy seems to be one result. Inadvertently the writer made a prohibited left turn near the Fountain of Diana the Huntress, at the entrance to Chapultepec Park. He was stopped by one of the policemen stationed at this traffic circle and his driver's license taken. This traffic officer conferred with his companion, letting the writer sit a while. Finally the second *agente de trafico* came over, explained that an infraction had been committed but that it was pardoned, and returned the license.

Still the traffic police of the Federal District do continue to take mordidas. To illustrate: again in 1961 the writer was driving a short distance on the Viaducto Alemán, a new divided highway with two lanes in either direction. Suddenly a motorcycle police-man appeared at the side of the car motioning to pull out. He explained that the legal speeds in each lane were obligatory—80 and 60 kilometers. The motorist had been driving 80 in the fast lane which was correct but then had shifted to the slow lane at the same speed. For this violation the usual fine was 100 pesos ($8), but since the violator was a *turista* the officer would reduce it to 50 payable to him. After giving him 50 pesos a receipt was requested. "For this it would be necessary to go to the office of the delegation," which happened to be impossible because of an appointment. "This is a mordida," the *turista* said. There was no denial. "It is difficult," rationalized the officer, "to buy expensive shoes and uniform on 1,100 pesos a month."

At first one gets the impression that the mordida is limited to policemen. Closer acquaintance with the problem convinces one, however, that it is widespread among government officials. Even in the army the eighteen-year-olds, all of whom were subject to draft in Mexico (July, 1945), sometimes found their lot easier if they gave mordidas to the colonel. Dr. Mendieta y Núñez in his book on public administration in Mexico makes the general situation clear in the following statement:

> The immorality of the bureaucracy which is in direct contact with the public or which exercises any sort of function which affects private interests is beyond any doubt. The immorality of those who manage the material interests of the State is no less

evident. The same public which condemns the hungry little thief who snatches a purse from the hand of some bourgeois señora on the streets of the city, laughs maliciously but with admiration when it speaks of some public functionary or prominent employee, a poor man yesterday and a potentate today, thanks to his bureaucratic accomplishments. . . . For the thief who fails, jail and ignominy; for the thief who triumphs, all the goods of the world.[3]

Since "white-collar crime," as defined by the late Professor Edwin H. Sutherland, refers to "a crime committed by a person of respectability and high social status in the course of his occupation,"[4] the "immorality" of the bureaucracy so vividly described by Dr. Mendieta would fall in this category. There was a deputy who within a few years was able to give two million pesos annually to charity. Other white-collar criminals made their money by dishonestly controlling the market for such items as pulque or sugar. Some ministers have left substantial deficits in the government departments over which they presided. In fact, the handling of money in a ministry is usually covered by a cloud. Only the head and an assistant or two know about it. When subordinates know too much about their chief's activities, it is possible for them to do as they please. If, on the contrary, the minister is honest, it is easier for the personnel to be honest.

A study of the 1945 home addresses of a sample of these big-time mordida collectors showed that all, who were still living in the metropolis and whose homes could be located, had residences in the better neighborhoods west and southwest of the center. More specifically, the colonias represented included the Lomas de Chapultepec, Roma, Colonia del Valle, Tacubaya, Condesa, Polanco, and Cuauhtemoc. This distribution was exactly the opposite of that for conventional criminals.

One day in 1945 at a leading tire factory a general came in with a priority for twenty truck tires. These tires were supposed to sell for 289.50 pesos ($61). Before the general left the factory he was offered 800 pesos for one of them. During World War II all tires manufactured by this company were purchased on priorities provided by either Economía Nacional or Defensa Nacional. The black market for tires in Mexico was supplied entirely from tires secured through the priorities of these two government departments.

Mexico City's Planning Commission is ordinarily interpreted as a product of civic enthusiasm. That it provides an excellent opportunity for substantial mordidas is indicated by the following statement of a property owner:

> The Planning Commission has proposed seven different projects involving this property of mine. Each was supported by maps and blueprints. They threatened to cut streets through the property. These threats were used as bases for mordidas. Over a period of years I finally got to the man who could decide. Each petty racketeer in the group around this boss got his mordidas. I paid one man who used to work for me 2,000 pesos for information on the others. I finally settled with 5,500 pesos to keep them from going through my property. They also collected from the other side of the street.

Not all government officials take mordidas. Some are honest. Dr. Manuel Gamio went to the United States for several years rather than continue as a high official and participate in Department of Education graft. Dr. Gustavo Baz, while minister of Health and Welfare, turned his salary over to the maternal and child-welfare centers. An increasing number of governors are reported to be honest. Among these could be included in 1961 the governors for the states of Mexico (Dr. Baz), Tamaulipas (Dr. Treviño Zapata), Tlaxcala (Joaquin Cisneros), Durango (Francisco Gonzales de la Vega), and Oaxaca. And some Mexicans have strong convictions against giving mordidas. Manuel Mesa A., a Mexican banker employed by the United Nations, spent a night in a police station rather than pay a mordida. Inspectors, are, however, notorious for their "bites." An inspector from Mexico City suggested to an honest businessman in Oaxaca a crooked way to keep books. In this case without even looking at the man's books he demanded and received a 200-peso mordida. From more important firms his "bite" was five times that.

The Mexican portion of the Inter-American Highway was not finished until 1950. The highway should, of course, have been achieved long before. Embezzlement by contractors (usually generals or other high political figures) and subcontractors helps to explain why the work was not accomplished during World War II. In 1963 the tourist could drive into Guatemala and return by way of the Inter-American Highway, but the "El Tapón" stretch just south of the border is subject to landslides and washed-out bridges. During the rainy season automobile travelers prefer the coast route. A returning motorist, for example, can drive from Guatemala City to Tapachula, Mexico, and have his

car transported to Tonalá or Ixtepec on a railway flatcar. Bringing a car from Guatemala into Mexico by this latter route had
its difficulties, as Mr. and Mrs. Emmet B. Martin discovered
back in 1949:

> First you must get the formal entry papers from customs.
> Then aided by a 10-peso mordida the railroad agent thinks he
> can get you a flatcar. Later there is another 5 pesos to the
> cashier at the railroad, we don't know why. The flatcar is ready
> at 2:00 P.M. and we drive on. There is next a 40-peso charge for
> thirty minutes of work by four men to tie the car on. (We had
> already bought 24 meters of rope for 26 pesos.) For another
> 120 pesos a watchman is hired to stay with the car a day and two
> nights en route from Tapachula to Ixtepec. We go by plane.
> Then we pay the station agent in Ixtepec 185.10 pesos, plus
> the change from 200 pesos, for freight—also to get the flatcar
> switched to the unloading dock. We give a young fellow 10 pesos
> to get the car docked and another 10 pesos when it is actually
> docked. Oh yes, we have a letter from a Texas oil man to a
> coffee exporter in Tapachula. He accepted 30 pesos for insignif-
> icant help! An American who would pay no mordidas had his
> car sidetracked for three days!

It is probable that mordidas are more prevalent in Mexico
City and vicinity than in other parts of the country. The experiences of automobile tourists like the Martins going to or from
Guatemala suggest, however, that mordidas tend to increase
when the person needing service is in a difficult situation in
relation to some law or regulation. We have seen how prison
employees prey on the inmates. The young American couple in
Mexico City who had their marriage date set and invitations out
were practically forced to pay the 50-peso mordida demanded
by a minor official before she would issue the license.

According to Sra. Pozas, the mordida is used as a problem-
solving technique by the residents of Atlapulco. If an individual
wishes to avoid being consigned as a prisoner to the delegation
authorities in Xochimilco, he must pay to the gendarmes at the
sub-delegation in Atlapulco from 5 to 50 pesos depending on the
seriousness of the offense. If he has already been consigned to
Xochimilco, the mordida is larger. If he has been sentenced, he
is able to cut the sentence by the same method.

It has become the custom in Atlapulco for a man who has no
land to acquire the parcel of a widow, if she has no son to work

it, by bribing the ejido authority with 50 pesos. Again, although every sanitary regulation may have been violated, hucksters who collect milk from houses that have cows can avoid having the milk on their trucks seized by paying the inspectors from 10 to 50 pesos varying with the quantity of milk. A desirable location on the market can be secured by a one- to ten-peso mordida to the man who collects the rentals for these locations. The conductor on the streetcar, before this form of transportation was discontinued, would give a lower price for carrying the flowers and vegetables to Mexico City if part of the amount saved was given to him. Sra. Pozas writes that many other pueblos in Mexico are subject to briberies such as these.

Further light on rural mordidas came from an agricultural-machine repairman, whom we shall call Don Enrique. This white-collar worker, whose underlings did the actual repair work, gave 10 per cent of his pay for labor to the manager of the state branch of the government agency for which he worked. Don Enrique's contribution, together with many others, made it possible for this manager to drive a new Nash which cost in Mexico $3,600 to $4,000. The zone chief in the same department held out two sacks of wheat of every ten from the 50 ejidos under his direction. Part of this went to the manager. The assistant to the zone chief got the spillings and driblets for his mordida. In addition to his legitimate family, the zone chief had a mistress with a family. He had built a $4,000 chalet for this girl friend who worked in a bank. Supporting two households made him unusually eager in the quest of mordidas.

Occasionally the method for paying a mordida is indirect. Such was the case of the man who, wishing certain mining rights, intentionally lost $5,000 worth of pesos to a Oaxaca official in a poker game.

In April, 1949, a fine-looking, elderly gentleman was sounding off in the lobby of the capital's Geneve Hotel about "these rotten Mexicans." A fellow American tried to quiet him. It seems the unhappy man was identified with an established American firm that has done water supply and irrigation projects all over the world. Not long before, his company had made a bid to provide water in a certain Mexican state. They asked the governor: "Do you want this to be a rock-bottom bid or do you want it to include graft money? Our company has never paid graft, but will, if necessary." The governor wanted a rock-bottom bid. He got it. Shortly after that the Americans struck water. They knew where to go. Politicos began "horning in" on it immediately. The company had to get a supreme court order, enforced by soldiers, to make them desist. When he went to get the million pesos contracted for, there were only 900,000. "Sorry, that is all we have." Somebody got the extra 100,000 and the company had to bear the loss.

Experiences such as this give point to a Mexican businessman's comment: "The majority of governors have a lot of money when they leave but have not made many improvements." It was alleged by Federico Holm that the large residence which is now the hotel nucleus of Oaxaca Courts was built by a former governor with $42,000 of illegitimate profits. Another former governor of Oaxaca not only left an empty treasury but also a $120,000 deficit when he was forced out of office by a popular uprising engineered by the local Chamber of Commerce. In contrast, one year after taking office Oaxaca's scholarly governor, Lic. Eduardo Vasconcelos, paid off the above debt and had more than $200,000 in the treasury. This was accomplished in addition to building roads, settling land disputes between villages, and establishing new libraries and schools.

It is important to remember that the mordida is not a phenomenon peculiar to Mexico, but, under different names, is widely distributed throughout the world. In Cuba it is customary for an attorney in a government position to do a job more quickly for what is called there a *busca* (perquisite) or a *tajada* (cut). In Peru an official will say: "*Dame mi ala*" ("give me my wing"). The Chinese want cumshaw money. Nikita Khrushchev has complained about bribery in the Soviet Union.[5] A distinguished Mexican scholar told the author of his experience in San Francisco while en route home from Japan. Because he was not using it till he got to Mexico, he wanted his trunk sealed. He arrived late at the customs office. Sorry, but they couldn't do anything for him. A man outside the door asked what was wrong. He could fix him up, but it would cost something. For five dollars the matter was properly arranged.

Petty stealing is not the problem with us in the United States that it is in Latin America. With our great mobility of population and our conflicting cultures, however, in the incidence of serious crimes against property and in the extent of bribery, both of public officials and of private persons, we rank high among the nations of the world. Edwin H. Sutherland, until his death "dean" of American criminologists, stated our problem in no uncertain language:

> In many cities and states an immense amount of white-collar bribery occurs in connection with the purchase of supplies, the making of contracts, the enforcement of regulations, and the enactment of legislation. It is involved when coal is purchased, when school books are purchased, when roads and buildings are constructed, when land is purchased for public purposes, when franchises are granted to railroads, bus companies, and other public-utility companies, and on hundreds of other occasions. Enforcement of regulations regarding insurance, banking, factories, housing, building construction, streets, garbage, public utilities, weights and measures, and most other important functions often is a matter of bargaining between agents of the state and the agencies subject to the law.
> Corruption is extremely prevalent also in private business. Buyers for department stores, hotels, factories, railways, and almost all other concerns which make purchases on a large scale accept and sometimes demand gifts or money payments.[6]

There is no adequate translation in English for the term *mordida,* but Nathan Whetten suggests that its scope includes graft and extortion as well as bribery:

> It might be referred to as "bribery" when government agents close their eyes to infractions of the law upon receipt of a stipulated sum of money from the offender; it could be called "graft" when business transactions require approval of government officials and they refuse to legalize a transaction until they have succeeded in exacting a fee for themselves or their superiors from the person wishing to do business; and it could be called "extortion" when government inspectors deliberately threaten to turn in false reports concerning innocent persons or firms unless they are paid a sum of money in return for making a true report.[7]

The widespread Mexican manifestation of dishonesty in the form of the mordida seems to be an outgrowth, among other factors, of tradition, attitude, and low salaries. Spanish Americans spent three hundred years during the colonial regime hating the government. The feeling became deeply rooted that anything one could acquire through public officials illegitimately was permissible. Businessmen complain that in many government offices in Mexico they cannot get anything done without putting down 20 or 50 pesos as a mordida. With this payment (sometimes much more) the work may be finished in the same afternoon.

A closely related factor is the attitude. When confronted with a flagrant case of graft the American characteristically becomes angry (like the engineer in the lobby of the Geneve), but the Mexican just laughs. Dr. Mendieta adds that he "laughs maliciously but with admiration." The uncle advises his nephew who is contemplating running for senator: "Don't become a senator; but if you do, steal." A changing post-revolutionary society still not only tolerates but expects stealing from its politicos.

Accentuating this custom and expectation is the rapid recent increase in the cost of living without corresponding increases in the salaries of government employees. On the large governmental staff for the state of Oaxaca there were in 1945 only three salaries of 500 pesos per month and three that were over this amount. The latter included the governor's which was 1,500 pesos. Most of the salaries were much lower, ranging down to the mozos who received 75 pesos monthly. A man with a wife and child could not live at a minimum of subsistence level for much less than 150 pesos a month. In Mexico City the economic pressure is, of course, even greater. When General Antonio Gómez Velasco doubled the salaries of his traffic officers preparatory to a drive against mordidas, he was moving in the right direction.

"A cabinet minister simply does not receive a salary high enough for his family to live on respectably, to say nothing about maintaining a standard of living commensurate with his position," writes Dr. Whetten in a letter. "Since upper-class Mexicans are very proud, they naturally will find ways and means of securing the essentials for maintaining standards of living whether the salary is adequate or not."

The mordida is so firmly entrenched in Mexican culture that it will be difficult to eradicate. Honesty will be encouraged when leaders at the top, commended by the groups that support them, set honorable examples for their subordinates. This last applies with equal force to the U.S.A.

With primitive beat the drummer on this church roof in Oaxaca is summoning to a fiesta. In the more isolated communities traditional forms of recreation endure, but commercialized attractions are gaining.

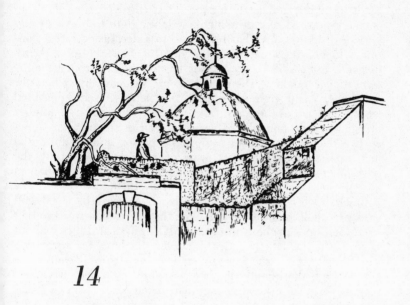

14

Revolution in Recreation

The play life of Old Mexico was centered in the leisurely social contacts and good music of the bi-weekly walk-arounds and in religious festivals with their colorful pageantry and costumed dances. In isolated communities these are still important. But Mexico is in a state of flux. The government is promoting athletics. Traditional ways of using leisure are declining and commercialized forms of play increasing.

In fact, one of the most remarkable changes in any Mexican

217

institution since the fighting Revolution of 1910-21 has been in this realm of recreation. The Revolution brought an increase in personal freedom. One outlet for this freedom was in play. If a person could excel in a sport, it gave him status in a group, or as the Mexicans say, *dignidad*. The economic and technological revolution that has characterized the last twenty years brought with it also an increasing number of semi-skilled and skilled jobs.

When one's work is felt to be menial, dull, and irksome, play tends to be pursued solely for the "kick" involved, and often becomes vicious. Heavy drinking and fighting are frequent during periods of leisure. This has been, and to a decreasing extent continues to be, the situation in the state of Oaxaca. But as work becomes more skilled, the use of leisure is likely to take on a recreational quality. There is still in Mexico City plenty of debauchery and fighting during the periods when unskilled laborers are not at their jobs, as is witnessed by the large number of injuries and homicides. There has been in recent years, however, a decline in offenses against the person and a substantial increase in the wholesome forms of play encouraged by the government. In the past, the rich alone enjoyed participation in athletic sports; now the masses can enjoy them.

Baseball was, to be sure, introduced at least by 1900 and soccer football long before that. The first basketball was brought from the States in the trunk of a YMCA physical director about 1907. Until the late twenties, however, facilities for recreation were limited ordinarily to members in private clubs. Teams were emphasized; the quality of play was high, but there were few players. By 1949 a great change had taken place. Numbers had increased so much that on the sport fields of the Federal District alone during that one year the government's Sport Promotion Administration (Acción Deportiva)[1] supervised seventy thousand persons and gave out to youths, workers, students, and even farmers, 199 trophies, 763 cups of different types, and 6,452 medals. There are still at least forty private sport clubs in the Federal District, but, although their fees vary, the average man does not belong.

About one-third of the Federal District players supervised by Acción Deportiva in 1949 were in soccer football and about one-sixth in baseball teams. Soccer[2] owes part of its popularity to its early introduction and part to the fact that only a ball is required. Padded uniforms are unnecessary. Even goal posts can be improvised with two rocks. No definite number is needed for a team. Three boys with a soccer football can have a lot of fun.

In 1961 the Sport Promotion Administration was supervising a total of more than 14,000 teams in the Federal District. These included around a thousand teams each for baseball and basketball; eight thousand for volleyball; 3,995 soccer teams with 43,945 players (mostly between ages 16 and 24); but only 30 softball and 15 American-style football teams. In addition, it supervised 6,800 athletes in track and field, swimming, *frontón* playing, boxing, roller skating, archery, and wrestling. Ciudad Deportiva, a "Sport City" located two miles southeast of the Zócalo, contains an impressive number of playing fields, courts, pools, and race tracks in its one mile square. It has been estimated that as many as half a million inhabitants of the Federal District enjoy sports in this public area on a weekend.

Since there are few adequate terms in Spanish for matters pertaining to a game like baseball, introduced from the United States, students of language have a lively curiosity in the increasing use of *"pochismo,"* a type of popular slang, by even the most conservative of the Mexico City newspapers. The following expressions have been noted in *Excelsior*: *un hit, el home run, jugar* (to play) *extra innings, el jardín central* (the infield), *el tercer* (third) *strike, el wild pitch*. The tendency seems to be for sporting terms to be accepted first in their English or English-Spanish forms and later to be spelled according to the rules of Spanish orthography. Eventually such terms as the following emerge: *jit, jonron, faul, tim*.[3]

The growing popularity of baseball in Mexico was shown when *Excelsior* for August 17, 1948, just after the death of "Babe" Ruth, devoted the major portion of three pages to pictures and news stories of his life. One of the cuts showed him in Mexico. Each page had a deep black headline concerning the "Bambino." Other papers carried similar stories.

In 1918 Enrique C. Aguirre, generally regarded as the pioneer of modern sports in Mexico, inspired a Methodist group to establish the first playground (*patio de recreo*) in the metropolis. In addition to private *patios de recreo*, there were by 1961 about a hundred and fifty public playgrounds for younger children scattered throughout the Federal District. They are maintained by Acción Deportiva. Unfortunately, these seldom have more supervision than that provided by a caretaker, and their use is so persistent and rough that the equipment is constantly in need of repair. Such was the case in 1949 in Parque España, west of Colonia Roma, where a treacherous slide had jagged holes, one at the top and one at the bottom. There were merely remnants of metal ropes where swings should have been. Playgrounds were in slightly better condition in 1961. Furthermore, by that year the idea had spread to all cities of the Republic.

Construction of the first sport park was started by Aguirre in March, 1929. It was a 40-acre tract (just north of Balbuena on Map IV) that had been used as a city dump. In spite of 250 tons of dumpings to be moved, it was completed in time for the spectacular sport parade that commemorates the Revolution on the third Sunday in November. It is known as Parque Venustiano Carranza. Since that time, in addition to Ciudad Deportiva mentioned above, four other extensive sport fields have been added.

With Major Antonio Haro Oliva, who in 1948 was the head of Acción Deportiva, the writer made a Sunday visit to Parque Carranza. In the big gymnasium a basketball game was in progress between the Treasury Department and the Jordan Hat Factory. A relatively new sight for Mexico, the players were girls in shorts, their uniforms in vivid colors. Athletes who use this gym come mostly from neighboring colonias which include Merced, Morelos, and Moctezuma. On Sunday afternoons wrestling and boxing matches are held here. On weekdays it is dated up for basketball from early morning to late at night.

Later there was a stop at an archery course where sixteen men and women, under the direction of an instructor, were using three targets. This was the first and only course of this kind in the public parks at that time. When the archers saw the major approaching, they gathered around and demanded that the targets be replaced. He later explained these demands by saying that Mexico is the only country where all the materials for games are furnished—uniforms, transportation, play equipment. So far, people have refused to play unless furnished all, or nearly all, of their equipment.

In 1948 the matter of giving everything to players seemed, in general, to be a headache for private sponsors, too.[4] The baseball team that was provided with uniforms wanted fancier ones the next year. No care was exercised in the use of equipment, no responsibility was shown on the part of players, and the maintenance of a team or sport proved to be more expensive than necessary. At that time most sport equipment had to be imported. By 1961 much of it was being manufactured in Mexico, which made it cheaper. Also, real wages had increased a little. Although uniforms were still being furnished by industrial groups, this practice was less necessary. Many industrialists feel, however, that to keep men out of trouble by aiding them to play is well worth the expense.

In 1948 there were twenty-seven fields for soccer football either in Parque Carranza or in the open area east and southeast of the park. On Sundays this great open space was covered with players. There were other vacant meadows on the outskirts of the city that were being used by the 106 physical education teachers in Acción Deportiva. Like the industrialists, many of these instructors believed that their program was keeping men from drinking. It was their experience that a man who has played a hard game is more ready for a shower than a drink. An exception, of course, is the person who was an habitual drinker before he started playing. Their statements agree, in part, with Covarrubius, who in writing about the "Pacific plains" of the Isthmus of Tehuantepec commented that "now young men pass Sunday playing soccer, baseball, or basketball instead of going to church or getting drunk."[5] *Mas deportes, menos vicios* (more sports, fewer vices) is the nation-wide slogan for recreation leaders.

Parque Carranza had also an excellent baseball field with concrete stands where games were played with teams from as far away as Los Angeles. It had a public movie house, sometimes used as a community meeting place; handball courts; courts for *fron-tenis* in which rackets somewhat heavier than for tennis are used, with similar balls; two swimming pools—one for men and one for women; a shooting range; and the National School of Physical and Premilitary Education.

Graduates of the National School could find jobs with Acción Deportiva or in various other recreational organizations, such as the Department of Physical Education (under the Board of Public Education). The latter handles all sports and recreational programs within elementary, secondary, normal, and higher public schools of the country with the one exception of the National University which is autonomous. The problem in Mexican schools, as in the United States, is that too much emphasis has been placed on searching out good performers and developing winning teams. The physical needs of the average student are neglected. The fact that as a rule the diet was poor in 1948, and that there were few agencies outside the school catering to the health and play requirements of children, combined to prevent the optimum in physical development. By 1961, with improvement in nutrition and more healthful living conditions, young people were growing taller than their parents.

That year the National School of Physical Education was operating in a new plant at Sport City. The school is still under political control but the director, José García Cervantes, has a master's degree from the Roger Williams YMCA College in Springfield, Massachusetts. There are 42 teachers, most of whom teach only twelve hours a week at a monthly salary of $104. Many teach also at the National University or in *Politécnico*. There were 400 students, half of them women. Graduation from *secundaria*, the equivalent of nine grades in the United States, is required for matriculation. Since a teacher of other subjects must take only three years in addition to *secundaria*, it is believed in Mexico that teachers of physical education need no more. Subjects like physiology, psychology, sociology, hygiene and nutrition, knowledge of the child and adolescent are taught as they apply to physical education. English is the only foreign language. The emphasis is on training in specific sports.[6]

An example of physical education work in the public schools may be seen in Atlapulco. Boys and girls in the fourth, fifth, and sixth grades learn to play volleyball, soccer football, basketball, baseball, and softball as part of their regular school program. After graduation the boys continue to participate in athletic sports, usually playing Sunday mornings, but occasionally returning early from the chinampas to play in the late afternoons. After the girls leave school they do not have this opportunity for play. They never leave their homes to participate in any sport. Parents prohibit such activity and the customs of the community strongly disapprove it. Why should a girl go out in the street to play when there is always something to do at home, like mending clothes, for example? On Sunday mornings it is proper for girls to attend mass and do the ironing.

Baseball was introduced to the central part of Oaxaca State about fifty years ago by the American miners at Taviche. Spanish merchants brought in soccer football. By 1949 baseball was slightly more popular than soccer. At various times one Sunday in Oaxaca City seventeen games of baseball were being played on the three available fields. As encouragement, buses gave a half-fare rate to visiting teams while the town where the games were played provided food. Boxing is also popular and "the fighting is as good as in New York City." Because of its simplicity and the few level spaces available, basketball is played more than any other game in the state.

"Relax, Señor, Relax"

Then there are the more individualized sports. In the early morning, almost any day, one may see men and women of the wealthy class riding horseback along the bridle trails which parallel the main boulevards of the capital. For those of more modest means cycling is a favorite Sunday diversion. Anyone traveling the highways out from Mexico City on a Sunday may pass men pedaling at full speed on their racing bicycles.

Hiking in the environs of Mexico City and mountain climbing are other favorite leisure-time activities. Surprisingly, hikes and explorations are becoming more and more popular for mixed groups, but organizations plan trips of all types and for all ages. Mountain climbing with competitions and establishment of records yields constant material for the newspapers.

Outdoor camping is approved in the Federal District, but its popularity is curtailed by the lack of personal security from murderous thieves or irresponsible drunks. There is no such thing in Mexico as an organized camping movement with educational intent. Some of the hiking clubs possess cabins. The Boy Scouts (*Exploradores*) own a large tract of land but did not have buildings in 1949, and made little use of the area. The YMCA alone boasts a camp (Camohmila Centro) with comfortable accommodations—two dormitories having a total capacity of forty beds, large dining room and kitchen, sanitary facilities, playfield, a director's cottage. Recognizing a unique educational opportunity, the "Y" is encouraging other agencies to establish camps.

García Cervantes, director of the National School of Physical Education, wants to build a belt of camps like Camohmila around Mexico City. These camps would take boys and girls (separated at first) out of the city during vacation periods and weekends. Teachers would be paid extra to serve as leaders. Some of the fathers and mothers from the Mexican counterpart of Parent-Teacher Associations would help in controlling the children.

Golf in Mexico has a longer history than camping. It was first played there in 1900 with bristly maguey plants as hazards. The

Mexico City Golf Club was incorporated in 1905, the clubhouse completed in 1907. During the Mexican Revolution the establishment was taken over and wrecked by the Zapatistas. The clubhouse was used as headquarters and barracks for troops. Some of the small suites were converted into stalls for favored horses. Full morocco from the furniture was used for saddle bags. Canvas and leather taken from golf bags were made into cartridge purses. "They turned golf clubs into swagger sticks and, casting chicken feathers to the breeze, remade the mattress ticking into uniforms."[7] Nevertheless, by 1938 the Mexico Golf Association included sixteen member clubs. With two exceptions, all of these were located either in or north of the Federal District. The swank Cuernavaca Golf Club, which is a few miles south, and the Alondra Golf Club in Minatitlán, an oil center in southern Veracruz, were the exceptions. By 1961 even Oaxaca had a golf course, used by the elite.

Chapultepec Golf Club on the heights west of the national capital is predominantly English and American in membership. The Azteca Club, a nine-hole course in Chapultepec Park, was in 1949 primarily a middle-class institution, popular with politicos. The area it occupied is now open to the general public as a park and is covered on a Sunday with family groups. The Mexico City Country Club with its 800 members is generally recognized as having the best laid-out and maintained greens and fairways of any golf course in the Republic. It is there every October that national championships are played. In the past these have usually been won by visiting "Anglos." Lockers and showers at the Country Club are luxurious. Although most of the caddies speak Spanish only, they are experts. What pleasanter way could be devised for learning a language? "Suelto, señor, suelto" ("Relax") and "Seguir con los brazos" ("Follow through") warns sixty-year-old Luis, one of the club's best caddies. Again, as in the early history of baseball, many English-language expressions have been taken over without change in spelling. Describing in a four-paragraph article the below-par golf that won the Mexican amateur championship in 1948 for Frank Stranahan of Toledo, Ohio, an *Excelsior* sports writer used the following terms: *el slice*, hole-in-one, *el drive, el bunker, el green*, approach, stroke, putt, *el match*, seven birdies. Also used was the equivalent Spanish term, *pajaritos* (little birds). A unique and satisfying feature of golf at this elevation is that with the same expenditure of energy, drives go about 25 per cent farther than they do at sea level.

Favorite Leisure-Time Activities

"How do you like to use your free time?" was a question put to a sample of eight occupational groups in the metropolis in August, 1947, by Dr. Laszlo Radvanyi, professor of economics at the National University. The results show what male Mexican urbanites like most to do with their leisure. Since those interviewed indicated an average of almost five preferred pastimes, the percentages actually add to 482. The findings are summarized in Table 8.[8]

The top ranking for "being with his family" is further evidence of the important role played by the family in Mexican society. This percentage rises to 58 among proprietors, directors, and managers and to 51 among private employees, but drops to 32 among students and to 30 among artisans. "Mexican artisans work all day in shops that are either in their homes or a stone's throw from home, and when day is done they want a change of scenery."[9] "Going to the movie" was the first choice for workers and small merchants and second preference for proprietors, directors and managers, artisans, and private employees. Seventy-six per cent of professional persons and 58 per cent of students consider the reading of books as one of their favorite diversions, but among manual workers (*obreros*) this percentage was only 33, among small merchants 25, and among artisans 21. The large number of bookstores in the metropolis is additional evidence of

TABLE 8. *Preferred Use of Free Time in Mexico City*

Rank	Pastime	Per cent	Rank	Pastime	Per cent
1	Being with his family	45	11	Attending fiestas	19
2	Going to the movie	44	12	Going to the theater	17
3	Reading books	42	13	Going to bullfights	17
4	Reading magazines or newspapers	41	14	Going to concerts	15
5	Learning something	38	15	Being alone	11
6	Listening to the radio	36	16	Playing cards, dominoes, etc.	10
7	Participating in sports	33	17	Other pastime	10
8	Going to see sport games	29	18	Going to see revues	9
9	Being with friends	27	19	Taking drinks	8
10	Making excursions	24	20	Going to the café	7

interest in books. The popularity of both engaging in and watching sports and also of making excursions gives an idea of the growing interest in the activities previously discussed. "With increase of income," wrote Dr. Radvanyi, "the liking for books, the theater, concerts, radio, and bullfights increases, but the interest in learning something, attending fiestas, participating in sports and playing cards, dominoes, etc., decreases. With increase in age the interest in learning something, going to the movies, attending fiestas, going to the café and being alone diminishes while the desire to be with his family increases considerably."[10]

FROM TRADITIONAL TO COMMERCIALIZED RECREATION

As fluidity of population increases, commercialized recreation gains in importance over traditional forms of play. With increasing contacts some of the customary leisure-time activities change; others die out. Fiestas may become festivals. Rings for bullfights are built larger; prices are higher; as many as six bulls may be killed in one exhibition. Whether the Mixteca handball native to Oaxaca will survive modern means of transportation and communication is a moot question. Under the same influences the delightful *serenata* tends to be forgotten and motion pictures become outstandingly popular.

The religious fiesta was a Mexican tradition long before the Conquest. But its character is altering today. Robert Redfield pointed out that whereas in the very religious, homogeneous, tribal village of X-Cacal, isolated in the forests of Quintana Roo, the fiesta is still a sacred occasion honoring the patron saint, in the coastal village of Tizimín north of Mérida it has degenerated into a secular festival.[11] Over a period of time, especially with increase in the number of persons on the move, the fiesta in any community will undergo some transition. "Paradoxically, the many splendid highways constructed during the last two decades spoil fiestas more than anything else," wrote Frances Toor. "It is only in the villages difficult of approach that the fiestas are still unspoiled and often lovely."[12]

The fiestas of Oaxaca State today represent a combination of the sacred and the secular. The story about the *santo* of San Juan Cópala, which was beaten and bathed after the hated but valuable outsiders had kissed it, has already been told. The annual fiesta of the Virgin of Solitude (*Soledad*), patron saint of Oaxaca, has, of course, its processionals and masses. Picturesque natives from the hinterland come to Oaxaca City for this December festival. A sprinkling of tourists, both Mexican and Anglo-American, also come. At this time, too, the *caballitos* (little horses, i.e., merry-go-round) and other commercialized amusements are set up in the Alameda. The small carnival stays several weeks, then moves to Carmen Alta, San Francisco, and La Merced when these churches have their fiestas. On the Isthmus of Tehuantepec, which has had more contact with foreigners than the rest of the state, fiestas are less sacred and more secular. Sra. Castillo who (in 1949) owned a store in Juchitán on the Isthmus, having lived there since 1923, commented: "Fiestas are only a matter of making money now." The "Spring Festival" in this town still is held on the day of the patron saint, but as Covarrubias pointed out, "it has lost its religious significance and has become a sort of national holiday for the *juchitecos.*"[13]

The variety of handball widely enjoyed by lower-class men in Oaxaca is known to them as *pelota mixteca* (Mixteca handball).[14] Räúl Bolaños Cacho, Director of Physical Education in Oaxaca State, has written a booklet outlining the official rules for this game. In the introduction he urges the farmers of the state to retain this vigorous sport of their Indian ancestors. He commented that it is played in all parts of the state except on the Isthmus "where through the influence of civilization they have resorted to baseball with true passion." In Miahuatlán, sixty miles south of the state capital, Mixteca handball is more popular than either soccer or basketball, ranking next to baseball as the favorite sport.

Swimming folkways seem to have evolved through opposite stages in the more Indian parts of Oaxaca State and in the Federal District. The writer was told that men and women bathe together in the nude in the Zapotec villages of Amatengo and Jalapa in Oaxaca. This was, of course, the pre-Spanish practice. In Miahuatlán he saw men and women bathing nude, near each other but in separate groups. At Tehuantepec the women used to bathe in the nude but too many clicking cameras made them self-conscious. Tapachula, the name of a town in Chiapas, means literally "Cover up, woman." The expression is said to have been used in early times when Spanish men approached.

In contrast, reflecting Spanish rather than Indian tradition, Enrique Aguirre was almost dismissed from the "Y" in Mexico City, and later from the National University, for having the men swim without suits. That custom prevails, however. For the past thirty years men and women have been swimming together—with suits, of course—in the great outdoor pool fed by mineral water from local springs in Cuautla, Morelos (elevation 4,200 feet). As transportation improved and people began to go more to Veracruz and Acapulco, the idea of the sexes swimming together at the beaches became acceptable. Yet when natatoriums were first opened to both sexes in the metropolis, it was only women of questionable character who swam with men. Later the practice came to be more generally accepted. As recently as 1949 during a girls' club meeting, however, the young women showed willingness to swim anywhere, but not with their boy friends. In more conservative Oaxaca City mixed swimming was not at all proper in 1949. In fact, the question was raised as to whether it was permissible for girls to swim under the guidance of a male instructor.

Every Mexican town has its plaza.[15] It is the square around which the town is built. Usually attractive, this little park with its bandstand in the center and broad sidewalk skirting the periphery is where the young people meet. In Cuernavaca, weather permitting, the band plays on Thursday and Sunday evenings. Facing each other as they pass, men and boys saunter one way around the plaza while women and girls stroll the other. The young ladies, often in bevies, dress for this occasion more than the lads. Older people watch from the benches. Occasionally a couple will pair off for the promenade, but this is not usual.

The Zócalo of Oaxaca City is frequented by young people at one or two o'clock Sunday afternoons and the "Llano" (Paseo Juárez on Map II) at five to six on Sundays or, during Lent, on Fridays. The Zócalo is especially popular Tuesday, Thursday, and Sunday evenings from seven to nine. Either Oaxaca's excellent municipal band or a group of marimba players provide music during all of these periods. Here young people may, at the present time, walk around in mixed groups. The ever-present chaperones occupy the concrete benches.[16]

By the time a city reaches the size of Guadalajara the *serenata*, as the Mexicans call this custom,[17] seems to disappear. There are too many competing amusements. The Zócalo, Mexico City's 600-year-old plaza, is occasionally the reviewing center for an impressive parade, as on the Day of the Revolution, but it has no serenata. The metropolis does, however, have Chapultepec

Park which is alive with people on a Sunday. Attired in European style—with colorful dresses and perhaps high heels for the women —members of the middle and lower classes predominate. The zoo in this park is always crowded on Sundays. The monkeys are interesting enough, but more interesting are the people watching them. "The show is not the show but they that go."[18] The types of visitors here vary from farmers in Indian-colonial dress to well-groomed metropolitans. Most members of the upper class, however, avoid the zoo. They prefer to ride horseback or in smooth-riding, perfectly polished limousines.

A part of the poor man's fun is sought in small carnivals (*ferias*). An ample, well-controlled, and relatively safe amusement center has been operating in Chapultepec Park since about 1945. This degree of safety and permanence is exceptional. Usually the owner of one of these mobile "fairs" chooses an empty lot near crowded slums as the place to set up his games and apparatus. For two or three months loud-speakers ballyhoo for customers. Prices are not high, but the ferris wheels, merry-go-rounds, and other equipment are often in dangerous repair. People patronize the feria for a time, then tire of it. Business slumps and the show moves on. This may be the only amusement a poor boy can afford which does not attempt to corrupt him. But sometimes even these ferias include puppet shows and tent comedies with *double entendre* and indecent scenes.

Although there are twenty types of recreational enterprises licensed for tax-collecting purposes in the Federal District, movies take in roughly two-thirds of all the money. In 1944 movies received forty-eight and one-half million pesos; bullfights, five and one-third; theaters, five; soccer, a little more than two; boxing and wrestling, a little less than two; and baseball, one and one-third.[19] The trend for the theaters has been down; for others, up. The income for bullfights, soccer, boxing and wrestling, and baseball was up from ten million in 1944 to eighteen million in 1947. These have been called "the Big Four of Mexico's flourishing professional sports business."[20] Mexico City's soccer stadium will seat 60,000 and the bull ring is the world's largest (1957).

Mexicans appreciate the finesse of gesture and the smoothness of form displayed by the actors as they dominate the bulls. It is the art of it which appeals. They are as wild as Anglo football fans when the bullfighter (*torero*) kneels at the moment the animal charges by him, when he swirls his cape gracefully and turns his back on the enemy, or when he allows the bull to come

so close that blood is left on his jacket. For an excellent perform-
ance such as this, they chant "olé!" and wave white handker-
chiefs as a sign they expect the judge to award him an ear from
the vanquished *toro*. But if the *torero* is clumsy and shows fear,
they hurl insults and cushions at him.

Nine times as important financially in the Federal District as
bullfights, however, motion pictures are a major dynamic in the
life of the metropolis. That they are also significant for other
Mexicans is suggested by the fact that about two-thirds of the
income from motion pictures in the Republic during 1943 was
received by movie houses outside the Federal District (three-
fifths in 1961). The type of picture preferred by these rural folk
is the ranch drama (*ranchera*). Some companies spend all of
their time producing pictures—made in two or three weeks—that
exploit the good-looking horseman (*charro*) and the pretty
daughter of the *hacendado* in a mixture of jealousies, shootings,
and kidnapings. Themes centering around the Mexican Revolution are also popular.

In 1955 there were only five metropolitan centers in Spanish
America with populations of over one million. Buenos Aires and
Mexico City were the most important. Argentina is, in fact,
Mexico's strongest rival in the production of Spanish-language
movies. To get a large distribution for a film, the appeal must
be to the provincial towns rather than to the metropolis. Lack of
education among the masses of Spanish America limits greatly
the level of show that will make money. In addition to the cow-
boy-type of picture already mentioned, slapstick comedies have
a wide appeal. Cantinflas, with his distinctive dress, facial ges-
tures, and language, is Mexico's Charlie Chaplin. In a play like
El Mago (The Magician), where many of his lines have a
double meaning, audiences go into spasms of laughter.

Movie fans in Mexico City like Cantinflas or a definitely Mexican theme if it is artistically achieved, but they prefer American
pictures. For several years the sound reels in these Hollywood
productions were changed and the pictures were exhibited with
a Spanish-speaking Clark Gable or Bette Davis. Since this failed
to appeal to city audiences, it was abandoned. In fact, many
urbanites prefer English dialogue for the opportunity it gives to
learn the language.

All classes in Oaxaca enjoy the movies. Middle- and upper-
class persons may attend two or three times a week. "Everybody
goes. There is nothing else to do." Since the words of earlier

films did not fit the lip movements of the American actors, educated people in Oaxaca did not like the Spanish "dubbing."[21] Conversely, because so many of them could not read, lower-class patrons preferred the dubbing, a method still being used in 1961. And yet even in 1949 provincial Oaxaca was showing a predominance of American films with English dialogue. Printed explanations in Spanish were inserted where needed.

Mexico City's Churubusco Studios, 50 per cent financed by the Radio Keith Orpheum Corporation and probably the best in the Republic,[22] produced more movies in 1948 than any other. Of their forty-five productions during the preceding year only one was in English. The plant is primarily a rental enterprise. Movies can be produced here more cheaply than in the United States. Cameras and sound equipment come from the States and are expensive, but personnel costs are much lower. An actor in Mexico is paid less, but due to the fact that his income tax is only 10 per cent without any surtaxes, he may net as much as a Hollywood star with three times the gross income.

It is the custom in Mexico for actors to come on the lot without having studied their parts. Many scenes have to be reshot because lines have been forgotten. Max Aub, chairman of the National Commission of Cinematography,[23] pointed out in 1949 that the Mexican movie industry does not put as much emphasis as the American on technical perfection. The "Latin temperament" would rather see the actor ad-lib and use his own experience and personality, thus making the picture more "true to life." For this reason the pictures are sometimes unusually good, and at other times outstandingly bad. Sr. Aub feels that the art in Mexican movies is, therefore, more personal and less professional than that of highly industrialized Hollywood.

The facts presented in this chapter show a revolutionary change in amateur sports from small membership in private clubs to large numbers of participants under public sponsorship. The private clubs are still important, of course, and in some activities, such as golf or polo, they dominate. Soccer, baseball, and basketball are more likely to be promoted by public organizations. Soccer, with a head start over baseball, has been able to maintain its lead in the Federal District. In the central valleys of Oaxaca State baseball is slightly more popular than soccer; on the Isthmus, more so. Basketball, promoted by zealous schoolteachers, is the most important game in that mountainous state where space is at a premium. With increase in geographical mobility, traditional forms of recreation decline and commercialized varieties flourish. The bullfights of the Federal District easily hold the lead in that metropolitan area for income taken in by professional sports, but movies are the big money-getters among all recreations. In some respects, and especially for the increasing number of skilled workers, the new play pattern encourages wholesome living; in others it lacks the leisurely charm of earlier days. But whatever one thinks, it has come to stay.

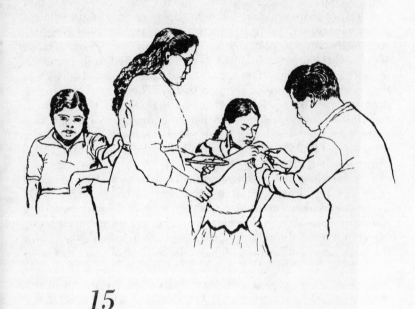

An experienced nurse shows the village teacher in Lachigoló how to vaccinate. With widespread inoculation smallpox is no longer a menace in Mexico.

15

The Dream of Health

There is a toast popular throughout Spanish America that translated reads: "Health and pesos and time to enjoy them!" In another of Dr. Radvanyi's polls a representative sample of the capital's residents were asked what they considered most important for their happiness. Health was mentioned by 76 per cent of those interviewed. Forty-six per cent said peace was a basic factor; 37 per cent, family life; 35 per cent, sufficient money to live without difficulty. Dr. Radvanyi observed that in France a

233

similar study ranked sufficient money more important than health.[1]

In Mexico the emphasis on health can be explained by the serious problems in that field. Although the crude death rate has been declining and is less than that in Chile and much less than that in the United Arab Republic (Egypt), it is above the rates for Uruguay, Argentina, or the United States. Rates for infant mortality, a more sensitive index to socioeconomic status, show a wider range (see Table 9). In this category, for 1960 Uruguay and Argentina are about twice as high as the United States; Mexico, three times as high; Chile and the United Arab Republic, more than five times. The health situation is reflected further in the youthful structure of the population. The proportion of children is large—for those under ten in 1940 almost twice that in the United States, but only 46 per cent more in 1960 due to a sharp increase in the birth rate north of the Rio Grande; and the proportion of older people is small—for those over 44 in 1960 about one-half that in the States.

The doubling of Mexico's population between 1930 and 1960 is, from a health standpoint, a good sign. In the period 1930-34 the average annual mortality rate per thousand inhabitants was 25.6. For 1956-58 it had dropped to 12.6. As in many progressing countries of the world, while the death rate has gone down the birth rate has remained high. By 1958 the death rate had been

TABLE 9. *Crude General and Infant Death Rates for Six Countries in 1945-49 and 1960**

Country	General death rates per 1,000 population		Infant deaths less than one year per 1,000 live births	
	1945-49 (average)	1960	1945-49 (average)	1960
Uruguay	8.6	8.0	57.0	49.1 †
Argentina	9.6	8.1	73.9	59.1 ‡
United States	10.0	9.5	33.3	25.6
Mexico	17.8	11.4	104.5	75.1
Chile	17.2	11.9	149.6	127.9
United Arab Republic	23.0	19.3 †	138.7	145.0 †

* From *Demographic Yearbook 1961* (New York: United Nations, 1962), pp. 269, 271, 225, and 227.

† 1958 figures; later figures not available.

‡ 1959 figure.

reduced to almost one-fourth of the birth rate. According to Gilberto Loyo, Mexican demographer, his country may have a population of 46,000,000 in 1970 and 64,000,000 by 1980.[2]

Communicable diseases have been a major cause of death in Mexico. The most frequent modes of transmission for these diseases are: contaminated food or water for typhoid, amoebiasis, and the dysenteries;[3] person-to-person contacts as for measles, smallpox, diphtheria, and syphilis; insect vectors such as the louse for typhus or the mosquito for malaria (see Table 10). With a reduction of one-half in the mortality rate during the 25-year period between 1932 and 1957, it is obvious that there has been improvement in the techniques for controlling these diseases. Although death rates for communicable diseases have been going down, it is interesting to note that rates for malignant tumors and for diseases of the heart have risen.

Pneumonia rates have also been high as a cause of death, but have declined sharply during the past twenty years. Many families, especially in the "cold country," have had inadequate shelter and clothing for the cool climate at the higher elevations.[4]

TABLE 10. *Average Mortality Rates in Mexico per 100,000 Population for Selected Communicable Diseases by Mode of Transmission, and for Diseases of Older Years, 1938-39 and 1957-58*[*]

Diseases	Average mortality rates	
	1938-39	1957-58
Communicable diseases by mode of transmission:		
Contaminated water or food †	531.34	241.19
Person-to-person contacts ‡	88.03	28.04
Insect vectors §	136.40	49.68
Diseases of older years:		
Malignant tumors	20.65	35.63
Heart diseases	51.83	70.30
Senility	105.03	133.73

[*] From José Alvarez Amézquita *et al.*, *Historia de la Salubridad y de la Asistencia En México*, Vol. IV, México, D. F.: Secretaría de Salubridad y Asistencia, 1960, pp. 381-91.

† Includes typhoid and paratyphoid, dysenteries, gastroenteritis.

‡ Includes syphilis, diphtheria, scarlet fever, smallpox, and measles. (Enumeration for smallpox stopped in 1953 when the rate dropped below .01 per 100,000 population.)

§ Includes typhus and malaria.

The availability of doctors varies widely. The 1956 distribution of physicians was one per 9,985 inhabitants in the state of Oaxaca, one per 600 in the Federal District.[5] These ratios are improving slowly.

HEALTH PROBLEMS IN OAXACA

From the standpoint of public health, Oaxaca is generally regarded by Mexican sanitation specialists as a backward state. The best available index to actual health conditions in the state is contained in an unpublished document, dated August 31, 1948, and commonly referred to as the Larumbe Report.[6] The following excerpts from this report, freely translated and adapted, show interesting aspects of the health situation in this area:

General Hygiene: The populations that rely on public sewage disposal are the following: Oaxaca City, to the extent of 80 per cent; Salina Cruz, 95 per cent, in very bad condition—the vent for this drainage flows into an interior cesspool constituting a danger to public health; Ixtepec City, 10 per cent; Huajuápam de Léon, 5 per cent; and finally Ejutla, 1 per cent. Actually, the conduits in Oaxaca, which were 60 centimeters wide, have been enlarged to 90 centimeters.

Oaxaca City has piped water which comes from three springs and passes through a plant where it is purified by the use of chlorine. Huajuápam de León, Tlaxiaco, Ixtlán, Villa Alta, Yalalag, Mitla, Pochutla, Miahuatlán, and Zimatlán are also supplied with water coming from springs; Ixtepec City, Salina Cruz, and Tuxtepec, with water from wells; and Ejutla, by means of filtration galleries. None of these waters, except that for Oaxaca City, receive any treatment; and the majority of them may be considered as not fit for drinking. Bacteriological examinations have revealed them to be contaminated.

With reference to garbage disposal, there are in the environs of Oaxaca City sixteen garbage dumps and for this reason there is a serious plague of flies, especially in the hot months. This municipal service depends on two trucks which are not adequate for the transport of the garbage. In the other communities of the state there is no garbage disposal, and each household throws its refuse where it thinks best.

Insects: Dangerous insects which are encountered in greatest abundance in the state are the following: The Anopheles mosquito (pseudopunctipennis), transmitter of malaria, is abundant on the Coast, the Isthmus, the Cañada (to the north), and in the districts contiguous to the state of Veracruz. In the districts of Ixtlán and Villa Alta (immediately north and northeast of

Oaxaca City), and to a lesser extent in other parts of the state, one finds flies of the genus *Simulium,* transmitters of onchocercosis, a parasitic disease which often causes blindness. The white louse (*pediculus vestimenti*) which transmits typhus, one finds more frequently in the places of very cold climate, where the activities of the louse substantially destroy the clothing of people. The lack of cleanliness on the part of these mountain dwellers encourages the louse.

Morbidity: Morbidity is figured for the period of four years from 1944 to 1947 inclusive. Unfortunately, it is very relative because of the limited extent of notification in comparison with reality. In Oaxaca City and districts of economic importance, where the influence of the medical world is felt, people report more or less, but in the rest of the state they fail to notify the Health Department in Oaxaca about cases of transmissible disease.

Making an analysis of the morbidity rates, we see that for the year 1947 malaria occupies the position of first importance with 169 cases per thousand, followed by intestinal parasites with 79, dysenteries 33, gonorrhea 25, whooping cough 24, syphilis 15, measles 8,[7] tuberculosis 5, typhoid and paratyphoid 3.

General and Specific Mortality: General mortality in the ten-year period (1938-47) covered by our study goes clearly downward. (Graphs are included which show a decline in general mortality from 28 to 22 per thousand inhabitants. They show in the same ten-year period a decline in mortality rate for whooping cough and the dysenteries of 8 per 10,000, a decline of 4 per 10,000 for typhoid, paratyphoid, and measles, but an increase of 9 per 10,000 for malaria.) Infant mortality in the state, with an average of 113 deaths per thousand births, is not ideal, but as compared with other jurisdictions maintains an acceptable (*sic*) rate.[8]

Food Habits: In the state of Oaxaca food is habitually eaten in three meals: breakfast between 8 and 10, dinner between 2 and 4, supper between 7 and 9. The first and third are practically equal, consisting of a cup of coffee with brown sugar (*panela*), one piece of bread, two *tortillas,* and a plate of beans. For dinner one partakes of some cooked cereal (corn or rice), meat stew, chile sauce, and beans. The average number of calories is a little over 1,000. The consumption of basic proteins is notoriously deficient and the same is true of fats. At the bottom of this general situation is the economic inability to acquire food. The above is more or less what people eat in the cities and towns. Nourishment is more deficient in the villages where it would be possible to say that food consists for the most part of carbohydrates, chile, and the fruits of the season.

Toxicomanias: Alcoholism in the state has caused much havoc for the people. It brings troubles not only to the afflicted persons but also to the social, economic, and moral order of which they are a part.

Deficiency Diseases: Seventy-five per cent of the indigenous population have deficient nourishment (*sic*). It is truly exceptional when an Indian eats eggs or drinks milk. He usually takes these products only in case of sickness. It is in the Mixteca Alta[9] that one sees the greatest prevalence of deficiency diseases. A higher-than-normal percentage of cataracts (which may be associated with vitamin deficiency) is found here in the age group 35 to 45. In addition, large numbers of children in this region die from underfeeding and the lack of indispensable vitamins.

The actual author of this Larumbe Report is Dr. Luis González Piñon, epidemiologist in the Oaxaca State Health Department. Every day he receives telegrams from leading towns listing the transmissible diseases in their districts. As the document indicates, there is much variability in the listing of these maladies. All deaths are reported, Dr. González affirms (others disagree with him on this point), but the "causes" often call for interpretation. For example, "causes" given on a sample of telegrams included vomiting and fever. Interpretations are, of course, aided by the fact that each region in the state has its distinctive pathologies whether they be malaria, onchocercosis, typhus, or diseases due to malnutrition.

Oaxaca City had 53 physicians in 1949, and the rest of the state, with a population of about 1.4 million, approximately the same number. Relatively more sick persons were seen by physicians in Oaxaca City than in Juchitán, for example, which had only four doctors for a population half as large. This situation would account in part for the apparently higher rate for syphilis or whooping cough in official 1948 reports for Oaxaca City. By 1961 the number of physicians in Oaxaca City, according to Dr. González, was approaching 100, while the total in the state was about twice that.

In 1948 the epidemiologist visited the small village of Rio Grande in the district of Juquila. It is located about eighty miles southwest of Oaxaca in the "hot country," near the Pacific. In the two weeks he was there four children died from the sting of the scorpion. If these creatures in the roofs of the jacales are cooled at night by storm winds from the Pacific, they may drop on the sleeping little ones. It is in the hot country, where the venom is more dangerous, that children die, although adults survive. The poison destroys the red corpuscles. If given injections of anti-scorpion serum, youngsters do not die. To preserve the serum for emergencies, there was by 1949 a refrigerator in one of the homes.

Oaxacans call their health department Salubridad.[10] The services of its postnatal clinic are free to mothers of the poor. In charge was the pediatrician, Dr. Guillermo Zárate Mijangos, now with Social Security serving a clientele in a higher socioeconomic bracket. Dr. Zárate had recently completed four years as intern and resident in Mexico City's Children's Hospital, one of the finest of its kind in Latin America. To the author's questions his first response was: "There are two basic problems here: (1) money, (2) education." While he examined the seven infants described below, he kept repeating this emphasis on non-medical factors.[11]

1. This child had bronchopneumonia last June. There had been no other appointment until November and several appointments since then had not been kept. "This is an illustration of the need for education. These mothers do not have the habit of consulting a doctor unless the child is sick."

2. "This infant was born in the maternity section of the General Hospital one month ago. It had bronchitis but weighed four kilos (almost nine pounds). Most mothers do not use this new maternity service. In fact, 50 per cent of the births in Oaxaca City are without either midwives or doctors. Babies are small and are usually born with little difficulty. Sometimes, however, labor is allowed to go on for twenty-four hours before calling a doctor. In the villages no professional help is used."

3. The third child had presented a problem of diarrhea brought on by too frequent feeding. When the feeding interval had been lengthened from two to three hours, the diarrhea stopped. Two factors are involved in such cases: (1) nourishment, (2) infection. The bacteria causing diarrhea in 80 to 90 per cent of the cases coming to Dr. Zárate's attention are of the genus *Shigella*.

4. A thirteen-month infant, still breast-fed only, seemed healthy to the mother but was not. The red blood corpuscles had become too large, indicating macrocytic anemia. "Up to eight months the child in the 'humble class' gets his nourishment entirely from the mother. Sometimes, in fact, mothers feed their babies from the breast for two or even three years. Unless breast feeding is supplemented beginning at eight months, weight usually starts to go down." A special diet was recommended for

this boy to improve his nutrition. The diet required four meals a day, each one including milk and bread; plus fruit at eight; soup, egg, beans, and *tortillas* at twelve; a sweet at four.

5. Although sixteen months old, this child weighed only fifteen and one-half pounds. He should have weighed twenty-two. A complex syndrome indicated pellagra, an endemic disease due to a deficiency in niacin. It would be necessary to work hard to effect a cure.

6. Other children living in the same *vecindad* as this child had the measles. Because of inadequate meals, poor sanitary conditions, and close contact between from ten to twenty children, epidemics spread easily in *vecindades*, the predominant form of housing in Oaxaca City.[12] This child had probably been exposed but did not show the symptoms yet. The measles problem was worse than usual in 1949; among the children he served in his private practice, Dr. Zárate had already seen 300 cases of it.

7. This baby was dirty. Not only his hands and face but his clothes were filthy. To the mother Dr. Zárate spoke sharply: "Wash him with soap before bringing him to the doctor." After the woman had gone, he said this was malaria. Every second day there had been fever. The day of the fever began with a chill, passed to high fever, then lowered again—all in a six-hour cycle. The prescription was paludrine. "Tomorrow he will be better."

Another health service in Oaxaca City is the venereal clinic. A 1944 federal government edict had put the treatment of prostitutes on the same basis as that for other patients. In 1961 there were 160 prostitutes registered in the municipal clinic. Each woman received thirty million units of penicillin weekly. This was intended to prevent her from being infectious for at least eight days. One physician commented that "penicillin is as familiar to people in Oaxaca as Coca-Cola." However, during the year preceding June, 1961, ten cases of venereal disease were contracted by inmates in the state prison from prostitutes who had visited them.

Typhoid fever is rarely seen among the indigenous peoples of Oaxaca, according to Dr. Manuel Rivera Toro, a leading private physician in the state capital (1949). This does not seem to apply to the Oaxacans of the central valleys, however, as will be seen later in the chapter. Soft drinks sold on the streets were dangerous sources of typhoid. In fact, the only safe soft drink bottled in Oaxaca at that time was Coca-Cola.

The exact incidence of active cases of tuberculosis and of deaths from this disease in Oaxaca was not known in 1949. Chest X-rays for the general population were unusual in Mexico City, unknown in Oaxaca. By 1961 persons found by X-ray and confirmed by laboratory tests to have tuberculosis were treated as ambulatory cases. Complete bed rest was out of the question. "The effect is too devastating on the man's family." The *ambulante* continues to work and the family is kept together. If the wife is found to be tuberculous, she also is treated. Various oral medications are used. Children in the family are vaccinated with live, attenuated bacilli.

Dr. Hyman Friedman, whom the author had met in Dr. Larumbe's office, had come from Texas in 1940 to study medicine at the National University. He was soon to complete his required five months of social service at Chilapa de Díaz, three hours south by horseback from Tamazulápan, a town on the International Highway. He had been studying a disease called tropical sprue, which appears to result from a defect in the digestion and absorption of starches and fats in a diet low in protein. It is usually fatal in six or eight months. Liver extract, folic acid, or protein cure it. Here was firsthand information concerning a deficiency disease in the Mixteca Alta.

In Chilapa de Díaz children lack eggs, milk, and meat. They lack lettuce, spinach, carrots, cabbage. They do get mother's milk for twelve to eighteen months. A woman from the neighboring village of Santo Domingo brought her son, a sprue victim, to Dr. Friedman. Apparently one and a half years previously she had noticed sprue symptoms, loss of appetite and a false fatness. Then the father returned from northern Mexico where he had become accustomed to better food. For three months the boy was fed eggs every day. When the father again departed, the boy did not get eggs. Now the symptoms had reappeared. The mother would not believe that it was just a matter of diet. She wanted her son cured with one injection. The doctor explained that without more protein in the food, such as renewing the egg supplement, it would take three weeks of expensive daily injections of folic acid and crude liver extract to cure the child. She returned to her lowly village and did not come back.

"The basic need in Oaxaca is not doctors," argued this troubled young American, "but what to eat, what to plant, how to raise animals." On this point he has the hearty support of most Oaxaca physicians.

Since the time of this conversation with Dr. Friedman a road has been completed from Tamazulápan southward for more than one hundred miles. With the coming of a road, burros tend to be replaced by buses. Helped by better transportation, men who made only three or four pesos per day near home can double their wages by working farther away. When it is necessary to travel eight hours by horse to reach a new school, teachers hesitate to make such a trip. With the road the school is readily accessible. Because of these roads, like the one south from Tamazulápan, the new highway from Oaxaca northward through the rugged Sierra region to Tuxtepec, and the motor route completed in 1962 from Oaxaca south to the Pacific Coast town of Puerto Escondido, a modification in the manner of life results. Improved diet reduces the prevalence of deficiency diseases; the incidence of typhus declines as people become more accustomed to taking baths.

From Dr. Larumbe that day in 1949, and from others in Oaxaca, letters of introduction were secured which gave gracious access to Mexican physicians in smaller centers. Dr. José Llaguno Gil, for example, was then head of Salubridad in Ejutla, forty miles south of Oaxaca on a rough gravel road. His office and home were a few doors from the colorful market place. A graduate of the Institute of Arts and Sciences in Oaxaca, with a certificate as Physician, Surgeon, and Obstetrician granted by the Governor in 1944, Llaguno had lived in Ejutla sixteen years.

The district of Ejutla, which includes the town and surrounding countryside, is a "zone of poverty and few resources." Even on market day only 5 per cent of the rural population visit the town. People are isolated, some having no contacts outside their own families. One *casita* may be two hours on foot from the next.

Only in the principal town, Ejutla, is the water good, according to Dr. Llaguno. Here it comes from a spring three kilometers away and is piped into the houses. "Two other places have 'running' water," the doctor commented wryly. "They are located on the Rio Atoyac."

Typhoid shots had been given selectively for five years: first to merchants of edibles; second to school children; third to clothing salesmen. A small number of persons have been inoculated of their own free will. Vaccination for smallpox began here in 1945.

As in many parts of the world, the number one medical

problem in Ejutla was malaria. In the town itself 70 per cent of the 5,000 residents had the parasites.

Diarrhea ranked next among the health problems. Amoebiasis was frequent in adults. Children have diarrhea because of the unhygienic conditions in which they live and carelessness with food. About one of ten infants die in the first year of life, approximately the same as the national infant mortality rate, hence probably underestimated. A few of these deaths are attributed to scarcity of food, the majority to poor sanitation.

Llaguno was the full-time doctor in this zone. In addition, a private medico worked part-time. Three nurses in the local Salubridad taught hygiene and helped with immunization, and with pre- and post-natal services. Since 1944 Ejutla has had a day nursery for thirty or forty children, three to six years of age. They are accepted without regard to economic need.

Like other Oaxaca doctors, Llaguno feels that the real problem is lack of education. There are many wizards and quacks. While we were talking, a quack in the market close by was broadcasting through a loud-speaker impossible claims for a certain nostrum. Such influences maintain the popular confusion. Some medicos even split fees with the wizards, a practice which aggravates the problem.

Next day everything was ready for a trip into the back country. In his sturdy car the doctor tore along the two blocks to the Health Center ("It is my habit to drive fast"), picked up a nurse and a mozo, bumped over the cobblestone streets of the central "Spanish" part of town, and was soon speeding through the encircling ring of Zapotec huts. Four or five miles south on the main road to Miahuatlán he turned west off the highway onto a narrow side lane which was rough and rocky. The most notable feature of this region—and the same is true in the municipality of Nuxaá and in the district of Miahuatlán—is that many families live in the midst of their fields away from any central village. As in pre-Spanish times, these isolated casitas cut down the necessity for walking long distances to till the crops. They are more sanitary, although less sociable, than the customary village of the present day.

About six miles from the main highway we came to San Agustín Amatengo, a community of 1,700 inhabitants, spread along both banks of the Atoyac River. Amatengo is famous for its mezcal, a kind of Oaxaca whiskey distilled by these farmers from the sweet cooked hearts of various cultivated species of agave. Since mezcal is for them an important export and they would lose economically by drinking it, the villagers actually consume less of their product than do people outside.

After moving cautiously down the rough, steep, winding lane to the river, we forded to the west bank and drove into a court-yard. The family the doctor came to see had the only *molino de nixtamal* on their side of the Atoyac. The mill, run by a Ford engine, was located in part of the large room that was used also for selling calico, for dining, and for sleeping. In one corner a *tapexco* of carrizo poles tied together and placed across two wooden horses served as bed for the head of the household. The census of 1940 reported that two out of every five persons in Amatengo slept on raised platforms like this.

The owner of the mill, whom we shall call Sr. Moreno, com-plained of regularly recurring periods of fever and chill, symptoms of malaria. Using a tiny alcohol stove, Dr. Llaguno sterilized his instruments and gave Moreno two injections. Llaguno often has to operate in dirt-floored dwellings like this—sometimes without a light. A servant then took the doctor to a neighboring casita where her husband was sick with malaria. "This case is from the same source," commented the doctor. Reed walls give no protec-tion from mosquitoes or any other insects. Llaguno recommended a diet of fruit juices, vegetables, and little meat. Without treat-ment, he explained, malaria is progressive; all functions become gradually worse. For the visit to the Moreno household, the doctor was paid twenty pesos plus the cost of the injections. Be-cause they are poor he charges no more.

In the meantime, accompanied by a daughter from the Moreno family, the nurse had been checking on the number in the neighborhood who had not been vaccinated for smallpox. We went out to see how the survey was progressing. We also were hungry. Although the census says that five out of every eight persons in Amatengo eat no wheat bread, we inquired in vain for tortillas served hot from a comal. Sra. Moreno did offer some over-ripe bananas and a few slices of pineapple, but the water, pulque, and bread placed on the fly-infested table were not touched by any of us.

At three in the afternoon, when we again drove through the Atoyac, a dozen women and girls were bathing nude in the shallow water on both sides of the ford. Farther up the river other naked brown bodies could be seen glistening in the sun. Whether these persons were men or women or both, we could not tell. According to the nurse, the two sexes bathe together in this village. That, of course, is the older way. As contacts with the outside world increase, however, males and females tend to separate. Even at this time two young men were sitting on the bank ogling the bathers. Already a bus somehow gets through to Amatengo three times a week. No doubt, as in Tehuantepec, nude bathing here will someday be a thing of the past.

Recently the World Health Organization has been pushing malaria control in many parts of the globe. By 1961 in Mexico the national campaign against malaria was making progress. Its principal objective is to break the life cycle of the mosquito. Measures are taken to kill the larvae in the breeding places and DDT is sprayed into the roofs of dwellings where mosquitoes like to hide. Prophylactic drugs are used in treating persons ill with the disease.

In the continuing campaign against smallpox it is now the policy to cover the entire state of Oaxaca. This is done in a five-year cycle of vaccinations. As a result, the jurisdiction reports only one or two cases a year. In 1934, admittedly an epidemic period, there were 8,000.

MEDICAL RESOURCES IN THE CAPITAL

Three blocks south of the Zócalo in Mexico City one finds the Hospital of Jesus. In its physical structure it is a curious combination of the old and the new. The older section on narrow Pino Suárez was built in 1525, the first hospital constructed in all of the Americas. Just a few years ago the remains of Hernán Cortés were discovered in the venerable church that shares the site. This ancient hospital with its attractive patios is now being used for the poor, some being served absolutely free. But that portion of the hospital facing the commercial Avenida 20 de Noviembre, is completely new. Here on the ground floor are many up-to-date shops while the upper stories house a modern hospital catering to private patients.

The entire hospital has for years been directed by Dr. Gustavo Baz, one of the few Mexicans who are members of the American College of Surgeons. Dr. Baz is, indeed, one of the most loved and revered physicians in the capital. During the Revolution he served as a general under Zapata and at the age of twenty-four became governor of the state of Mexico. His office at the Hospital of Jesus is decorated with beautiful bronzes and with paintings by outstanding Mexican artists. In 1961 he was again governor of Mexico, but continued to make frequent visits to his hospital. The widening of Pino Suárez has cut eight feet from the older side. The plan now is to cut eight more feet and build a new narrow structure on the east front.

Not only does Mexico City have the oldest hospital in the Western Hemisphere, it has also one of the most modern. Its National Institute of Cardiology is a world center for scientific study of the heart. Although the United States and Europe have plans for institutions similar to this, by 1950 at least, these projects had not yet been achieved. The fifteen selected interns in the Mexican institute came from the United States, Canada, England, France, and Latin America, and were staying from eighteen to twenty-four months.

The hospital for this institute[13] was completed in 1944 on a site adjacent to the Children's Hospital. It had 140 beds—42 for women, 42 for men, the rest for children. Eighty-two per cent of the patients pay nothing or a very small amount. Only 4 or 5 per cent pay the full fee. The principal cardiac problem is rheumatic heart disease. In the huge General Hospital across the street, where economically underprivileged patients receive a poor quality of medical treatment, 60 per cent of the cardiac cases are of this type. For private cardiac patients the percentage with rheumatic heart disease is 35.

Separate from the main cardiac hospital is a smaller building devoted entirely to research. Constructed according to the specifications of Dr. Arturo Rosenblueth, it was made possible by a 1946 gift of 400,000 pesos ($80,000) from Manuel Suárez, the first private grant for research in Mexico. This building was completed May 14, 1948, exactly one year prior to the writer's talk with Dr. Rosenblueth. The Rockefeller Foundation gave the money for equipment and continued to make it possible for Rosenblueth to spend six months of each year at the Massachusetts Institute of Technology in Cambridge and for his friend, Dr. Norbert Wiener, the M.I.T. mathematician, to spend six months with Rosenblueth in Mexico. Not limited to the study of the heart in their researches, they were working together on the physiology of the nervous system. The laboratory used by Rosenblueth at the National Institute of Cardiology had six recording machines to measure electrical charges as they are passed through live tissue. In fact, many electrical instruments were being employed in this research.

The National Institute of Cardiology is controlled by a self-perpetuating board. Most of its expenses are covered by private grants. It receives some financial assistance from the government and the only government control derives from that fact. The Hospital for Diseases of Nutrition, located a short distance away, is also autonomous.

The National Medical School in Mexico was about equal in quality, thought Dr. Rosenblueth, to "class-B" medical schools in the United States (at present this category is not used in the U.S.A.). It had 3,000 unselected students (6,644 in 1958), which is too many. All of the medical schools in the state capitals combined had about one-third of this number (less than one-fourth in 1961). In 1949 Buenos Aires had the only class-A medical school in Latin America. The United States had eleven grade-A medical schools out of a total of eighty-two.[14] Ten or fifteen more were acceptable, he thought.

The National Institute of Cardiology, and the Hospital for Diseases of Nutrition which follows the same international policy in the selection of interns, are supplying a need that is met in the United States by grade-A medical schools. Whereas M.C., *médico cirujano* (physician and surgeon), is the usual degree in Mexico, these two institutions are giving the degree of M.D. in cardiology, surgery, or gastrology. It is alleged by a reliable source that a minimum of ten years of full-time practical work in the special field is required. The Children's Hospital, next door to the Institute of Cardiology, has increased its research program since 1948. Its new research center near Cuernavaca focuses on problems of children in rural areas.

The Director of the 88-bed Hospital for Diseases of Nutrition was Dr. Salvador Zubirán, former president of the National University. Dr. Zubirán explained that his hospital deals with the damage done by undernourishment. Here clinical and laboratory observations are made on manifestations of malnutrition in patients. Special attention is given to changes in the liver, in the composition of the blood, and in the nervous system. The head resident showed colored slides illustrating symptoms of malnutrition, e.g., scaly skin, eruptions, black spots on the tongue, whiteness of the area next to the teeth. A little lady of sixty, formerly a rural schoolteacher, now a patient in the hospital, actually had scaly hands, a sore on her leg, and whiteness of gums around the teeth. Roughly stated, her diet had been: *atole* (cornmeal gruel) and bread for breakfast, rice and soup for dinner, *atole* again for supper. Tortillas and frijoles were not included and, of course, no meat, eggs, or milk.

South of these three hospitals a new medical center has been constructed with a capacity of 2,115 beds. The buildings are designed not merely as hospitals for the treatment of various medical problems, but also for training and research.

The first Mexican maternal and child-welfare centers were established in 1937, according to Dr. Enelda Fox, who was formerly director of child-welfare social services in Mexico City under Public Assistance. The method used was to organize simultaneously a voluntary committee of wealthy women and a club of poor mothers. Since it was not difficult to persuade doctors to give a few hours and drug stores to give medicines, it was easy to start a clinic. A day nursery was more expensive but could be initiated by serving dinner only, the other meals to be added later.

During the Camacho regime Dr. Fox led a group of women who requested help from the President's wealthy brother, General Maximino Avila Camacho, in establishing a maternal and child-welfare center that would be a model for the country. The general complied. After his sudden death, funds were granted by his wife—at the insistence of President Camacho—to help continue the center.

On a visit to this impressive institution, known as the Maternal and Infant Center General Camacho, the director, Dr. Antonio Candano, assured us that it is indeed the best place in the Republic for such service. Specialists, like Dr. Larumbe of Oaxaca, are trained here for work in other communities. For the children and their mothers there is a wide variety of medical and social facilities including an auditorium where, for the modest charge of eight cents American, programs combine entertainment with instruction. At times this lecture room is used for giving sex education to older boys and girls.

The Center is located across a boulevard from Los Pinos, the Mexican "White House," but it is also adjacent to the community of Tacubaya, with a 1950 population of 140,000. Tuberculosis, syphilis, and other infectious diseases which have especially high incidence in the poorer part of Tacubaya are treated here. It was estimated that 7 per cent of the children of Tacubaya had syphilis, 12 per cent of the mothers.

Nine social workers and 60 nurses were employed here in 1948. The nurses are graduates from the National University with further minimum training of six months at the Children's Hospital. They received $50 a month for six hours of work daily but were permitted to supplement this by work elsewhere, usually earning a total of $100. They were called *sanitarias*, female health officers, which helped them to avoid the generally low status of nurses in Latin America.

To prevent the spread of infection each child or mother entering the Center was given a preliminary examination. A social worker contacted the client next. Even if it was no more than five centavos (one cent), something was paid for every benefit. An average of 250 children were served in the spacious dining room of the day nursery. The playground was popular. The medical and dental offices, the waiting room, the laboratory, the wing that provided temporary shelter for abandoned mothers, the delivery rooms—all were strictly modern in equipment and functional in architecture. "Why delivery rooms?" it may be asked. In the more prosperous northern part of Tacubaya mothers gave birth to babies at home; but not in the southern part. Temporary shacks were unfit for the birth process.

Dr. Candano found himself increasingly interested in the economic life of the zone from which clients came. Medical problems cannot be solved adequately, he concluded, without attention to the low economic level of the patients.

Visits to homes in the poorer part of Tacubaya helped to make this situation vivid. Señoritas Sánchez and Leje took the writer with them one morning into the poverty-stricken area. The immaculate *sanitarias*, uniformed in crisp white, topped with capes of navy blue, were in striking contrast to the squalor of the slum. The first place visited was a *cobacha*. This means that a bit of ground was rented for about eight pesos a month and on this plot a shack was constructed of whatever was available—in this instance, boards and cartons for siding with tar paper roofing. The earth sufficed as floor. A cluster of perhaps ten such hovels gave the impression of a small "Hooverville." Everything about the cobacha seemed dirty, unkempt, and dark. Sanitary facilities were in the open air. There was, however, a double bed, and a candle burned before "La Morena," the brown Virgin of Guadalupe. The mother in this cobacha had given birth to a baby in the Center fifteen days before. She was examined, the baby was checked, and an appointment was made for her to visit the Center twenty-six days later.

"The poor of Tacubaya are not so poor as those in Peralvillo" (two miles north of the business center), said Srta. Sánchez. One wondered, however, with Dr. Candano how much long-time good could be accomplished by this magnificent Center unless an effort was made to attract industries to this zone or in some way provide a higher level of living for the families served. A child left at the nursery at 7:00 A.M. and cared for hygienically all day loses the value of this care when the mother takes him to a *pulquería* at 6:00 P.M. and gives him a snack of dirty food to munch. Like the dredge at Veracruz: what it takes out during the day, the ocean puts back at night. Certainly without careful follow-up on each case, such as these nurses were providing, much of the value from the Center would be lost.

The program in 1961 remained approximately the same, but Tacubaya had changed. With the growth of the city and the cutting of a boulevard through the northern section, land values had increased. The very poor who lived in Tacubaya in 1948 had moved outward to cheaper areas.

Both public and private health enterprises conducted in any part of the Republic are likely to get direction from Mexico City. For example, three men working with DDT and oil to destroy mosquito larvae at Salina Cruz on the Isthmus of Tehuantepec were employed by an anti-malaria bureau located in the national capital more than five hundred miles away. Campaigns against typhus, tuberculosis, syphilis, and onchocercosis also center in government bureaus situated in the metropolis.

Private physicians may live in the capital and serve clinics or hospitals a considerable distance away. This was true of the young anesthetist and surgeon, Dr. Angel Calvo de la Torre. Dr. Calvo graduated from the National Medical School, interned at the Hospital of Jesus under Dr. Baz, and spent one and one-half years in England during World War II where he became an accomplished anesthetist. A group of nuns and a priest who knew Dr. Calvo were pushed out of Mixcoac in the southwest corner of Mexico City by another Catholic group. They took refuge in Zitácuaro, one hundred miles west on the highway to Morelia and Guadalajara. Soon they sent an S.O.S. to Calvo to come and help them. He said that if they could set up a hospital for him, he would. In fifteen days these energetic people got some of the conflicting groups of the town together—not the

Protestants, but conservative Catholics and radical pro-government persons—and prepared a temporary clinic. Accompanied usually by an assistant, Dr. Calvo drove his old French car to Zitácuaro on Thursdays and Sundays to perform operations. The nuns acted as nurses.

Franciscan and Carmelite nuns were cooperating to make the Sanatorio a success. Realizing that it was too small, they had already acquired a piece of land with a spacious house in the center. Here a larger hospital was established. President Alemán himself had helped the venture with the gift of a *camioneta*.

Turning from free enterprise to "socialized medicine," the Mexican Institute of Social Security, commonly referred to as "Seguro Social," is now an important branch of the Mexican government. Little by little it has come to be accepted by workers and by many employers. It helps to protect workers from the insecurities arising out of disease, work accidents, invalidism, old age, and death. Usually the employer pays 50 per cent of the expense; the blue-collar or white-collar worker, 25 per cent; the government, 25 per cent. For industrial accidents and occupational diseases the employer pays all of the expense. Seguro Social helps when a man marries. If a registered person becomes ill, medicines, medical care, and 60 per cent of the salary are provided. After the death of the wage earner, it gives pensions to the family. Although this organization covers workers in city factories, only a few groups of wage-earning campesinos are benefited.

In the battle against disease Mexicans have been helped by the Institute of Inter-American Affairs, a branch of the U.S. Department of State. The American staff of this institute included in 1949 an administrator, a business manager, a medical director, two sanitary engineers, and a construction engineer. Projects were financed about two-thirds by the United States and one-third by Mexico. Construction of a modern water system, for instance, was usually requested by Salubridad. After completion it would be turned over for operation to Hydraulic Resources (Recursos Hidralicos), a dynamic branch of the Mexican government.

Just a mile east of the Inter-American Highway near the southern border of the state of Hidalgo is the village of Huitzila. Here in 1939 the state government had dug a fifty-meter well, but no pump or pipes had been installed. Led by a young and energetic municipal president this small farming community applied to Salubridad for help. The problem was referred to the Institute of Inter-American Affairs. At the time of our visit the Institute had bought a pump and pipes and was in process of building a concrete reserve tank on the hill above the village. The Institute was also furnishing skilled counsel and paying a foreman. Townspeople (620 in 1940) supplied the unskilled labor by a system of drafting. They also furnished land for the pump house and reservoir. Each householder would pay 40 pesos for his separate water connection. Five connections in a distance of 100 meters was the minimum number permitted. Pesos for the connections were coming in slowly but would no doubt be accelerated when people could actually see the water.

Huitzila is in the heart of the maguey country where much of the nation's pulque is produced. Charles S. Pineo, the construction engineer, and the writer watched the process of harvesting the "honey water" from the maguey, looked at the work on the reservoir, and then visited a home across the dusty lane. Near this dwelling, shaded by pepper trees and rows of organ cactus, and less than one hundred feet from the new, carefully designed storage tank, was a hole in the ground about twenty feet square. It was deep enough to hold four feet of water. Since the season was almost November, however, and the rains had practically ceased, the hole contained only a few inches of water and this was covered with a coating of green algae. In the dry season they push back the algae to use water that is half mud. For centuries Huitzila had depended on rain water caught in holes like this.

Another activity of the Institute of Inter-American Affairs has been the building of health centers. An elaborate center was constructed in the slaughterhouse district about two kilometers northeast of Mexico City's Zócalo. And one was built in Xochimilco sixteen miles south of the Zócalo. This town with its famous canals had a population of 20,711 in 1950; the delegation of Xochimilco, 47,109. There were 36 on this health center staff (1949). Included were six physicians (three of them part-time), fifteen nurses, and five home visitors—all Mexican.

Typhoid shots were being given in Xochimilco on a systematic block-by-block basis. A nurse would visit all the dwellings in the block announcing that injections would be given in a certain house at a certain time. In one instance about twenty individuals took the shots. They showed no fear, nor did they wince during the injection.

Returning to the Health Center we watched a group of school children file into an auditorium where they saw two Walt Disney health movies.

In 1961 the Xochimilco and slaughterhouse district centers were reported to be operating without help from the United States, like the other health centers in the Federal District. The Rockefeller Foundation had in the beginning pioneered with this health work in Xochimilco by maintaining, in cooperation with the Mexican government, a clinic with one part-time doctor, two nurses, a sanitation officer, and a mozo. The records of this clinic over the ten-year period of its operation, 1937-1946, give a clear picture of the general and infant mortality rates for the delegation. The average general mortality per thousand was 27; the infant mortality, 409. (General mortality in the United States for this decade was a little more than one-third of this figure; infant mortality, less than one-tenth.) Recorded cases of infectious and parasitic diseases during the year preceding our visit to the more elaborate Health Center (November, 1948) provide the following totals: gonorrhea 159, syphilis 156, tuberculosis 146, malaria 114, whooping cough 108, amoebiasis 96, measles 36, smallpox 22, chickenpox 22, typhoid and paratyphoid 20, *orejones* (ear trouble) 19, itch 18, diphtheria 14, undulant fever 12, ophthalmia 10, scarlet fever 9, poliomyelitis 4, meningitis 2, erysipelas 1, rabies 1. The epidemiologist asserted that there were, in addition to amoebae, many types of parasites which produce dysentery, the principal cause of infant mortality. Polluted drinking water, lack of sanitation in the homes, and failure to wash hands before eating are preventable factors.

Another health activity sponsored by the Rockefeller Foundation in the Xochimilco area was a study by Dr. Wilbur G. Downs. It was a study of the particular variety of anopheles mosquito that lives in the region between Xochimilco town and Mixquic, a village about sixteen miles east. This region includes Atlapulco. By August, 1948, Dr. Downs had learned enough about the habits of this malaria-carrying pest to be sure of a control. At first, people were non-cooperative. Xochimilco is near Mexico City and this section of the Federal District had been invaded by carpetbaggers ever since the time of Cortés. Any bright young man who wanted to try some questionable racket made an effort to put it over on the natives of this region. Another factor making for difficulty in the villages has been the custom of drinking pulque early in the day. By afternoon there was danger from drunks. Whenever a drunk began to bother, Dr. Downs and his helpers quit at once. Occasionally they have gone out at night to enter houses and capture mosquitoes but only when accompanied by the president of the municipality.

Two experiments in control were made by Dr. Downs: one in Tlaxialtemalco, a village of 156 houses near Atlapulco, and another in Mixquic with 600 homes. Since the owners of four out of five houses in Tlaxialtemalco refused permission to spray with DDT, only the fifth was sprayed. Not long afterwards, however, others came and requested spraying. The people of Mixquic, according to Dr. Downs, were completely sold to the program. "DDT speaks for itself," he said. They "put on a party" for the doctor and his Mexican government associates. They also wrote a letter of appreciation to President Alemán. In Mixquic "I could sleep in the middle of the highway and my billfold would not be touched," he averred. A woman in Mixquic laughingly offered him her baby at a very cheap price. This was the first time a joking attitude had been taken toward the doctor by a native in the Xochimilco area. It was an indication of success.

THE NEED FOR EDUCATION

Madame Calderón de la Barca wrote from Mexico: "The smallpox has been very common lately, but it is owing to the carelessness of the common people, or rather to their prejudice against having their children vaccinated."[15] This was in 1840. And yet in very recent years there was still resistance to vaccination in isolated sierra villages of Oaxaca. When vaccinators arrived in some settlements, the natives would run for the mountains. Many physicians in Oaxaca State agree with Dr. Zárate in saying that the most urgent problems are lack of money and education. Of the two, ignorance is usually regarded by medicos as the more basic.

The following excerpts from a letter illustrate this conviction. An army captain asked Dr. Vera Castro of Tlacolula to describe health conditions in his zone. The doctor answered in part:

> The lack of education is very important in making dysentery and typhoid endemic. The high proportion of illiteracy is the primary factor which explains why people do not understand that by such simple methods as boiling the drinking water, bathing daily, washing the clothes and dishes in daily use, they may in large measure prevent the onslaught of these sufferings.

While the nurses in Tlacolula were vaccinating members of a family for smallpox in 1949, Dr. Vera Castro and the author walked to the back of the cactus-fenced lot. Here was much human fecal matter left on the ground for the sun to dry. During the rainy season it would soak down through the soil into the family's twenty-foot unprotected well and might then become a source of dysentery or typhoid. Again in 1961 Dr. Vera Castro, who now has a private practice in the town, asserted that the sanitary situation was "more or less the same." Almost all the inhabitants have wells and the majority are not protected from contamination.

On a six-day trip to the Isthmus of Tehuantepec the first interview was with a colorful American of seventy years who had settled there, married a *tehuana* and raised a large family. He was at the time of the interview suffering from undulant fever, which may, of course, be contracted from unpasteurized milk. "I drink only beer or Tehuacán (bottled soda water) now," he said. "Need something I can take the top off. Don't even trust my wife to boil milk. She gets to talking with someone and the fire goes out. The milk is served as boiled when it is not."

An interesting and effective device for health education was first used in Peru by Dr. David Glusker. He prepared a series of eight fables on important health topics using the imagery that appears in children's stories in Latin America, familiar symbols from folklore and religion. This series of fables was then published by the ministry of health. The method has since been employed in Costa Rica, Brazil, and Mexico. The results were highly encouraging. For example, in the face of the occurrence of smallpox, there was resistance to vaccination. At one school thirty of one hundred children and one teacher refused immunization. "The Tragedy of Young Mrs. Gomez and Her Beloved Daughter, Serapía," an immunization story, was read and all thirty as well as the teacher went to the hospital for vaccination.[16]

According to President Adolfo López Mateos, Mexico's major problems are lack of education, lack of money, and lack of health. Of these the most crucial is lack of education. And to Dr. Carlos Vejar Lacave, Director of the Central Library for Seguro Social, "learning to read is less important than learning to live." In rural areas Mexicans still sleep, cook, and eat on the ground. For better health they should lift their beds, cook on something higher, eat on a table. They also need more protein in the diet;

they need to learn cleanliness; and they need to know how to avoid parasites.

Educated Mexicans seek the help of doctors more readily, but most physicians live in large cities. In round numbers, of the 20,000 *medicos* in Mexico, the Federal District has 9,000; other large cities, 6,000; rural areas and smaller cities with a total of 18 million persons, 5,000. Men with medical training do not want to live or practice in the country. Good dwellings for their families are not available. There is no refrigeration or heating. And the campesinos are very poor.

In recent years the emphasis has been on preventing illness. Smallpox is practically conquered. Under the influence of the National Commission for the Eradication of Malaria, the incidence of that disease is decreasing sharply. The main victories have been in the control of communicable diseases, but as in the United States, with the drop in these illnesses and the rising life expectancy, deaths from cancer and heart diseases tend to increase. When one million new Mexicans are being added to the population each year, progress is hard to come by, but if the drive to educate the common people and raise their standard of living continues, Mexico's dream of health will someday come true.

At nineteen a Mexico City house-maid is learning to write her name. Since few servants are able to record one's message, telephoning in the metropolis is sometimes difficult.

16

'The House of the People'

A Mexican friend says: "My country is like an old Ford; it makes a terrific noise, but it's going ahead." The most obvious scientific advance is in the field of medicine. Some Mexican physicians have won international reputations in their specialties. But the need for education is felt by these doctors to be even more basic than the need for physicians. Without literacy the people cannot understand the teachings about hygiene. Without education for the masses, not only will health problems remain serious, but efficient functioning of such enterprises as modern factories and large-scale irrigation projects will continue to be hampered.

The national campaign against illiteracy has been a dramatic battle. In 1910 at the end of the Díaz dictatorship 70 per cent of the population ten years of age and over could neither read nor write. By 1960 this percentage had been cut to 38. With the exception of the Federal District, literacy decreases by belts as one moves south from the Border toward the more Indian-colonial, Guerrero-Oaxaca-Chiapas zone. Of the Federal District population six years of age and over in 1940, one in four was illiterate as compared with almost three in five for the country as a whole, and four in five for Oaxaca State. By 1950 these ratios were, respectively, less than one in five, more than two in five, and three in five. The rate for Oaxaca City was 35 per cent in 1940, 28 in 1950. Dr. Whetten found a statistically significant correlation ($+.75$) between rates for illiteracy and rates for "Indianism." "The district in which the city of Oaxaca is located," he writes, "is the only district in that state where less than 75 per cent are living at the Indian-colonial level."[1]

The Catholic Church has in some instances opposed the literacy campaign. In 1949 the priest in the town of Mitla was an agreeable young man educated in Paris and Rome. He was preceded, however, by a padre definitely hostile to education for the common people. The extreme of that point of view appeared during the Cárdenas regime (1934-40) when bands of Catholic Cristeros actually murdered schoolteachers. In their 1948 message to the clergy, the bishops came out positively with the statement that "we must continue with great intensity the campaign against illiteracy," but this exhortation has not been followed by many parish priests.

The army has helped in the fight to make the country literate. In 1949 all eighteen-year-old conscripts who did not know how to read and write were required to attend classes twice a week.

Probably the most important factor retarding the campaign is the absence of any real need for literacy in the isolated villages. Where there are no newspapers and few letters, why should one learn to read?

However, one of the slogans of the Revolution had been "land and books." The village school was a partial answer. Villagers were expected to provide a site, a building, and equipment. Teachers' salaries were paid by the government. Enthusiasm for the school today is reflected in the widely used designation, "the house of the people."

The law now requires attendance of all children six to fourteen years of age, but this is still more of an ideal than an actuality. Many communities do not yet have schools. Half of the pupils enrolled in the elementary schools, 1942, were in the first grade, one-fifth in the second grade, one-eighth in the third. In rural schools where usually only three or four of the six primary grades were available, two-thirds of the pupils were in the first grade.

By 1958 29 per cent of the pupils in urban elementary schools were in the first grade; 9 per cent in the sixth. In the Federal District these percentages were 25 and 11; in the state of Oaxaca, 30 and 9. Looking at this problem in a different way, for the same year 38 per cent of the school-age children (6 to 14) in the Republic were not receiving education. The percentage in the Federal District was 16; in the state of Oaxaca, 55. Still, between 1950 and 1958, the number of scholars in Mexico increased twice as fast as the population.[2] Beginning in 1959 a school building crusade was initiated by President Lopez Mateos. During 1961 alone, nearly 3,000 of the new "instant" schools were "put up by local people, mostly volunteers."[3]

PUBLIC SCHOOLS IN OAXACA STATE

While getting acquainted with Oaxaca State, the author visited eight primary schools. The four-grade *primaria* in the village of Nuxaá was described in Chapter III. Two others were of special interest.

One of these, the *primaria* in Ejutla, shows some of the problems in Mexico's elementary schools. Although the town had about 600 children of school age (approximately 1,000 in 1961), the total matriculation during the preceding year was 273, and the average attendance was 201 (in 1961, 570). Attendance was distributed by grades in 1948 and in 1961 as follows:

Grade	Boys		Girls	
	1948	1961	1948	1961
1	26	89	25	74
2	33	69	20	70
3	21	44	14	57
4	20	23	13	26
5	9	47	6	33
6	8	25	6	13
	117	297	84	273

It will be noted that in 1948 although boys and girls were almost equal in numbers at first, girls dropped out more rapidly. If there had to be a choice in a family, the boy was usually favored. Many parents felt that two years were enough—at least for girls. As in all Latin America, it was the policy to educate boys first, girls if possible. In 1961 this tendency was not evident prior to the fifth and sixth grades.

Then there was Centro Escolar Morelos in Oaxaca City. It is located just below the Inter-American Highway on the northwest edge of town. The 418 students came mostly from the peripheral barrio of Xochimilco and from the district to the west called Ex-Marquesado. In contrast to the pupils in Nuxaá, who were all born within their *municipio*, three out of every ten of the sixty-nine Morelos youngsters in the fifth and sixth grades were born outside Oaxaca City. All of the pupils in Nuxaá lived in homes that were owned by their parents; about half of those in Oaxaca. In Nuxaá two out of ten pupils and in Oaxaca five out of ten included meat in their reports on the food consumed each day. A study made later of a comparable group in Mexico City revealed that eight out of ten had some meat daily. Another food that appears more frequently in family menus as one moves from village to town to national capital is wheat bread.

Of the secondary schools visited in Oaxaca State the most interesting was the new combination secondary and normal school in Oaxaca City. The *secundaria* in Mexico corresponds in grades to our junior high school. The *normal* gives a three-year additional course which prepares for teaching. The Oaxaca Secondary School had, in 1949, 153 full-time students—82 first year (our seventh grade), 46 second, 25 third. In the Oaxaca Normal School there were 58 "professional" students—18 first year (our tenth grade); 27 second (students came in from other schools); 13 third. It is evident that the drop-out rate for both schools is high.

No text was available for the second-year English class. This is a common situation, not only in Mexico but in other Latin-American countries. The teacher regularly put on the board about fifteen English statements. Spanish equivalents were dictated later. The sentences for the first day of the visit covered food and household situations, e.g., "The salt is wet," "The bread is fresh," "The meat is tough (tender)." Understandable mistakes are made by students in trying to pronounce English vowel sounds.

At the next meeting of the class questions were dictated. The most interesting point that came out was the difference in backgrounds for the boys and girls. There were eighteen boys and twenty-four girls making a sex ratio in the class of 75.[4] Since English is a required subject, this group included all the second-year students present on that day. Some of these girls no doubt planned to be teachers. In any case, the monthly income of the father was sharply higher for the girls—twelve over $52 as compared with three for boys. Homes of girls were a little more likely to be owned but, if rented, the monthly rental was markedly higher—six of $6 and over in contrast to one for boys. In general, then, the economic position of the girls was higher. Since boys tend to be educated first, a more comfortable financial status seems to be necessary if girls are also educated.

PUBLIC SCHOOLS IN WORKING-CLASS NEIGHBORHOODS OF MEXICO CITY

Escuela Dr. Mora is a primary school in the northern part of poverty-stricken Colonia Morelos (where during the 1950's two of Oscar Lewis' *Five Families*[5] were living). The director, in 1948, Dr. Teofilo Pérez y Pérez, regularly worked in his private medical clinic during the morning, guided the school's second session in the afternoon (1:30 to 6:30 P.M.), returning to his clinic in the evening. This session was for boys—about 800 of them. The number of classes in each grade decreased regularly from first to sixth. There were five rooms of first graders, four of second, three of third, two of fourth, and one each of fifth and sixth. Whereas in the town of Ejutla 7 per cent of the pupils were in the sixth grade, here only 4.5 per cent were. The poverty of the neighborhood is undoubtedly reflected in this drop-out rate.

Dr. Pérez made the sixth-grade class available for eighteen questions similar to those used in Oaxaca. He helped the boys to answer accurately. In the process of clarifying each question the director brought out significant points. Many of these boys worked during the morning to earn money for the family. Some of them had only two meals a day. A few went barefoot, but none wore huaraches. "Huaraches are symbols of 'Indian' status," he said. "After their wearers have lived for a time in the city, sandals are discarded for shoes."

The mean age for the boys was about what one would expect in the States (12.4). It was two years lower than that of sixth graders in the Centro Escolar Morelos of Oaxaca (14.5). It was lower than that of the third graders in Nuxaá (13.1). Education comes more slowly in provincial areas. All but five monthly family incomes were between $13 and $48. Three-quarters of the homes were rented. Usually "home" consisted of from one to three rooms in a vecindad secured for a monthly sum of less than $4.50. One cubicle number, added to the street number in a boy's address, was 86; another 130. These suggested the rabbit-warren character of family housing in many of the tenements of this colonia.

Bread, soup, beans, milk, coffee, and meat, in that order, were included in the meals served in these homes. Tortillas and fruit were eaten in less than half of the homes; eggs, in only seven. Fresh vegetables were not reported by any. The following items, usually referred to as *antojitos* ("little desires"), were customarily eaten by these boys away from home: enchiladas (20), *tacos* (14),[6] *paletas* (13),[7] cakes (10), sweets (8), *sopes* (7).[8] Obviously the diet of these boys could not be measured accurately by the foods consumed at home.

The number of movies attended each month ranged from none to ten (one case at each extreme). The average was five. Remember, from the discussion in Chapter XIV, the widespread popularity of movies made in the United States and exhibited with Spanish explanations. Consider the low economic status of the families who send boys to the sixth grade of Escuela Dr. Mora and it becomes apparent how influential Hollywood must be in producing stereotypes of Anglo-American behavior and in creating desires for material progress in the proletariat of the metropolis.

A 1956 study by Oscar Lewis of 157 households in what he calls the "Casa Grande" vecindad in this neighborhood showed that 49 per cent used knives and forks rather than tortillas for eating, 55 per cent had gas stoves and 21 per cent owned television sets.[9] The movies and other urbanizing influences together with improvement in real income for skilled workmen were at least bringing some superficial changes.

Six blocks west of Dr. Mora Primary School, in a working-class area somewhat higher economically than Colonia Morelos, was Secundaria No. 16. This secondary school faced the Plaza of Tlaltelolco where Cortés saw a great pyramid and market when he first arrived in Tenochtitlán in 1519. With the help of the director, Sr. Pedro Díaz, and of Srta. Flora Pérez, who was teaching a first-year (seventh grade) geography class, the same eighteen questions were dictated to forty-three boys.[10] In general the answers reflected the slightly better economic position of residents in Tlaltelolco as compared with Morelos.[11] Movies, for example, were less popular. Perhaps these boys had a wider array of leisure-time activities from which to choose. Milk, meat, fruit, and fresh vegetables were used more frequently and coffee less.[12] It is clear that if data like these were available for representative public and private schools in the various areas of the city, sharp differences would be noted.[13]

"Cultural Missions"

Only when Indian groups are better known will real advances be made in their education. This was the conclusion of Dr. Gamio. With cultural evolution at various stages—from the primitive Lacandones of Chiapas, whose mode of living is similar to that of thousands of years ago, to modern civilized man—education should be adapted to the social setting. To be successful, it has to be integral. Major aspects of community life should be improved at the same time.

An approach to this ideal is suggested by the very name, "cultural missions." These are attempts to raise the standard of life in specific communities. They are actually examples of adult education with a Mexican flourish. Professor Guillermo Bonilla y Segura, who headed this government effort (1949), stated in an interview that the missions help to improve the character of an entire region. They combat indolence, apathy, and neglect of children. They influence cookery and hygiene in the homes. Recreational activities such as music, dancing, and sports are encouraged. The fight against illiteracy is pushed. From three to ten communities are included in a single cultural mission. Since the aim is a general change in the life of the people, and the point of view is organic, from one to three years is spent in each region.[14]

In the western part of the state of Mexico, some twenty-two miles north of Valle de Bravo, is the interesting old town of Villa Donato Guerra.[15] Here in 1948 Carlos Auriel Ramírez, head of Rural Cultural Mission No. 3, was working. He graciously told what the activities were. Preparatory to the establishment of a rural mission in a given community, various places are surveyed. In a likely village the people are called together. "Do you want to have a mission?" they are asked. "What can you do to help?

We are now in such and such a place. Transportation must be furnished." Salaries of the five workers (the number of staff members varies somewhat in different missions, depending on the services rendered) are paid by the federal government. Housing is provided by the community.

The expense of renovating the sport field in Villa Donato Guerra would be carried by the little town. A basketball court would probably be included. Encouraged by a priest and in preparation for a fiesta to be held during the following month, three miles of very rough road approaching the village were being smoothed. The local school had but three grades. This mission was planning to expand these to six.[16] One of the workers on Cultural Mission No. 3 helps women in the making of clothing. She also goes into the homes and notes conditions. If a *cocina* is unsanitary, she reports this to the nurse who visits and helps the woman make her kitchen more hygienic. The agriculturalist gives information on the prevention of hoof-and-mouth disease, helps to import a good quality of avocado, apple, orange, pear, or peach tree, and teaches how to spray.[17]

On the negative side, it was pointed out in 1949 by Alfonso Villa Rojas that some of the rural cultural missions located in the basin of the Papaloapan River had failed. It was felt by Villa Rojas and Dr. Gamio that the employment of anthropologists might help make the missions more effective. In a program which promotes changes it is indeed important to know the cultural background of each group. An anthropologist can suggest ways for making progress without disrupting traditional values.

Villa Rojas himself was later given an opportunity to demonstrate the contribution that could be made by anthropologists when he was placed in charge of moving 600 families (3,000 individuals) from the area about to be flooded by the President Alemán Dam to new communities in the state of Veracruz.[18] Most of these people were illiterate Mazatecos, 30 per cent monolingual, 100 per cent infested with parasites. The first machines ever seen by them were the bulldozers used in the construction of the dam. During 1952 and 1953, Villa Rojas and two assistants trained in anthropology held informal orientation sessions with the teachers and medicos sent into the area in order to give these professionals an understanding of the customs and attitudes of the Mazatecos. One illustration: because their use fitted in with superstitions about the importance of a person's blood, free injections by the doctors were popular, but due in part to rumors that vaccinations for smallpox were designed to sterilize, the latter were resisted.

Finally, in the spring of 1953 the women, who were the last to leave, were transported with their children, animals, and movable belongings to entirely new homes in the expropriated areas that had been prepared for them. Every transplanted family received fifteen hectares of land in addition to the new house, and each male over sixteen was paid five pesos a day (52 cents American) until the first harvest. Three cultural mission groups worked together with teachers and doctors to raise the standard of life of these preliterates. The initial adjustment to the new ways was better than expected. Evidence from the field of recreation includes the notation that a Mazateco basketball team soon became regional champions.

EDUCATION AT THE UNIVERSITY LEVEL

On three successive evenings in October, 1948, the writer gave lectures in Spanish at the National University's School of Law, which at that time was located three blocks north of the Zócalo in Mexico City. The third 50-minute lecture was one of the hardest he had ever attempted. Two big side doors seemed never to be closed, and there was much clamor in the patio. Students would barge in, listen a while, then go noisily out. Sometimes they even talked out loud in the lecture room. Because he would not have been backed by the University's weak administration, the chairman could not ask for quiet. The whole affair, although in itself a minor happening, was evidence of the lack of discipline which characterized the University.

In 1945 a faculty member had asked about career professors in the United States, i.e., university teachers who devote all of their time to academic work. The National University was considering the idea. Paid only a nominal sum—as little as 80 pesos ($16) per month for lectures on neurology in the Medical School, for example—their professors were expected to earn their living in some other way. A law professor or a medical professor might support himself by private practice. Up to October, 1948, twenty-five career positions, from instructor to professor, had been created. Of these the Law School had six. Each career professor signs a contract which specifies that he will not work at anything else. This development marks an important step in improving the quality of instruction and research at the National University.

One of the professors traced the history of faculty-student relations during the past two decades approximately as follows:

Whereas the old Latin-American universities were ruled by the church, it was the tradition of the nineteenth and the early part of the twentieth centuries that they be supported and controlled by the state. This is also the custom in Central Europe. As official institutions the Latin-American universities became bureaucratized. Scholars considered themselves public officials. There was too much administration by established rule. The universities were not sufficiently alive.

Beginning about 1923 many groups of students urged reform. They wanted more flexibility, more fresh air from the outside, autonomy. Often the official in charge of a university did not understand either pedagogy or scientific problems. The absurd idea (*sic*) spread to most Latin-American countries that students should intervene in the rule of the university. The students thought that half-student, half-faculty committees would be fair. They talked about a university demos of teachers, students, and graduates.

Students in Mexico became possessed with this democratic virus. When exams grew harder or study schedules richer, they staged strikes. In 1928 or 1929 a great party of students struck for autonomy and failed. There was a second violent strike in 1933 or 1934. The minister of education, Narciso Bassols, was a Marxist. He was close to communism. He intended to make the university Marxist. But a large majority at the university was composed of Catholics and Liberals, a group similar to the British Liberals. It was this majority which organized the second strike and preserved liberty of thought at the university. Bassols did succeed in making the university autonomous. The joker was that it had a very small budget.

From 1934 to 1944 there was a student revolution every two years. With each, the rector and the dean were changed and the rules were reformed. In 1944 the riot was more serious. Two rival rectors and two rival deans were the outcome. The President of the Republic intervened and asked the competing officials to resign. He called together the seven former rectors of the preceding twelve-year period and asked them to work out a way to get the university out of trouble. They met for fifteen days, many hours each day. They succeeded in electing a temporary rector, Alfonso Caso, whose task was to study reorganization. Caso accepted the rectorship only for the time necessary to make the reform. He wrote an organic law for the university which was approved by the President and made a statute by Congress. The university was to be ruled by a permanent Governing Board of fifteen persons chosen by a representative assembly composed of professors (three-quarters) and of students (one-quarter). The men elected were outstanding scholars. Vacancies were to be filled by the Governing Board itself. The Board was to appoint rectors and deans. The incentive to revolution was gone, it was thought.

"We lived in peace for a year." In November, 1945, there was another violent strike. Lic. Genaro Fernández McGregor, the rector, remained. The new statute works, it was believed. After three months the rector resigned. The new rector was Salvador Zubirán, "the best rector the university ever had." He performed "miracles." It had not been the custom in Mexico for private individuals to help support the university. Zubirán succeeded in getting ten million pesos (two million dollars) from private sources. This gave new life to all the schools. Zubirán kept order. The university was improving every day. Plans were made for a new university to care for 25,000 students. A site was acquired on the Pedregal, a lava flow just south of the city.

Zubirán did not care to work out any policy with the students. All the others, except Alfonso Caso, had catered to students. In April, 1948, a new riot broke out. Zubirán tried then to stave off trouble by making concessions to the rioters. He hoped to satisfy them, but failed. They seditiously occupied the building containing the rector's office, held him as a prisoner four or five hours, insulted him, threw him to the floor, beat him.

The strike lasted four weeks. During this time there were neither classes nor activities. Many American students supported by the G.I. Bill transferred to the Mexico City College, a private institution which started on a shoestring but began to boom in 1946—with the aid of the veterans. Zubirán resigned. The Governing Board found a new person to accept the job. The new rector does not rule the university. He is afraid of riots. Many of the improvements made by Zubirán have been lost. The group of students who beat up the rector remained unpunished. Later, however, when the same students insulted the Law School dean, they were expelled. Afterwards this dean had to resign because the rector would not support him! The six expelled students tried to get reinstated, but the court confirmed the dean!

Today "University City" on the Pedregal is a reality. A team of 156 architects and the country's top painters, sculptors, and designers produced by 1953 a brand-new home for the oldest American university and at the same time built an artistic masterpiece. Most notable from an aesthetic standpoint is the Central Library, its high, straight outer walls vividly set with natural-stone mosaics which depict the history of Mexico during the pre-Hispanic, colonial, and modern periods. Originally it was planned that the inner surfaces of these walls would be covered with shelves sufficient to house two million books. Volumes from the National Library that were to have been transported here, however, have been retained in the city center where they are accessible to a larger group of readers. Since for this reason the actual number of volumes housed in this magnificent structure is small, each school or faculty is left to gather its own collection of books.

From an academic standpoint, the university's prestige has been sufficient to persuade the distinguished Mexico City lawyers, physicians, and businessmen who comprise about 90 per cent of the faculty to continue as part-time professors although the university is now eleven miles away from their courts, hospitals, and board rooms. Of the 5,000 members on the academic staff in 1961, 4,500 were part-time. They received approximately seven dollars for each hour of teaching. Five hundred were full-time teachers or researchers or a combination of the two. A top-ranking career professor received about $400 a month. Contrary to the original plan for such men, many supplemented their salaries by writing textbooks or newspaper articles, or giving outside lectures for which they were paid, but the situation had improved substantially since 1948. The strongly entrenched tradition of token payments for university professors had been broken.

Not counting the preparatory schools or the summer session, the total enrollment at the National University for 1961 was 39,471. The heaviest registrations were in the faculties of medicine (7,642), engineering (6,440), and law (6,194), and in the schools of commerce and administration (4,436) and chemical science (2,669). There were approximately 1,300 women among the medical students, 1,000 in commerce and administration, 700 in chemical science, and 1,600 in the smaller faculty of philosophy and literature. Of those following a professional career at the National University, about one-fifth are women.[19]

Returning to the problem of student discipline, it is significant that during the seven-month period which began March, 1961, there were four student strikes in the countries of Haiti, Colombia, and Peru; four student demonstrations in Guatemala, Peru, and Chile; "chaotic extra-curricular political activity" in the city of Puebla, Mexico; and in Morelia, Mexico, student action so violent that the Mexican-American Cultural Institute was wrecked and burned and its director was forced to flee for his life.[20] During this same period on the campus of the Mexican National University the statue of Miguel Alemán (under whose administration University City had been constructed) was undergoing repairs because of damage from student bombs. In an article on "Student Politics in Latin America" S. Walter Washington gives three explanations for these strikes and demonstrations. He says that Latin Americans have respect for young people with education and will follow their leadership; that the increasing number of students who come from the poorer classes are impatient for social reform; and finally that Latin American populations in general are young and volatile.[21]

The university professor who was quoted earlier on student strikes summarized the 1961 situation in Mexico roughly as follows:

> Dr. Nabor Carrillo Flores, an internationally famous specialist in underground mechanics, was rector of the National University for eight years. He was responsible for moving the University from the old quarters near the Zócalo to the Pedregal. Unfortunately he spent a lot of money paying professional student leaders to quiet disturbances which they themselves had created. Discipline became worse and worse.
>
> The new rector, Dr. Ignacio Chavez, is the cardiologist who set up the National Institute of Cardiology, best in the world. After he was chosen head of the University by a neutral board, a few professional leaders started a riot, occupied the administration building, and threatened to prevent the new leader from entering. This "noise" crumbled and vanished. However, at 1:00 A.M. on the day in March when Dr. Chavez was to be sworn into office one of these leaders appeared at his home. The young man exhibited 40,000 pesos ($3,200) and said that Dr. Chavez could have more if he did not accept the position. Chavez threw him out. The inauguration took place, but in an atmosphere poisoned by the use of ampules of ammonia and other chemicals.
>
> There is a small but very active minority of communists and fellow travelers among the students. They have succeeded in exciting many other students, not with communism, but with anti-Americanism. Still, after less than three months under Chavez discipline is much better.

Mexico has experienced a fundamental revolution. Tangible progress such as the increasing control of communicable diseases, the rising percentage of literacy, the building of 3,000 new primary schools each year, the construction of a magnificent university, all are interpreted as a continuation of that revolution. It is natural for Mexicans to be sympathetic with the struggles in a country like Cuba and to be hostile toward Americans. In spite of a high drop-out rate in the elementary schools—free distribution of textbooks and notebooks initiated in 1960 may help to reduce this—and in spite of occasional evidence of lack of discipline at the university level, one gets the impression that Mexico is gradually building up an educated citizenry and a group of professionals who are intelligent, know what their country needs and are active in working toward practical goals.

Oaxaca's aqueduct constructed in 1727 is crossed by power lines. During recent hydroelectric developments anthropologists and other professionals have helped to incorporate even preliterate groups like the Mazatecos into the national life.

17

Understanding the Mexicans

Anyone gets more out of a sojourn in Mexico if he gives attention to a particular aspect of its life, whether it be ruins of past civilizations, churches and ex-convents, paintings, native dances, or colorful birds.[1] Although many persons in Mexico City know some English, in towns and villages a knowledge of Spanish is indispensable. For social research, specialized training in the chosen field is, of course, fundamental. Important work has already been done by Mexicans in various branches of social science, notably in anthropology and archeology. In the long run most social investigation should, and will, be done by Mexican scholars. Students south of the Border are being trained increasingly in research techniques. A wider provision in our country of scholarships and fellowships for Latin Americans would help to meet the need. The University of Texas and the University of Florida, to mention only two schools, are pioneering in this direction. Until more opportunities for advanced study of this type in the United States and Mexico are developed, however, Mexico will continue to offer challenging possibilities to Anglo-American social scientists who wish to do field research.

Described below are some promising opportunities. These are presented under nine headings.

1. *Social Change.* It is clear that Mexican institutions are changing and changing differentially. The rate of change varies between institutions and between aspects of the same institution. Changes in athletic sports, health practices, percentage of illiteracy, and methods of work have been more rapid, for example, than changes in the folk religion. The material culture of the family has been altered considerably and the status of women is rising, while the average size of family shows practically no tendency to change. Statistical indices that will measure the rates of change are needed.

The principal method used in the field work on which this book is based was to compare selected aspects of certain social institutions in isolated agricultural villages with the provincial town of Oaxaca, and again with Mexico City. It was assumed that the village would show the least change; the town, more; the metropolis, most. This assumption, insofar as the communities studied are concerned, has been supported by the facts.

We have seen that the rate of social change varies in different social classes. The predominant lower class usually shows the least change; the upper class more; the middle class most. The Mazatecos of Oaxaca State provide an exception to this rule. Subjected to traumatic experiences by the building of a great dam in their territory, these people of the lower-lower class seem initially to have made a good adjustment to the impact of modern civilization. Are these primitives changing in ways similar to the natives of the Admiralty Islands who are reported by Margaret Mead to have moved 2,000 years in a short period and without social disorganization?[2] To what extent, under the influence of rapid industrialization, are other indigenous groups of Mexico being incorporated into the national life?[3]

2. *New Ecological Patterns.* In the cities of Mexico the better homes were in the past characteristically located near the central plaza, while the least desirable residential areas were on the periphery. Usually today the small towns of Oaxaca State have Spanish-style centers and Zapotec or Mixtec margins. The plaza-centered pattern still persists in Oaxaca City. It is changing in Mérida, which is twice as large, and changing more markedly in Guadalajara with almost eleven times the population. In the latter city the better districts are moving westward, with one new upper-class *colonia* near the country club to the northwest, but the poorest districts still remain at some distance east of the central plaza.[4] Under the influence of rapidly growing numbers, new industries, and improvements in the means of transportation, Mexico City seems to be shifting toward a basic configuration similar, in some respects, to that in large cities of the United States. The better residential districts are now, for example, three to eleven miles from the center of highest land values. In other ways, however, Mexico City is sharply different. There are no areas of homeless men. High-land-value slums, with men and women in about equal numbers, do form a poverty-stricken "horseshoe" around the north and east sides of the central business district, it is true; but in contrast to Anglo-American cities, there are also large, low-land-value slums in a broken circle on the periphery of the metropolis.

Airphoto maps made by the Compañía Aerofoto S.A. at intervals since 1932 afford an index to observable changes in the ecological structure of Mexico City, but they are no substitute for detailed life histories of specific peripheral slums. How do these slums get started? In their development what has been the role of the "parachutists" who just "fall" into the open spaces? And through what stages do they pass as these aggregations of squatters evolve into proletarian neighborhoods?

Table 6 shows the rates for juvenile delinquents in the Federal District by delegations. These rates were based on the place of arrest. What would be shown by a rate map based on the home addresses of boy delinquents and for smaller areas than police delegations? Would peripheral slums be designated as important criminogenic zones?

Estimates of the circulation of metropolitan as compared with local newspapers provide a rough index of the extent to which

Mexico City dominates the country economically. Another method used by the late R. D. McKenzie for delineating metropolitan regions is the number of railroad tickets sold to competing cities from various stations.[5] How far from Mexico City would it be necessary to go to find a majority of tickets for Guadalajara or Monterrey?

3. *The Changing Family.* We have seen that inventions and techniques arrive first in Mexico City; later, in Oaxaca City; still later, if at all, in the small outlying towns and agricultural villages. Improved transportation, like the coming of the train to Oaxaca, is an important factor influencing the speed of diffusion. Privileged classes of the cities change their housekeeping habits more rapidly than underprivileged, and urban workers shift more quickly than campesinos. A careful study of trends and variations in the sales of specific items of household equipment in representative communities would be interesting. What articles are accepted quickly, slowly, or not at all? What relation is there between purchasing habits and socioeconomic status?

Marriages between American men and Mexican women seem to have a greater chance of success than marriages between Mexican men and American women. In the latter the roles which husband and wife expect to play may be very different from the roles which they do actually play. The dominance of the male is traditional in Mexico. The freedom of the female is probably greater in the United States than in any other country. Conflict is the natural result. A systematic and yet intimate study of a series of Mexican-American marriages would be both interesting and significant.

Fathers who abandon wives and small children are a problem to child welfare workers in the capital. How is this situation related to the migration from village to city? Has the loss of village controls demoralized these men? How is it related to *machismo*? Under what circumstances does a migrant become a *pelado* (bum) and under what conditions does he become a respected citizen? What principles should be followed by Mexican social case workers in dealing with abandoned mothers? With problems so different in Latin America are mere translations of social work books from north of the Rio Grande adequate?

4. *Personnel Problems in Mexico.* Perplexing situations like unwise squandering of money, or absenteeism and inefficiency, particularly on Mondays and Tuesdays, are present in both provincial town and modern city. These problems seem to have

some relationship to the tradition that permits a man to maintain two or more families, the wide incidence of alcoholism, and the low level of education. The hostility of many young Catholics toward the mistress custom suggests a possible decline in this practice. The alleged low incidence in Mexico of mental diseases growing out of syphilitic infection of the central nervous system and the alleged high incidence of psychoses related to alcoholism pose challenging research questions for psychiatry. A critical study might be made of social services like those provided at "Industrial City," or of procedures such as that at the glass factory which requires a man to buy basic commodities for his family early in the week.[6]

5. *Resurgence for What?* A sympathetic and yet critical study of Protestant struggles in Catholic Mexico would be in itself both interesting and worthwhile. Why, for one thing, are Protestant leaders so conservative? Is it because of the conflict with Romanism or something else? In any case, more important for research than the small Protestant group would be further study of the resurgence of the Catholic Church. How many new Catholic churches have been constructed in recent years? Is this merely another drive for political power, or does it represent a revival of the early apostolic spirit? To what extent has the competition with Protestants stimulated a more socialized approach to the problems of campesino and worker? Are the occasional examples of cooperation between Evangelicals and Catholics increasing?

6. *Government.* Miguel Alemán was the first president since Juárez to complete the full six-year term of his office without having been himself a general. Adolfo Ruiz Cortines did the same, and now civilian Adolfo López Mateos gives promise of reaching the end of his term undisturbed. In 1945 the number of generals in active service was reduced from 682 to 84, the number of colonels from 500 to 65. "Mexico has solved the problem of militarism," writes Edwin Lieuwen. "That is a major reason why it has become one of Latin America's most progressive nations."[7] It has been proved that dominance by individual leaders need not be a permanent aspect of political life in Mexico and doctrines are becoming more important.

There has been much lip service to the moralization of government departments. Under what circumstances is honesty most likely to be the policy? How can the mordida be most effectively discouraged?

The custom of permitting conjugal visits in Mexican jails and prisons has been described, and an attempt has been made to explain the practice. Would another study also show a high participation in the custom by "square Johns" and politicians? Would additional empirical data support the idea that it is used as a means of maintaining inmate morale in an otherwise almost intolerable situation? Under what circumstances in Mexico did the custom originate and take root?

An analysis of recent trends in the rates for homicide and suicide would be enlightening. The incidence of murder dropped 45 per cent in a twenty-year period. The average annual rate per 100,000 in 1936-38 was 60.6; in 1956-58, 33.1. As reported by Arthur L. Wood in *Crime and Aggression in Changing Ceylon: A Sociological Study of Homicide, Suicide and Economic Crime,* the mean annual homicide rate (1951-56) for thirty-six countries was 1.7; for suicide it was 8.5. Mexico's homicide rate at that time (39.1) was the highest among the thirty-six countries that had reliable statistics, and its suicide rate (1.1) was next to the lowest. According to the United Nations' *Demographic Yearbook 1961,* the mean annual 1957-58 rate for suicide in Mexico had risen to 1.7.

It is probable that during the twenty-year period when the homicide rate was diminishing so dramatically, suicides were slowly increasing. In these years Mexico's middle class with its lower homicide and higher suicide rate had been increasing too. Will homicide continue to decrease in Mexico during its transition stage and suicide to increase, as in Ceylon?[8]

7. *Fiesta to Festival.* As mobility increases, commercialized types of recreation become more important than traditional forms of play. The fiesta becomes a festival, Mixteca handball declines, and the *serenata* drops out completely. At what point in the evolution of a city does the *serenata* disappear? Do the movies, the big money-getters in the field of commercialized recreation, have anything to do with the loss of interest in the "walk-around"? And conversely, is the economic and technological revolution of the last twenty years, with its increase in the number of skilled occupations, responsible for the recent upward trend in active utilization of leisure time?

8. *Magic to Medicine.* The most valuable source of information for any community in Oaxaca proved to be the doctor. He was usually the best educated man in town. He not only knew the health problems, but he saw them in relation to the supersti-

tions, illiteracy, and poverty of his patients, A struggle between the more or less modern medicine of the small-town physician and the magical notions of primitive wizards goes on every day in backward communities. This makes material for vivid drama as Steinbeck has shown in *Forgotten Village*. It could lend itself neatly to social science research.

Perhaps the economic factor in health could be studied more easily in Mexico City. If general and specific mortality rates could be figured for the homes of the deceased rather than the places where they died, as at present, sharp differences would appear between a ward high in economic status, such as VIII, and a ward like I, which is low.

With the present downward trend of communicable diseases, Mexico should become a more healthful country for both residents and visitors.

9. *The Fight against Illiteracy.* Mexicans are continuing their national campaign against illiteracy. They have built many elementary schools in recent years. They have attempted to change whole communities with their cultural missions. A 1950 study concludes that the missions "are doing an excellent job with the funds and materials with which they have to work."[9]

Interesting for research would be the important role of the Latin-American university student in politics. What are the factors associated with success or with failure in student strikes or demonstrations? What do they accomplish? What part is played by militant leftist or rightist minorities?

Now thinking of ourselves, sixty years ago in the United States we rode behind dobbin, jerked along in quaint little streetcars, or walked. Even in the cities there was the sound of horses' hoofs on the pavement to announce the morning milk delivery and warn the housewife to get out the pan. As in Mexican towns today, if the woman had an attractive daughter, the boy could pour a generous quart. Although steam "donkey" engines were in general use throughout the dense forests of the Pacific Northwest, ox-team logging was still relatively common. There were then many isolated communities in our country. Today with automobiles, airplanes, widely distributed newspapers, telephones, radios, and television sets it would indeed be difficult to find a person who was not familiar with the issues in the presidential campaign of 1960. But in Mexico right now, as we have seen, there are thousands of isolated hamlets with their thatched huts, oxcarts, wooden plows, burros, chickens, and pigs.

Among many of these people there is little knowledge or understanding of federal government.

Even mountain villages do, however, have schools and eager teachers are helping the people to progress. In one hamlet, for example, four boys walked past. They had been sent home by the teacher. They were followed by an even larger group of girls. This was an example of what teachers call practical hygiene. At the beginning of each school day students are examined for cleanliness. If their hands are dirty, they are sent home to wash.

To what extent are the primitive Indian groups of Mexico learning Spanish? Are they too being taught practical hygiene or will they die out in the near future like the Lacandones and Seris, "who formerly numbered thousands and today do not total even 500 members together"?[10]

As Mexicans Might See Us

A major value in studying another culture is that it throws a flood of light on the traveler's own country. As the United States moves into a position of world leadership, it becomes increasingly important that our social scientists gain the insight which comes from familiarity with the language and traditions of at least one foreign people. And indeed for all Americans seeing ourselves as others see us is enlightening, to say the least.

After struggling with the alien tongue, getting acquainted with representative communities, learning some of the basic customs, one's reactions to American life during the first days and weeks in the homeland are to a certain extent similar to those experienced by a visiting citizen from the foreign country. There is, of course, a bias in the warm feeling of happiness at being back in "the good old U.S.A." There is also an absence of the discrimination on the basis of race or accent which those who belong to that country may encounter. Just what do Mexicans actually think of us? On the whole they find our country less colorful than their own, with less appeal for the artist, more standardized, and with climates less conducive to out-of-door living. And they find our people less appreciative of music. A small window into that world of Mexican attitudes may be opened by a few of our impressions on the 1949 drive from Laredo to Seattle.

At a little restaurant in Carrizo Springs, Texas,[11] on the way to Los Angeles, lunch was served and eaten and the bill paid in twenty-five minutes. This never happened in Mexico. The same thing occurred with dinner at Sonora. It took just twenty minutes. The restaurant was busy and noisy, but efficient. A Mexican would miss his leisurely way of eating.

Highways in Texas are smoother than those in Mexico. Road signs are more frequent. Gas station attendants wipe off the windshield without being asked and without expecting tips. In most stations extra items like windshield wipers are available for sale. But no highway in the United States is as interesting as the one from Mexico City to Laredo.

The shop windows of Sonora, however, were fascinating. The town had a population only slightly over 2,500 in 1950. Perhaps there was nothing unusual for the Anglo in these displays, but the grocery stores were comparable to the supermarkets of Mexico City's better residential areas. Oaxaca City with eighteen times the population was just beginning to use electric refrigerators and gas stoves like those exhibited in the windows. Oaxaca Courts had a washing machine but most laundry work in that provincial region was still done by hand. Oaxaca City did have car agencies, movies, and billiard halls comparable to those in Sonora. In fact, Ejutla, population 5,000, had a motion-picture theater, but that was exceptional in a town so small. Usually a Mexican town must have 10,000 or more inhabitants before it reaches the degree of urbanization represented by Sonora.

In the morning a day later at the progressive little city of Roswell, New Mexico, there was a crowd of teen-age girls in levis and slacks ready to go on an outing. Although customs are changing, especially in the metropolis, few girls in Mexico would dress that way. But how great the freedom enjoyed by girls in the United States! And how numerous the opportunities provided them for outdoor recreation!

The descendants of aboriginal Americans observed in and near Gallup seemed to have strong feelings of inferiority. In contrast, Mexicans do menial work with dignity and a smile. The Navajos and Hopis out on their Arizona reservations, however, show little demoralization and a high degree of persistence in the old languages and traditions. Their cultures are, in fact, the most distinctive of any within continental United States. They are proud of their unique heritages.

Streamlined passenger trains and long freights pulled by four-unit Diesel engines, like those on the Santa Fe, are just not seen in Mexico. The smaller trains of that country with older equipment are in the habit of leaving on time, but arriving late. Railroaders there are paid time and a half for overtime.

One is impressed with the tremendous flow of traffic during the afternoon peak in Los Angeles. Two cars for every five persons in 1950. In spite of this, pedestrians have the right of way in cross-walks. Cars keep their lanes better than in Mexico City. There is very little honking of horns. Many service stations are huge affairs. Car washing is reduced to a science. Stores in the newer parts have parking areas as big as football fields. This third-largest metropolitan area in the United States (four and one-sixth millions in 1950) is remarkable for the way it sprawls over the landscape. The reason? Automobiles.

When they are at home during the day, the members of a certain well-to-do family in Los Angeles leave their cars outside unlocked. At night they do lock the house, but the back door is merely a screen. In seventeen years no burglar has invaded. Some of the homes in this neighborhood near the Wilshire "Miracle Mile" have been broken into, it is true. These had become known as places with expensive furnishings. But at this ménage the garden hose is left outside all the time and only a clothespin is used to "lock" the garage doors. Such habits would be incomprehensible in the Mexican capital.

Now up through the redwoods and along the Oregon coast. Evergreen ferns, log dumps and sawmills, "lumberjack dinners," rivers with water in them, fresh crabs for sale, ocean beaches without a soul in sight—to most Mexicans these would be strange indeed. Our neighbors to the south would respond, however, to the friendly warmth of farmers and fishermen on Lopez Island (where this book was written), for they themselves are friendly and warm.

Renovating a town house in Seattle afforded interesting contacts with city workmen. A series of specialized craftsmen gave, on the whole, a very favorable impression. One marveled at the speed and skill with which they worked. How long would it have taken Mexican workmen to do these jobs? One also marveled at their wages. An electrician earning $95 American a week (1950) was receiving substantially more, and probably was living more comfortably, than the governor of the state of Oaxaca.

In our effort to understand the Mexicans, it is important to remember that although close in distance, they are far in culture. They are products of a different tradition. Our borderlands are, however, somewhat Mexicanized just as Mexico's "porch" is partly Americanized. The nature of our social contacts with Spanish Americans, especially in these border states, is not merely important for Mexico and for us; it is being watched by all of Latin America. If we can succeed in maintaining friendly relations here, the impact will be felt around the world.

Notes

Chapter I

1. Important institutions have been omitted; but those included are all fields in which the author has either taught courses, published papers, or had a long-time special interest.

2. Due to the building of a faster highway between Piedras Negras on the Rio Grande and Mexico City, through Saltillo, San Luis Potosí, and Querétaro, Tamazunchale has shown little change since 1949. In contrast, "the entire tempo of Querétaro became one of optimistic, energetic progress," writes Andrew H. Whiteford in *Two Cities of Latin America* (Beloit, Wisconsin: Logan Museum of Anthropology, 1960, p. 11). "New hotels were built along the road, automobile agencies and service stations appeared, and new factories and processing plants were constructed."

3. *Life in Mexico* (New York: E. P. Dutton, 1931), p. 355.

4. *Tepoztlán, A Mexican Village: A Study of Folk Life* (Chicago: University of Chicago Press, 1930). Stuart Chase featured this village in *Mexico—A Study of Two Americas* (New York: Macmillan, 1931). He emphasized the contrast between our machine civilization and the handicraft culture of the Mexican village. More recently Oscar Lewis published a book entitled *Life in a Mexican Village: Tepoztlán Restudied* (Urbana: Univerity of Illinois Press, 1951), in which new facts about family life appear.

5. New York: The Viking Press, 1941, p. 7.

6. See *Tepoztlán: Village in Mexico* (New York: Holt, Rinehart and Winston, Inc., 1960), Chapter 8.

7. For a vivid picture of the hardships and isolation of the Mixe, the importance of their village groups, and their hostility to outsiders, see Ralph L. Beals, *Ethnology of the Western Mixe* (Berkeley and Los Angeles: University of California Press, 1945), pp. 7-8, 16-17, 18-19.

8. See Alfonso Villa Rojas, *Los Mazatecos y el Problema Indígena de la Cuenca del Papaloapan* (México, D.F.: Instituto Nacional Indigenista, 1955), pp. 91-94.

9. *Septimo Censo General de Población: 1950* (México, D.F.: Dirección General de Estadistica, 1953).

10. See John P. Gillin, "Some Signposts for Policy," Chapter 1 in *Social Change in Latin America Today* (New York: Random House, 1961), for a helpful discussion of social values held by all middle-class Latin Americans.

Chapter II

1. "Mexico" is used by Mexicans to mean either country, state, or city, the context determining which.

2. Manuel Gamio, "Geographic and Social Handicaps," in *Mexico Today, the Annals of the American Academy of Political and Social Science,* CCVIII (March, 1940), 4.

3. Data from Preston E. James, *Latin America* (New York: Odyssey Press, 1942). Most of the long tongue of Baja California and large sec-

tions of Sonora and Chihuahua have less than 7.5 inches annually. See Map I for location of place names.

4. *Ibid.*

5. In 1950, for one-third of the 1,200,000 persons in the state of Oaxaca five years of age and over, and for one-fifth of the 440,000 five years of age and over in Yucatan, the mother tongue was an Indian language. While the proportion of such persons throughout the Republic had increased slightly during the decade 1950 to 1960, in Oaxaca it had increased from one-third to two-fifths and in Yucatan from one-fifth to one-fourth.

6. "The Indian in Mexico," *Mexico Today, the Annals,* CCVIII (March, 1940), 132-33, 143.

7. Since probably not more than one Mexican in a hundred has obvious Negro ancestry, the Negro is not included in this discussion.

8. For a scholarly discussion of this point of view, see the article, "Definición del Indio y lo Indio," by Alfonso Caso in *America Indígena* (October, 1948), Vol. VIII, No. 4.

9. *Rural Mexico* (Chicago: University of Chicago Press, 1948), p. 367. See pp. 360-71 for a detailed explanation by Dr. Whetten of his index of Indian-colonial culture.

10. *North from Mexico: The Spanish-Speaking People of the United States* (Philadelphia and New York: J. B. Lippincott, 1949), p. 48.

11. Whetten, *op. cit.,* pp. 298-300.

12. *The Wind That Swept Mexico* (New York: Harper and Brothers, 1943), p. 51.

13. Whetten, *op. cit.,* p. 144. See Part II in Whetten, "The Relation of the People to the Land," for a detailed, careful study of this problem.

14. These facts about Ejido Guadiana were reported personally to the author in September of 1948 immediately after Barnard and Lucero completed their field work.

15. Whetten, *op. cit.,* pp. 563, 572.

16. See Ifigenia M. de Navarette, *La Distribución del Ingreso y el Desarrollo Económico de México* (México, D.F.: Instituto de Investigaciones Económicas, 1960), pp. 85, 94, 95.

Chapter III

1. Although connected by highway with Oaxaca City in 1962, Puerto Escondido did not yet have a direct truck road to Miahuatlán.

2. The state of Oaxaca contains one-quarter of the *municipios* of the Republic. The average population of these 572 "counties" in 1950 was 2,484. The *municipio* is larger in other states. It is sometimes referred to as a "municipality." See Whetten, *op. cit.,* pp. 524-34. The 1960 census includes detailed information for the state's 27 "ex-districts," but not for *municipios.*

Chapter IV

1. The civilizations that centered on Monte Albán may be classified roughly into four epochs. The "Archaic" period was around 400 B.C. The dancing figures that characterize this epoch are stone relief sculptures of human beings, each with a bodily deformity such as twisted feet, or a

head too flat or elongated. These *danzantes* were found underneath the remains of the second epoch which extended from the first to the fifth centuries A.D. Pottery of the second period is similar to that in the pre-Maya ruins of Guatemala. Upside-down heads in the carvings of this period indicate tribes that had been conquered.

The third epoch evidenced on Monte Albán (fifth to eleventh centuries A.D.) marked the height of Zapotec influence. It was during this period that the magnificent stone mosaics and tombs of Mitla, 32 miles to the east, were built. The fourth epoch (eleventh to fifteenth centuries) is the so-called Mixtec period. Tomb 7, in which the archeologist Alfonso Caso found the exquisite jewels now on exhibit in the Oaxaca Museum, was built by the Zapotecs but later used by the Mixtecs.

2. Asael T. Hansen, "The Ecology of a Latin-American City," in E. B. Reuter (ed.), *Race and Culture Contacts* (New York: McGraw-Hill Book Co., 1934), pp. 124-42; Norman S. Hayner, "Mexico City: Its Growth and Configuration," *American Journal of Sociology*, L (January, 1945), 295-304, and "Differential Social Change in a Mexican Town," *Social Forces*, XXVI (May, 1948), 381-90; Olen E. Leonard, "La Paz, Bolivia: Its Population and Growth," *American Sociological Review*, XIII (August, 1948), 448-54; Harry B. and Audrey E. Hawthorn, "Stratification in a Latin-American City," *Social Forces*, XXVII (October, 1948), 19-29, and "The Shape of a City: Some Observations on Sucre, Bolivia," *Sociology and Social Research*, XXXIII (November-December, 1948), 87-91; Theodore Caplow, "The Social Ecology of Guatemala City," *Social Forces*, XXVIII (December, 1949), 113-33; Floyd and Lillian Ota Dotson, "Ecological Trends in the City of Guadalajara, Mexico," *Social Forces*, XXXII (May, 1954), 367-74; Andrew H. Whiteford, *Two Cities of Latin America: A Comparative Description of Social Classes* (Beloit, Wisconsin: The Logan Museum of Anthropology, 1960).

3. "Estructura Social de la Ciudad de Oaxaca," *Revista Mexicana de Sociología*, XX (Sept.-Dec., 1958), pp. 767-80.

4. This distinction between the rich and the comfortable families was made on a purely economic basis by a member of the old upper class who knows Oaxaca well. It will be noted that the geographical distribution of the two groups shows little divergence.

5. See W. Lloyd Warner, *Social Class in America* (Chicago: Harper and Brothers, 1960).

6. This item not available in 1950 and 1960 censuses.

7. By 1950 in Oaxaca City three persons in five wore shoes; in Ocotlán, one person in five; in Lachigoló, one in twenty-five.

Chapter V

1. See Ernest W. Burgess, "The Growth of a City: an Introduction to a Research Project," *Publications of the American Sociological Society*, Vol. XVIII (1924), and James A. Quinn, *Human Ecology* (New York: Prentice-Hall, 1950), Chapter 6.

2. *Report on the World Situation Including Studies of Urbanization in Underdeveloped Areas*, p. 183.

3. Eric R. Wolf in *Sons of the Shaking Earth* (Chicago: University of

Chicago Press, 1959) writes as follows on page 131: "The Mexican (Aztec) town (Tenochtitlán), built in 1344 or 1345, rose in the shadow of an older city, Tlatelolco, probably in existence since the early Militarist period (900 A.D.)."

4. See Daniel Moreno, *Los Factores Demográficos En La Planeación Económica,* (México, D.F.: Cámara Nacional de la Industria de la Transformación, 1918), p. 67.

5. Dan Stanislawski, "Early Spanish Town Planning in the New World," *The Geographical Review,* Vol. XXXVII, No. 1, 1947, p. 98.

6. *Encyclopedia Americana.*

7. A statue affectionately referred to as the Caballito (Little Horse). See inset on Map IV.

8. *Colonia* is used in Mexico much as the term "addition" is used in the United States. It seems also to carry an implication similar to the English word "neighborhood." See Map IV for the location of streets and colonias mentioned in the discussion.

9. William H. Hessler, "The Dilemma of Sr. López Mateos," *The Reporter* (Sept. 15, 1960), p. 21. In May, 1961, Alfonso Villaseñor, director of the Pemex Travel Club, said that some 750,000 tourists came to Mexico in 1959 and spent $637,000,000.

10. The exact numbers reported by the various censuses since 1900 were: 1900, Mexico City, 344,721, and Federal District, 541, 516; 1910, 471,066 and 720,743; 1921, 615,376 and 906,063; 1930, 1,029,068 and 1,229,576; 1940, 1,448,422 and 1,757,530; 1950, 2,233,709 and 3,050,442; 1960, 2,832,133 and 4,870,876.

11. See International Urban Research, *The World's Metropolitan Areas* (Berkeley and Los Angeles: University of California Press, 1959), pp. 27-30, for criteria used to determine inclusion of administrative divisions contiguous to the principal city, and pp. 43 and 75 for data on the Mexico City metropolitan area, 1950. Added to the city itself were the delegations of Atzcapotzalco, Gustavo A. Madero, Ixtacalco, Ixtapalapa, Coyoacán, and Obregón in the Federal District and the "counties" of Naucalpan and Tlalnepantla in the state of Mexico.

12. An objective index of this tremendous expansion is the skyrocketing of land values. After the Revolution, the value of property dropped. In 1923 it began to climb very slowly. The year 1940 marked the beginning of a rapid increase. The average 1940 value of land per square meter along the Avenida Juárez was 400 pesos (80 dollars); by 1948 it had risen to 2,400 pesos (350 dollars); and by 1961 it was more than 6,000 pesos (480 dollars) all the way to Insurgentes and Reforma. and more than 4,500 pesos (360 dollars) as far as Chapultepec Park. Roma and Juárez, leading residential colonias before the Revolution, rose from 40 per square meter to about 250 to more than 1,000. For interesting details see Edmundo Flores, "El Crecimiento de la Ciudad de México: Causas y Efectos Económicos," *Investigación Económica,* Vol. XIX, Second Quarter of 1959, Map 2, p. 269. Professor Flores' actual figures seem too low.

13. Secretaria de Industria y Comercio, Dirección General de Estadística, *Anuario Estadística de los Estados Unidos Mexicanos, 1958-1959* (México D.F., 1960), pp. 603-4.

14. Kingsley Davis, in a paper on "The Causes and Effects of the Primacy of the Primate City," presented Nov. 14, 1962, to the Thirteenth

National Congress of Sociology at Hermosillo, Sonora, Mexico, showed that the heavy concentration of cultural and economic life in one city is the usual pattern in Latin American countries.

15. Based on an unpublished paper by Arnold S. Linsky entitled "Some Generalizations Concerning Primate Cities." See also Clyde Eugene Browning, "The Structure of the Mexico City Central Business District: A Study in Comparative Urban Geography," unpublished Ph.D. thesis in geography, University of Washington, Seattle, 1958, pp. 59-63.

16. *Mexico: The Making of a Nation* (New York: Foreign Policy Association, 1942), pp. 35-36.

17. *Part I, Mexico*, edited by Ronald Hilton (Stanford and Chicago: A. N. Marquis, 1946). More recent data of this type are not available.

18. Circulation estimates were provided in 1948 by José Castillot, columnist for various provincial newspapers, formerly president of *Excelsior*, one of the two leading metropolitan dailies. Puebla, eighty miles east of Mexico City over a 10,500-foot pass, had a distribution of twenty thousand metropolitan papers and only about ten thousand for a paper published by the independent chain of García Vanseca. Clearly it is dominated by the metropolis. In Oaxaca about fifteen hundred papers from Mexico City were circulated, but perhaps three thousand of the four-page *Provincial*. The dominance of the metropolis was not as obvious here. Four hundred miles to the west Guadalajara received two thousand Mexico City papers daily but *Informador* and *El Sol* (also of the García Vanseca chain) each sold twenty thousand copies every day. This apparently is a separate region of dominance. The same was true for Torreón (two thousand from the metropolis, *El Siglo de Torreón* about eighteen thousand); for Monterrey (three to four thousand from Mexico City, *El Porvenir* twenty thousand and *El Norte* fifteen thousand); and for Tampico (three to four thousand from the capital, *El Mundo* eighteen thousand and another local newspaper four to five thousand). In Sr. Castillot's home city of Campeche only four to five hundred papers were received from Mexico City in comparison with a circulation of twenty-two to twenty-three thousand for the *Diaria de Yucatán*.

19. For these estimates I am indebted to a North-American-trained engineer, appraiser for a leading mortgage loan company, who modestly wishes his name omitted. He made the 1948 estimates shortly after attending a meeting of representatives from all the leading banks. At this meeting commercial land values were the central topic of discussion. Unfortunately the writer was unable to locate this appraiser in 1961.

20. See article cited in Note 12 above. By 1961 the values given on Map IV had increased sharply. In addition to the actual increase reflecting the rapid growth of the metropolis, there was an artificial increase due to the devaluation of the peso. In 1943 and also in 1941 it took only 4.85 pesos to make one dollar; in October, 1948, 6.90 pesos; by 1961, 12.50 pesos. It took more than five 1961 pesos to equal two 1941 pesos. Since the American dollar had about half the purchasing power in 1961 that it had twenty years before, the Mexican peso was worth about one-fifth what it was in 1941. For most purposes in this book, it seemed better to use dollar equivalents rather than pesos.

21. *México en el Tiempo: Fisionomía de una Ciudad* (México D.F.: Talleres Tipograficos de Excelsior, 1945), p. 50.

22. The sex ratio for the Republic was 97.4 in 1940 and 99.5 in 1960. In the past, more males died early, often violently, or migrated to the United States. The lower sex ratio for cities is to be accounted for by the greater occupational opportunities for women. In 1940, for example, about 67,000 women were employed in domestic service in Mexico City—13 per cent of the total gainfully employed population. (This item was not available from later censuses.)

23. The first half of the word Cuauhtémoc on Map V is in Nueva Anzures.

24. Following the European pattern, Mexicans change a street name at intervals in space and frequently also at intervals in time. Beginning on the north the Cuauhtémoc-Guerrero avenue, for example, included the following street names: Guerrero, Rosales, Bucareli, Cuauhtémoc, and División Norte. A few years ago Avenida Cuauhtémoc was called Calzada Piedad. The change reflects the tendency to glorify pre-Cortesian heroes.

25. The writer is indebted to Abogado Adolfo Zamora, formerly General Director of the Banco Nacional Hipotecario Urbano, for the opportunity to study this map. Abogado Zamora also contributed the map which is the basis for Map III.

26. Some of the two-story Spanish-colonial private houses (*residencias*) have deteriorated to the point where they are now used by many families, each occupying one or more rooms. The term *casa de vecindad* is used to describe such a tenement. This term means literally "a neighborhood house," but it does not have the connotation of "settlement house" that its literal translation has in the United States. One-story structures have also been built especially to serve as *vecindades*. From ten to two hundred family dwelling units of one or more rooms open on a common patio. There is but one exit to the street for the entire vecindad. A water faucet, a set of *lavaderos*, or washing places, and a group of toilets are shared by all families. Two of the *Five Families* (New York: Basic Books, Inc., 1959) described so vividly by Oscar Lewis, lived in vecindades.

27. Banco Nacional Hipotecario Urbano y de Obras Públicas, *El Problema de la Habitación* (México, D.F., 1949). In 1952 the same bank published a more detailed report of this study under the title: *Estudios 6, El Problema de la Habitación en la Ciudad de México*. See also the 1958 study by Architect Sánchez for the National Housing Institute on *The Horseshoe of Slums (Herradura de Tugurios)*.

28. See Arq. Mario Pani, "Conjunto Urbana Nonoalco–Tlaltelolco: Regeneración Urbanistica de la Ciudad de México," *Arquitectura México,* XXII (December, 1960), 183-224.

29. Between 1950 and 1960 the delegation Gustavo A. Madero (La Villa on Map V) increased 282 per cent to a total of 579,180.

30. Instituto Nacional de Vivienda, p. 9, and Map (Plano) No. 4.

31. See Floyd Dotson and Lillian Ota Dotson, "Urban Centralization and Decentralization in Mexico," *Rural Sociology,* XXI (March, 1956), 41-49.

Chapter VI

1. *Something of Myself, for My Friends Known and Unknown* (London: Macmillan, 1937), p. 131.

2. The rapidity with which the city is sinking varies in different places

from as little as two to as much as thirty centimeters a year. One can imagine what this does to sewers. See Ing. José A. Cuevas, "El Subsuelo de la Ciudad de México; Importancia de Conocerlo Antes de Emprender Obras de Replaneación," *Arquitectura y Decoración*, Agosto, 1938.

3. In 1961 we visited the apartment house in which we had lived during 1948 and found the tenant who had occupied the apartment next to ours. She remembered us. Our maid, Elena, had gone to the States two years after we left and had married an American of Mexican origin, owner of taverns in two southwestern cities. Her son, now in high school, plans to study law. In fact, Elena herself had visited this *señora* only two weeks before.

4. It was based on occupations listed in the school records which varied greatly from the occupations as more accurately revealed by the brief interviews with 150.

5. For breakfast there is coffee with milk, bread, beans, *tortillas;* for dinner, soup, meat stew with vegetables or potatoes, *tortillas,* and beans; for supper, black coffee with bread.

6. Señorita Guadalupe Ramírez, one of the first lady mayors in Mexico. On a visit with her to villages in the delegation we were impressed by the strong affection of the common people for the *delegada*. Two months later she died suddenly in her office in Xochimilco. Native women took turns watching over the body until the time of burial. She had been so beloved that Casas Alemán, Governor of the Federal District, appointed her sister, Señorita María Elena Ramírez, to take her place.

7. For interesting facts about the heavy internal migration to the cities of Mexico—a trend also in other Latin American countries—see the testimony by Nathan L. Whetten to the House Committee on the Judiciary about "Population Trends in Mexico" (Washington D.C.: U.S. Government Printing Office, 1963). See also "Migration and Urbanization—the *'barriadas'* of Lima: an example of integration into urban life" by José Matos Mar (Chapter VI in *Urbanization in Latin America* edited by Philip M. Hauser —New York: Columbia University Press, 1961).

8. As Anita Brenner has said, the *petate* is "the cheapest, most common, and oldest household possession." *Idols behind Altars* (New York: Payson and Clarke, 1929), p. 123.

9. "An Approach to the Nutrition Problems of Other Nations; Mexican Dietary," *Science,* CII (July 13, 1945), 42-44.

10. In the 1960 census so-called *ex-distritos* are used as the basis for detailed statistical breakdowns rather than *municipios* as in 1940 and 1950.

11. Young women in a Oaxaca private school gave a low rating to "temperance in use of liquor" as a trait desired in a husband—3.08 as compared with an intersample mean of 1.84. See Table 4.

12. Editorial Acrópolis, México, 1946. In 1961 Dr. Cervantes was still living in the same house but was engaged exclusively in private practice.

Chapter VII

1. The actual distribution of the schedules was done in Oaxaca by Jaime Ortiz Dietz, President of Catholic Youth, and in Mexico City by Enrique González Hernández, secretary to the Central Board of Mexican Catholic Action.

2. See pages 62-68 (New York: Columbia University Press, 1944) for a detailed discussion of attitudes toward courtship and marriage. See also John and Mavis Biesanz, "Mate Selection Standards of Costa Rican Students," *Social Forces*, XXII (December, 1943), 194-99.

3. Using the Biesanz questionnaire, Ferdinand T. Johnson made a comparable 1951 study of Garfield High School students in Seattle. The modal income for their parents, as reported by these students, was in the $3,000 to $5,000 range.

4. These young men were in a private school and, like the girls from Oaxaca, came from middle- and lower-class homes.

5. Pearsonian r's show that the ratings by the various groups of young men are significantly correlated beyond the .001 level. In contrast, the ratings for the young women in the Mexico City private (Catholic) and public schools are not significantly correlated. The biggest difference is for chastity (1.19 and 3.89 as compared with the intersample mean of 2.27).

6. American boys concur with their Latin counterparts, but American girls disagree with the *señoritas* by giving the "at least equal social status" item the low importance quotient of 3.09.

7. Elizabeth Treviño, *My Heart Lies South: The Story of My Mexican Marriage* (New York: Crowell, 1953).

8. Comparable data not available for 1950 and 1960.

9. Aida Thompson, "Pilot-politico," *Independent Woman*, April, 1948, pp. 101, 102.

10. From mimeographed report on this conference prepared by Dr. Dorothy H. Veen, Pennsylvania Division, American Association of University Women, p. 9.

11. *Ibid.*, p. 11.

12. *Time*, October 12, 1959.

13. Sra. Pozas used the plural (*novias*) in discussing the basis for a break by the girl.

14. Divorce and marriage figures based on the *Anuario Estadistico de los Estados Unidos Mexicanos 1958-1959* (México, D.F.: Secretaría de Industria y Comercio: Dirección General de Estadistica, 1960), pp. 68-74.

15. For the three large cities of the central plateau the average number of widowers to every 100 widows in 1940 was 15.5; for Oaxaca, Morelia, Toluca, Uruapan, and Pachuca, it was 20.9; for Tepoztlán (Morelos), Pátzcuaro (Michoacán), Tecolotlán (Jalisco), and Ixmilquilpan (Hidalgo), it was 28.0. These percentages for 1950 were 15.8, 19.5, and 27.6. The proportion in Ward VIII for 1950 was 11.8; for Ward I, 18.3; for Xochimilco, 31.1. The corresponding percentages for 1960 were 15.0, 23.5, 32.6.

16. An unpublished study by Charles A. McBride of 2,189 families in which children were attending secondary schools in 18 metropolitan and two rural communities of the Federal District indicated that the average percentage of families with both father and mother was 72, but that in the two village schools the percentage was 83. McBride also found that the proportion of broken families was highest in the more disorganized areas near the central business district and decreased as one moved outward.

17. Lewis, *op. cit.*, p. 16.

Chapter VIII

1. *Mexico South* (New York: Alfred A. Knopf, 1947), p. 294.

2. *Censo Industrial 1956: Resumen General,* Tomo 3 (México D.F.: Dirección General de Estadistica, 1959), p. 8.

3. Brenner, *op. cit.,* p. 31. See also John Skeaping, *The Big Tree of Mexico* (Bloomington: Indiana University Press, 1953), Chapter 11, "The Potters of Coyotepec."

4. In 1956 there were in Oaxaca City and immediate environs 46 pottery-making places employing a total of 124 workers (*Censo Industrial 1956,* p. 9).

5. "José Cruz Ortega me llamo aunque no lo quieras creer soy macho y a la berdad amo y nunca se retroceder si la prueva quieres hacer comigo ya savras a que save mi filo." The confusion of b's and v's is in the original.

6. Serapes and tapetes are, of course, woven in many other Mexican communities. Villages near Toluca, 40 miles west of Mexico City, Texcoco, 28 miles east and north from the metropolis, and Santa Ana Chiautempán in the state of Tlaxcala are well known for this handicraft. In response to tourist demand, the aesthetic level of the designs has been lowered in some of the products and the quality of weaving has occasionally deteriorated. In all of these weaving centers, however, good quality serapes and rugs are still available for the discriminating visitor.

7. See Norman S. Hayner, "Taming the Lumberjack," *American Sociological Review,* X (April, 1945), 217-25.

8. See Wilbert E. Moore, *Industrialization and Labor* (Ithaca and New York: Cornell University Press, 1951), Chapters 10 and 11, for more data on the villages and factories of the Atlixco region.

9. Alfonso Villa Rojas, "Kinship and Nagualism in a Tzeltal Community, Southeastern Mexico," *American Anthropologist,* XLIX (October-December, 1947), 83-86.

10. *Ley Federal del Trabajo* (Mexico, D.F., 1948), Art. 58.

11. *Mexico 1960: Facts, Figures, Trends* (México, D.F.: Banco Nacional de Comercio Exterior S.A., 1960), p. 155.

12. In Mexican Spanish the same word, *camión,* is used for both truck and bus.

13. *Industrial Revolution in Mexico* (Berkeley and Los Angeles: University of California Press, 1950), pp. 182-83.

Chapter IX

1. See Ernest Gruening, *Mexico and Its Heritage* (New York: D. Appleton-Century, 1928), p. 271.

2. To achieve a reasonable degree of detachment for the present study neither extreme was suitable. A combination of sympathetic understanding with an effort to be scientific was needed. Finally, Enrique González Hernández agreed to help. He was an engineering student at the National University and secretary to the Central Board of Acción Católica Mexicana. He therefore combined in an unusual degree training in a scientific approach and sympathetic familiarity with the inner workings of the Mexican Catholic Church.

3. See Alfonso Villa Rojas, *The Maya of East Central Quintana Roo* (Washington, D.C.: Carnegie Institution of Washington, Pub. 559, 1956) and Robert Redfield and Alfonso Villa Rojas, *Notes on the Ethnography of Tzeltal Communities of Chiapas* (Washington, D.C.: Carnegie Institution of Washington, Pub. 509, 1939).

4. Beals, *op. cit.*

5. Translated from *Rarámuri: Mi Diario Tarahumara* (México, D.F.: Talleres Tipográficos de Excelsior, 1948), pp. 106-7. Baez-Camargo, a Protestant, gives the Jesuit mission among the Tarahumara a high rating.

6. *Life*, January 9, 1950, p. 62. See also Gruening, *op. cit.*, p. 232, for a photo of an idol in the church cloister in the village of Milpa Alta, ten miles from Atlapulco.

7. *Idols behind Altars* (New York: Payson and Clarke, 1929), pp. 154-55. Reprinted by permission of Anita Brenner, who owns the copyright. See also Gruening, *op. cit.*, p. 238.

8. This neighborhood has been renamed Villa Gustavo A. Madero after the first revolutionary president, but the name doesn't seem to stick. The expression "La Villa" is often used as a compromise.

9. *"El cura es la voz de Dios."*

10. Almost one-third (31.6 per cent) of all persons in the state living together as husband and wife in 1950 were united in marriage by priests only.

11. See G. Báez-Camargo and Kenneth G. Grubb, *Religion in the Republic of Mexico* (London and New York: World Dominion Press, 1935), p. 86.

12. See Gruening, *op. cit.*, p. 229.

13. R. P. Galindo M., Sp.S., *El Problema Más Grave de México* (México, D.F., 1946).

14. *L'Observatore Romano*, December 25, 1942. The archdiocese of Mexico includes the Distrito Federal and the state of Mexico; the archdiocese of Oaxaca does not include the Mixteca or the Isthmus.

15. The archdiocese of Oaxaca included 119 parishes in 1945 with 882 churches and chapels.

16. Reported by Archbishop Martínez in *Time* magazine, May 9, 1955.

17. By June, 1961, there were 26 first-year students at a site northeast of Oaxaca City and 100 in the main institution.

18. See Chapter XV.

19. Four hundred years before John Dewey, Fray Pedro de Gante had an activity school using the Aztec language and relating the teaching to the current life of his Indian students.

20. *Christian Century*, LXVI (April 27, 1949), and letter to the author.

21. Hugh Nelson also made the following case study of El Chilar in the Cañada region of Oaxaca:

El Chilar, a village of about six hundred inhabitants, is located in the canyon of the headwaters of the Papaloapan River in the district of Cuicatlán. It is an agency of the village of Dominguillo which lies about five miles further up the river. El Chilar is so named for the chili which it produces, though it is also a center for the growing and shipping of tropical fruits and tomatoes. Not an old village, it came into being when the haciendas were divided by the federal government —a distribution of land which drew settlers in from many areas. These newcomers along with the families that had tilled the soil as peons of the haciendas formed the new village.

El Chilar soon took on a distinctive character due to a large element of undisciplined and criminal inhabitants. It came to be known as the center of crime and delinquency in the area designated "La Cañada" with a reputation based on fact. Few traveling men attempted to sell their wares in El Chilar, and if they did venture to enter, they were careful to be gone by nightfall as it was probable that they would be robbed or killed by the vicious inhabitants. The town jail was usually full of delinquents and many cases of criminal action were processed in the head town of the district, Cuicatlán. There were gang leaders who were feared throughout the whole area and who lived their criminal lives with freedom in the village.

There are no figures on the consumption of alcoholic liquors, but old residents say that weekends were times for drunken brawls, and that there were always drunks lying stupified on the streets of the village.

Of religious attempts for social betterment there were none. Nominally the populace was Roman Catholic and on the occasions when the priest visited the church there were many who attended mass. The annual saint's day was a spectacle of most ungodly drunkenness and brawling. The priest did no more than to perform his liturgical duties, receive the collection, and depart.

Then an eighteen-year-old Bible School student named Felipe Herrera came to El Chilar during his vacation to evangelize. He had walked fifty miles to get there. For several weeks he held simple services every night. When some of those attending finally announced their determination to join the evangelical faith, trouble began. Sra. Dolores, who had permitted the meetings to be held in her new home, was beaten before friends and family on the main street.

There were several years of violence as the villagers resisted the development of the new influence, but week by week new names were added to the congregation of believers and frequently they were names of men well known for their criminal behavior. Finally when peace was established the opponents of change admitted defeat and settled back to live as best they could with the Evangelicals.

Today there are only fifty-five members of the Presbyterian church in El Chilar with a community of sympathizers that numbers about two hundred—approximately one-third of the population of the village. So far as I could determine, there are no other factors than the new religion which might have caused such great social change in El Chilar. Other villages, such as Dominguillo, remain as they were twenty years ago. The jail in El Chilar is almost never used—so little, in fact, that should it have an occupant, the people fear for him lest he be bitten by a scorpion living in the uncared-for room. Drinking has not stopped altogether, but public opinion has so changed toward drunkenness that seldom does one find a drunk on the street. Those who drink go to other villages to pursue their carousing. The public school has more than doubled. The local minister is influential in helping to provide books for the students. He also has stimulated an interest in better Spanish usage by means of contests with cash prizes. In the last one, sixty non-sympathizing citizens participated. A number of young people have gone to Puebla, Oaxaca, and México to continue their schooling.

Public health has improved. There are two residents who dispense medicine and nursing care; one is a trained nurse and the pastor's wife. She is now teaching a group of girls to vaccinate and give injections in order to extend the influence of her small clinic.

There are several mills for grinding the masa used in making tortillas and much interest is shown in acquiring modern agricultural implements. Some pure-blooded chickens have been introduced by the missionary from Oaxaca and are being raised with good results. Lands eroded by the river are being reclaimed by the cultivation of rice. The Aftosa control commission which visited the village recently declared that they found there the finest cooperation in the whole area.

The first change was that of the attitude of individuals. With personal living standards radically altered for the good, it became possible for ideas of community betterment to take root. When fathers could concentrate on their jobs and not waste their incomes, more money was available for improvement of homes and for family and community welfare. Mothers became more receptive to health measures which benefited their families. More stable homes led to more children, increased school attendance, and better school facilities. El Chilar is now making another name for herself!

22. *Instituciones Protestantes en México* (México, D.F.: Editorial Jus, 1962), p. 179. See also by the same author, *Protestantismo Mexicano: Su Desarrollo y Estado Actual* (México, D.F.: Editorial Jus, 1961).

23. More than 150 years ago Indians who participated in the Revolution for Independence believed that Spaniards had tails.

24. "Exhortación del Episcopado Nacional al Clero y a los Católicos para Aliviar la Situación de los Campesinos Mexicanos," México, D.F.: March 28, 1948.

25. See "Blueprint for Hungry Nations" in *New York Times Magazine,* January 1, 1950, pp. 8, 9, 27.

26. A notable exception is Monsignor Méndez Arceo who has done away with most of the images in his cathedral in Cuernavaca and has substituted Scriptural quotations in their places. It is reported further that he is encouraging study of the Bible in his diocese.

Chapter X

1. See Ching-Yueh Yen, "Crime in Relation to Social Change in China," *American Journal of Sociology,* XL (November, 1934), 298-308.

2. This court, established in 1926, has three judges, each specializing in certain types of cases. One must be a physician, another a lawyer, and the third a woman educator. Similar courts were founded in Monterrey (1934) and in Guadalajara (1936). Juvenile courts have been started in other cities of the Republic, but not in Oaxaca. (From Lic. Solis Quiroga.)

3. See Clifford R. Shaw and Henry D. McKay, *Juvenile Delinquency and Urban Areas* (Chicago: University of Chicago Press, 1942), pp. 137-39.

4. Shaw and McKay, *Social Factors in Juvenile Delinquency* (Washington, D.C.: U.S. Government Printing Office, 1931), pp. 69-71.

5. See Chapter V.

6. See Departamento de Acción Educativa Eficiencia y Catastros Sociales: *La Mendicidad en México, beneficiencia publica del Distrito Federal,* 1931. (Copy available in Biblioteca Nacional.) This is a pioneer monograph, but a more up-to-date and scientific study is needed. *Pobres,* poor persons, is the usual name for beggars in Mexico. Calling them *pobres* rather than *mendigos,* beggars, is the key to the situation. Most Mexicans pity these people. They feel that one should give to them.

7. For this correlation between vice resorts and girl delinquency see Walter C. Reckless, *Vice in Chicago* (Chicago: University of Chicago Press, 1933), pp. 217-24.

8. The reputation of this street, formerly named after one of the Latin-American republics, became so unsavory that the consul from that country objected and the name was changed.

9. See Benjamín Argüelles, "La Delincuencia de los Adultos y los Menores en el D.F.," *Prevención Social,* Año I, No. 1 and 2 (June and July, 1943).

10. See Lincoln Steffens, *Autobiography* (New York: Harcourt, Brace, 1931), Part II, Chapter 7, "The Underworld," for description of a comparable situation in New York City many years ago.

11. Sra. Esperanza Balmeceda de Josefé, sometime head of the Department of Social Investigations at the Juvenile Court, provided data on the relation between occupations and juvenile delinquency.

12. A few girls were included in the series.

13. One of her sons took a training course in Montevideo, Uruguay, for work in the Y.M.C.A.

Chapter XI

1. *"Si el indio es inferior, lo es por pobre y no por indio."*

2. *"Salida el dinero y los timbres no se permite reclamación."*

3. Alfonso Quiroz Cuarón, José Gómez Robleda, Benjamín Argüelles: *Tendencia y Ritmo de la Criminalidad en México, D.F.* (México, D.F.: Instituto de Investigaciones Estadísticas, 1939), pp. 16, 22, 24, 27, 110-13.

4. Alfonso Quiroz Cuarón, *La Criminalidad en la República Mexicana* (México, D.F.: Instituto de Investigaciones Sociales de la Universidad Nacional, 1958), pp. 33-35.

5. *El Crimen, El Hombre, y El Medio: Principios de Geografía Criminal para la República Mexicana* (México, D.F.: Ediciones Ciceron, 1938).

6. Quiroz Cuarón, *op. cit.,* pp. 69, 80.

7. By 1961 Dr. Quiroz Cuarón had twenty investigators and a force of 105 uniformed police. Salaries ranged from one hundred to three hundred dollars per month.

8. Picking pockets has been for many years an important criminal activity in Spain. It is probable that some of the techniques for skillful execution of this variety of thievery were imported long ago from the mother country.

9. As a youth Tostado was a butcher in the slaughterhouse. It is

alleged that by 1943 he had bought off most of the judges responsible for criminal proceedings. There were many campaigns against him in the newspapers. Later he was not the only man in this racket. He had three or four sons.

In 1961 Tostado and sons were operating in a small park in front of the "preventive jail" on Lecumberri Street. Dr. Quiroz Cuarón reports that Tostado speeds justice for many respectable people who get into some such difficulty as an auto accident.

10. Statements by the investigators were supplemented in this answer by the experience of the author's assistant, José Antonio Méndez, who was not only trained in criminal law but was also employed by a loan company. There was no point of disagreement between the two sources.

11. In 1961 a drug laboratory was added to the central office of the Federal Judicial Police. Marijuana, morphine, heroin, and cocaine in that order of frequency are analyzed. The force was increased and the program was strengthened by a grant from the United States. Helicopters are now used in a special campaign against marijuana. But opium poppy growing increases (*Federal Probation*, XXVII [June, 1963], 80).

Chapter XII

1. A keen interest in correctional institutions has led the author to visit more than 130 in nine different countries; twelve of them several times; two, fifty times; one, ninety times.

2. See Norman S. Hayner, "German Correctional Procedures: Impact of the Occupation," *National Probation and Parole Association Journal*, I (October, 1955), 167-73, and "Notes on the Spanish Correctional System," *Federal Probation*, XIX (December, 1955), 48-51. The latter includes a comparison between Spanish and Mexican prisons. See also the author's "English Schools for Young Offenders," *Journal of Criminal Law and Criminology*, XXVI (January-February, 1937), 696-705 and "Correctional Systems and National Values," *British Journal of Criminology*, III (October, 1962), 163-70.

3. Lecumberri is the east-west street which ends at the penitentiary portal.

4. See José Räúl Aguilar, *Los Métodos Criminales en México: Como Defendernos* (México, D.F.: Ediciones Lux, n.d.), for a 34-page and yet incomplete, dictionary of the jargon of the Mexico City underworld.

5. The similarity in architecture to the old Eastern State Penitentiary at Philadelphia (Barnes and Teeters, *New Horizons in Criminology*, First Edition, New York: Prentice-Hall, 1943, p. 510) is unmistakable. This pattern probably came to Mexico by way of Europe where the Pennsylvania system had a large influence. It is interesting that a prison constructed in 1910 could be so influenced by one built in 1829.

6. A department of the government whose major function is to execute the sentences pronounced by the federal criminal courts. Unfortunately it has no jurisdiction over the administration of the penitentiary which is politically controlled.

7. In 1948 a Catholic youth organization sponsored a service project which provided a better quality of utensil for some of these men. By 1950 the prison administration supplied plates.

8. For a series of photographs showing some aspects of a conjugal visit in this penitentiary, see *Life*, October 27, 1941, pp. 49-50. In the South American country of Colombia inmates may leave the prison for two hours every two weeks, under guard, to meet their wives at a designated rooming house. See Negley K. Teeters, *Penology from Panama to Cape Horn* (Philadelphia: Temple University, 1946), pp. 33-34.

Dr. Teeters told the writer in 1951 that Perón had introduced sex visits into Argentina. In Buenos Aires a special building had been added to the prison for this purpose. The woman came into this building from the street, the man from the prison. No prostitutes were permitted—only wives. Both signed a statement that they were willing to have a sex visit. When she entered the building, the woman was identified by a male attendant. She was then turned over to a female employee. There was a quick medical exam. She then waited in a pleasingly furnished lounging room. At the same time the man entered a lounging room on the prison side. Although each was given a key, the woman went into an attractive bedroom first. This was one of twelve such rooms that were available. The couple was allowed two hours. The visit was, of course, private, but attendants were alert for any sign of dissension. Although data was not available on the actual extent to which this privilege was exercised, every man approved by the prison's diagnostic clinic was allowed a conjugal visit once in two weeks. If permission was denied by the clinic, he might even appeal his case to a higher authority.

With the change of administration in 1955, conjugal visits were discontinued in Argentina and a system of home visits substituted. These "transitory departures" are usually for twelve or twenty-four hours, occasionally for forty-eight. They are granted not only for serious illness or death of relatives as in the United States, but also for the celebration of family events, such as birthdays of wife or children, for strengthening family ties, and near the end of a sentence, for making arrangements about work and lodging. Depending on the degree of security risk he presents, a convict may go out under guard, under the supervision of a relative or friend, or on his own word of honor. To be eligible for a home visit, lifers must have served at least fifteen years; other prisoners, half of their sentences. They must also have a good record in the prison and a favorable prognosis for success after release. During April and May, 1956, from one of the three federal penitentiaries of Buenos Aires, 234 home leaves were granted to 159 prisoners. Due to an error in selection, there was one *fracaso* (failure).—Based on information sent to Ruth Shonle Cavan in 1956 by J. Carlos García Basalo, Inspector General of Penal Institutions.

9. Based on a 1937 unpublished manuscript by Sr. Dr. Don Räul González Enríquez entitled "Visitas Conyugales en la Penitenciaría del Distrito Federal." Dr. González Enríquez was the physician in charge of these visits from 1935 to 1939.

10. Homosexuals are to be found in this penitentiary but are segregated. "Marriages" among inmates of the same sex do occur as in prisons north of the Rio Grande.

11. See Norman S. Hayner, *Proceedings of the Seventy-first Annual Congress of the American Prison Association*, 1941, pp. 121-30. See also Ruth Shonle Cavan and Eugene S. Zemans, "Marital Relationships of

Prisoners in Twenty-eight Countries," *Journal of Criminal Law, Criminology and Police Science*, XLIX (July-August, 1958), 133-39.

12. See article on "Family Prison" in *Cosmopolitan* for March, 1960, and also the more scholarly paper by Columbus B. Hopper in the *Journal of Criminal Law, Criminology and Police Science*, LIII (September, 1962), 340-43.

13. See Robert Redfield, *Tepoztlán* (Chicago: University of Chicago Press, 1930), p. 1.

14. In 1945 Mornard was a trusted prisoner whom the writer was permitted to interview. Dressed in a brown coat, civilian pants, and black pointed shoes, he did not look like a convict. He spoke English quite well and showed an intelligent although somewhat biased grasp of prison problems. "Relations are informal and friendly between guards and inmates," he said. "The more intimate form of Spanish verbs is used in addressing each other." It was not until after the interview that the author was told who he was.

15. April 3, 1950, pp. 106-15.

16. "La Reorganización Penitenciaría," *Revista Jurídica Veracruzana*, Tomo V (1948), No. 5, pp. 307-8.

17. Report prepared by the Secretariat (A/CONF. 17/20), p. 65.

18. For a detailed description of these inmate roles, see Clarence C. Schrag, "Social Types in a Prison Community" (unpublished Master's thesis, Department of Sociology, University of Washington, 1944). A recent excellent revision of this classification by Dr. Schrag in the *Pacific Sociological Review*, IV (Spring, 1961), 11-16. is entitled "A Preliminary Criminal Typology."

19. See discussion of "Personalism, a Central Value" by John P. Gillin in Richard N. Adams *et al.*, *Social Change in Latin America Today* (New York: Random House, 1960), pp. 29-33.

20. See Gresham M. Sykes, *The Society of Captives* (Princeton, New Jersey: Princeton University Press, 1958), "Wolves, Punks, and Fags," pp. 95-99.

21. See Hayner, *op. cit.*, *British Journal of Criminology*.

22. They are permitted in Cuba, Guatemala, Honduras, Salvador, Colombia, and Peru, and in selected prisons of Sweden and Yugoslavia.

23. Hopper, *op. cit.*, pp. 342-43. In a letter dated May 15, 1964, Austin MacCormick refers to this institution as "one of the most primitive prisons in the country."

Chapter XIII

1. Alfonso Quiroz Cuarón, José Gómez Robleda, Benjamin Argüelles, *op. cit.*, pp. 134-35.

2. Based on Irving Tragen's six weeks of talking with people in the poorer sections of Mexico City; 1947 data increased 20 per cent for 1949 conditions.

3. Lucio Mendieta y Núñez, *La Administración pública en México* (México, D.F.: La Imprenta Universitaria, 1942), p. 296.

4. *White Collar Crime* (New York: Dryden Press, 1949), p. 9.

5. See "Bankrupt Socialism" in *Barron's*, XLII (December 24, 1962), 1.

6. Edwin H. Sutherland and Donald R. Cressey, *Principles of Criminol-*

:

ogy, Sixth Edition (Philadelphia: J. B. Lippincott, 1960) pp. 44-46. Copyright 1960 by J. B. Lippincott Company. Permission given by this company to reprint. Adapted slightly by Dr. Cressey from Dr. Sutherland's 1947 edition.

7. Nathan L. Whetten, *Rural Mexico* (Chicago: The University of Chicago Press, 1948), pp. 545-46. Copywright 1948 by the University of Chicago. Permission granted to reprint.

Chapter XIV

1. Dirección General de Acción Deportiva, commonly referred to as Acción Deportiva.

2. Called *futbol* by the Mexicans. American-style football is called *futbol americano.*

3. See William E. Wilson, "A Note on 'Pochismo,'" *The Modern Language Journal,* XXX (October, 1946), 345-46.

4. The head of the boys department at the "Y" tried to help a friend, who had a new and promising business, organize his workers into a baseball team. Players were provided with good quality equipment and the company pickup was placed at their disposal for transportation to the field. In discussing plans they conceded that they could forget about uniforms for a few months, but that something would have to be done about them eventually. They were not satisfied with playing ball on Saturday afternoons and asked that they be given, in addition, Thursday afternoons. When this request was denied, they called off the whole project.

5. Covarrubias, *op. cit.,* p. 336.

6. Physical education is becoming more important in the military service. Each year about 257,000 eighteen-year-old men are required to take military training. To meet this obligation they have only to serve on Sundays. The Mexican Army is ordering an increasing number of these young draftees to take physical education along with their military training. García Cervantes is sending second- and third-year students to help. In addition to setting-up exercises, the program includes the more important aspects of track and field.

7. Harry Wright, *A Short History of Golf in Mexico and the Mexico City Country Club* (New York, 1938).

8. Adapted from Laszlo Radvanyi, "Resultados de Mediciones Estadísticas por el Método de Muestro Estratificado: El Empleo del Tiempo Libre," August, 1947 (mimeographed). No comparable studies were available at a later date.

9. "Mexico's Leisure Hours," *Mexican American Review,* November, 1947, p. 20.

10. *Ibid.,* p. 2.

11. See *The Folk Culture of Yucatan* (Chicago: University of Chicago Press, 1941), Chapter 10, "Holy Day to Holiday."

12. *Treasury of Mexican Folkways* (New York: Crown Publishers, 1947), p. 109.

13. Covarrubias, *op. cit.,* p. 379.

14. Also called *mano fría* (cold hand).

15. Although villages sometimes have central plazas too, these are rarely important in the village life. At Atlapulco the plaza is less used

than the *embarcaderos,* the public washing place, or even, in the past, the streetcar terminal.

16. See Charles Macomb Flandrau, *Viva Mexico!* (New York: D. Appleton, 1908), pp. 277-78, for a vivid description of what the plaza meant to the people of pre-revolutionary Mexico.

17. See John and Mavis Biesanz, *op. cit.,* pp. 51-53, for the origin of the *serenata* or *retreta* and its status in the town of Heredia, Costa Rica.

18. Emily Dickinson, *Love Poems and Others* (Mt. Vernon, New York: Peter Pauper Press), p. 72.

19. Gobierno del Distrito Federal: *Memoria 1944-45* (México, D.F., 1945). Pesos were 4.85 to one dollar in 1944 and in 1947.

20. "Sports: A Big Business," *Mexican American Review,* March, 1948. Among the minor sports, bowling—established about 1930—seems to be gaining most rapidly in popularity. There is, however, only one bowling alley in the entire state of Oaxaca.

21. The term "dubbing" is used in the motion-picture industry for the introduction of a voice—in this case Spanish-speaking—other than that of the actor. The Mexicans call the substitute voice a *doblaje,* or double.

22. The National Commission of Cinematography estimated the 1946-1948 investment for land, buildings, and equipment in these studios at 3.3 million dollars. The total investment of this type in Mexico was 13 millions. Tepeyac studios had an investment of 2.8 millions; Azteca, of 2.5.

23. Interviewed for this book by Juan Pascoe, Jr., the author's assistant for the study of trends in recreation. In spite of the increase in television stations in the Republic from 10 in 1957 to 18 in 1959, the number of movies produced and the number of movie theaters remained about the same during these years, while the monetary return to these theaters increased. (Data from *Anuario Estadístico de los Estados Unidos Mexicanos, op. cit.,* pp. 287, 288, 297.) Argentine movies are more likely to be shown on television than in theaters.

Chapter XV

1. "Resultados de Mediciones Estadísticas por el Metodo de Muestro Estratificado: Mediciones de los Sentimientos de Felicidad de la Población Metropolitana." Instituto Cientifico de la Opinion Pública Mexicana (México, D.F., November, 1947).

2. *La Población de México: 1950-1980 Investigación Económica,* First Quarter, 1960, p. 29.

Data on Mexican death and birth rates from *Anuario Estadístico de los Estados Unidos Mexicanos, op. cit.,* pp. 82 and 89. See also Daniel Moreno, *Los Factores Demográficos en la Planeación Económica* (México, D.F.: Cámara Nacional de la Industria de la Transformación, 1958), Chapter IV, "Dinámica de la Población."

Due to more adequate registration, statistics for cities in Mexico are more complete than those for smaller communities. The apparently large differences between general and infant death rates in urban areas and those in rural areas become less when inadequate registration in the smaller places is considered.

3. Deaths from the dysenteries, enteritis, typhoid and paratyphoid—so-called "diarrheal diseases"—declined from 537 per 100,000 population or

23.4 per cent of the Republic's mortality in 1939 to 231 or 18.5 per cent in 1958. See J. Alvarez Amézquita, M. E. Bustamante, A. L. Picazos, and F. F. del Castillo, *Historia de la Salubridad y de la Asistencia en México,* Vol. IV, pp. 286, 381, 382, 389.

4. Pneumonia deaths declined from 417 per 100,000 in 1939 to 186 in 1958. *Ibid.,* pp. 286, 388.

5. Secretaría de Salubridad y Asistencia, Comisión Nacional de Hospitales, *Censo y Planificación de Hospitales* (México, D.F., Republica Mexicana, 1958), pp. 204, 260.

6. "Informe de la Situación Sanitaria Que Prevalece en la Actualidad y Los Recursos con Que se Cuenta en el Estado de Oaxaca." This report was signed in 1948 by the late Dr. José E. Larumbe, at that time head of the Coordinated Services of Health and Welfare for the state.

7. Measles follows the usual three-year cycle. Peak years were 1940, 1943, 1946, and 1949.

8. The reader should remember that the registration of both births and deaths in the smaller places in Mexico is inadequate. The infant mortality rate for the Republic in 1943 was given as 117 per 1,000 live births.

9. The mountainous region northwest of Oaxaca City where the village of Nuxaá is located.

10. Since Health and Welfare are combined in Mexico, the complete official title of this department is Servicios Coordinados de Salubridad y Asistencia.

11. February 7 and 9, 1949.

12. See Chapter V, Note 9, for a general statement about this type of housing. The opportunity to accompany Sra. Enequita Cruz, a nurse, as she vaccinated for smallpox and gave shots for typhoid, whooping cough, and diphtheria in five *vecindades* convinced the author that there is much a sociologist can learn from an experienced nurse.

13. Mention must be made of the magnificent murals by Diego Rivera which adorn two interior walls, two stories high, at the entrance of the institute. These great frescoes review the history of cardiology. The murals are largely action portraits vividly depicting the men who developed cardiology from Galen to Paul Dudley White of Harvard. Over the first wall a lurid light is thrown by the Spanish physiologist, Miguel Serveto (1509-1553), burning at the stake.

14. According to Rosenblueth, the following medical schools were included in the class-A list: Harvard, Cornell, Pennsylvania, Michigan, Chicago, Northwestern, Illinois, Minnesota, Washington University in St. Louis, Tulane, Stanford. It was anticipated that the University of Washington in Seattle would soon be added.

15. Madame Calderón de la Barca, *op. cit.,* p. 258.

16. David S. Glusker, M.D., and Solon Núñez Frutos, M.D., "Fables in Health Education," *Journal of Health and Physical Education,* XV (April, 1944).

Chapter XVI

1. Whetten, *op. cit.,* pp. 360-69. In 1940, 58 per cent of the Mexicans six years of age or more were illiterate; by 1950 this had been cut to 43 per cent; by 1960, to 38 per cent. Comparable percentages for the

Federal District were 26 to 18 to 17; for the state of Oaxaca, 80 to 61 to 59.

2. *Anuario Estadístico de los Estados Unidos Mexicanos 1958-1959, op. cit.*, pp. 150-52.

3. See Robert S. Strother, "Mexico's Amazing 'Instant' Schools," *Reader's Digest,* August, 1962, pp. 162-66.

4. The sex ratio for the 5,966 primary-school pupils in Oaxaca de Juárez (1948) was 126. The sex ratio for the 189 teachers, however, was 60. By 1961 the primary-school enrollment had increased to 12,759 with a sex ratio of 102. In the sixth grade the sex ratio increased to 115.

5. Lewis, *op. cit.*, pp. 5-6. The home of Sanchez' second wife in free union, Lupita, and her children, described in this book, is in the northeast periphery of the metropolis. The home of his deceased first wife in free union, Lenore, described in *The Children of Sanchez* (New York: Random House, 1961), was in the "Casa Grande" of Colonia Morelas.

6. A *taco* is a Mexican sandwich using a rolled tortilla in place of bread.

7. A *paleta* is a candy or ice made in the form of a spade like our "all-day sucker."

8. A *sope* is a tortilla mixed with other food items such as bits of meat.

9. Lewis, *op. cit.*, p. 13.

10. These questions included the following: (1) Name. (2) Sex. (3) Age. (4) Place of birth. (5) Home address. (6) Number of brothers and sisters. (7) Number of brothers and sisters who have died. (8) Is your home owned or rented? (9) If rented, how much do you pay each month? (10) How many rooms in your home? (11) Food included in each one of your daily meals. (12) Food eaten outside your home. (13) Occupation of your father. (14) Monthly salary of your father. (15) Occupation of your mother. (16) Places which you know outside Mexico City. (17) How many times each month do you go to the movies? (18) With whom do you go?

11. Secundaria No. 16 has recently (1961) been torn down to make way for the Nonoalco-Tlaltelolco housing project described in Chapter V.

12. Guided by Srta. Martin, the attractive visiting teacher for Secundaria No. 16, the homes of two boys from the geography class were visited. Alberto lived in cubicle three at Allende 177. It was one of thirty-four cubicles in this vecindad. The rent was $3.50 a month. His sister, Ester, graduate of another secundaria, was at home when we called. The bedroom, lighted only from the door, contained two double beds with chests for storing clothes. There was a radio. A tiny outer patio was made gay with pots of blooming plants and a parrot of many hues. On one side of this entrance there was a small kitchen with oil stove and table. There was also a private toilet. This was the home shared by a mother, two sisters, and a brother. The father neither lived with them nor helped financially.

13. An attempt at a city-wide survey of socioeconomic status was made for this book during 1949 by Charles McBride, a graduate student in sociology from the University of Texas. The data had been collected by Srta. Castro, supervisor of visiting teachers for the Federal District. About two thousand families of children from eighteen of the capital's secondary schools had been investigated. From this material McBride worked out a socioeconomic index for each school. The following items were used to

compute this index: (1) the percentage of professional workers, (2) the percentage of families with a monthly income of more than 100 pesos ($14.00) per person, (3) the percentage of families paying a monthly rental of 100 pesos or more, (4) the number of bedrooms per 100 persons, (5) the number of beds per 100 persons. Each of these items was divided by the appropriate average for all the schools. The results were added and divided by five. The final is an index number representing the relative socioeconomic status for the families represented in each school.

Although the ecological value of these indices is weakened by the fact that many students were found, on later examination, to be living in areas outside the neighborhoods where they attended school, the results were consistent with the data shown on Map V, Homes of Intellectuals and the Poor. The nine schools located west of the "Cuauhtémoc line" had indices over 100 except No. 15 in the working-class district east of Tacuba and No. 17 which served the Tacubaya slum; and the nine schools to the east of this line under 100 except No. 13 which is far to the south near Churubusco. Secundaria No. 5 in Morelos had the lowest index of all, 60; No. 16 in Tlaltelolco had 82; No. 3 in Roma had the highest, 152. Most families in the best neighborhoods, however, send their children to private schools. The many buses used in transporting pupils to and from these private schools are, as any visitor will tell you, a distinctive feature of the metropolis.

14. Professor Bonilla died in 1960 and his place was taken by Professor José Avila Garabay. Professor Avila reported that the cultural mission program is continuing but less money is available now for its campaign against illiteracy. The current emphasis in education is on the construction of new primary schools. In 1959, 751 new *primarias* were built in the Republic—248 in the Federal District and 14 in the state of Oaxaca.

15. Formerly called Asunción Malacatepec.

16. En route to Villa Donato Guerra we had stopped in Amanalco de Becerro where a former mission had engineered an additional schoolhouse for the fourth, fifth, and sixth grades.

17. For a description of similar methods in the Pátzcuaro area of Mexico see *New Horizons at Tzentzenhuaro: One Year of Work at a Fundamental Education Centre for Latin America* (Nijmegen, Holland: UNESCO, 1953). This has become an important center for training selected individuals in the techniques of community development.

18. See Alfonso Villa Rojas, *Los Mazatecos y el Problema Indígena de la Cuenca del Papaloapan* (México, D.F.: Instituto Nacional Indigenista, 1955).

19. Figures on the enrollment of women are based on an address by Dr. Ignacio Chavez, rector of the National University, to the annual conference of the International Federation of University Women in Mexico City, July, 1962.

20. Based on *Hispanic American Report*, XIV (1961), published by the Institute of Hispanic American and Luso-Brazilian Studies, Stanford University.

21. S. Walter Washington, "Student Politics in Latin America: the Venezuelan Example," *Foreign Affairs*, XXXVII (April, 1959), 463.

Chapter XVII

1. While staying at Oaxaca Courts during January, February, and March of 1949 we identified fifty species of birds, including the pileolated warbler which migrates to Mexico from Western United States. Some of the others were: the cañon wren ("wall jumper" to the Mexicans) whose cascade of liquid notes reverberating against a building is one of the most distinctive and delightful sounds of the Central Plateau; the caracara hawk, called "king of the buzzards" in Mexico because of his ability to lord it over the vultures; the blue grosbeak; the vermillion (venturilla) and the Derby (*Tito fué*) flycatchers; the western gnatcatcher; the linnet ("sparrow with red head" to the Oaxacans); and another migrant from the American West, the violet-green swallow.

2. *New Lives for Old* (New York: Morrow, 1956).

3. For a partial answer to this question, see James L. Garrard, "Education of the Indians of Mexico as a Factor in Their Incorporation into Modern Mexican Society," unpublished doctoral thesis, University of Washington, 1956.

4. See the housing area map for Guadalajara in Floyd and Lillian Dotson, "Ecological Trends in the City of Guadalajara, Mexico," *Social Forces*, XXXII (May, 1954), 367-74.

5. *The Metropolitan Community* (New York: McGraw-Hill, 1933). See especially Chapter 8, "Newspaper Circulation and Metropolitan Regions," and Chapter 10, "The Structure and Orientation of Settlement."

6. Vidriera México, S.A. in Mexico City.

7. *Arms and Politics in Latin America* (New York: Frederick A. Praeger, 1961), p. 121.

8. *Transactions of the American Philosophical Society*, New Series, Vol. 51, Part 8, pp. 54-56.

9. Lloyd H. Hughes, *The Mexican Cultural Mission Program* (Monographs on Fundamental Education III, UNESCO, Paris, 1950).

10. Manuel Gamio, "Primitive Indian Groups," *Boletín Indigenista*, XIV (June, 1954), 87.

11. Carrizo, it will be recalled, is the bamboo-like reed widely used in Mexico for the sides of jacales. The hybrid character of this town name is symbolic of the Anglo-Spanish culture of the borderlands.

Index

Index

Abandonment, a city problem, 131
Abdala, Annuar, 42
abuelita, defined, 98
Adult crime:
 being a prostitute not a crime, 175
 more stealing in Mexico City, 182-83, 175-76
 police tripled at night in Oaxaca City, 180
 spot maps show close relation between *pulquerías* and *lesiones* (injuries to person), 176
 stealing increases with Inter-American Highway, 180
 thieves well known to police, 176, 294
 violent crimes and stealing in state of Oaxaca, 179-80
Aguirre, Enrique C., 219, 220, 227
Alcoholism:
 heavy drinking traditional in Oaxaca, 106, 135
 Monday the day off in Mexico City, 143
 a problem in Oaxaca, 237-38
 young Oaxaqueñas give low rating to "temperance in use of liquor," 288
Alemán, Casas, 288
Alemán, Miguel, 195, 251, 254, 269, 275
almuerzo, defined, 102
Alvarado, Pedro de, 53
Alvarez Amézquita, José, 235, 300
Aragón, Austreberto, 137
Archeology:
 Mitla, stone mosaics and tombs, 284
 Monte Albán, 40, 283-84
 Tenochtitlán, 52-53
 Tlatelolco, 62
Argüelles, Benjamín, 294, 297
Aub, Max, 231
Auriel Ramírez, Carlos, 263
Avila Camacho, Manuel, 144, 156, 248

Avila Camacho, Maximino, 248
Avila Garabay, José, 302

Báez-Camargo, G., 153, 157, 162-63, 291
Bailey, Helen Miller, 37
Bargaining folkways, 41
Barnard, Robert C., 30-31, 283
Barnes, Harry Elmer, 295
Bassols, Narciso, 266
Baz, Gustavo, 211, 245, 250
Beals, Ralph L., 148, 282, 291
Beggars:
 called *pobres* (poor persons) rather than *mendigos* (beggars), 294
 children as beggars, 88-89
 concentration in the city center, 174
Bellon, Sr., 135
Biesanz, John, 114, 289, 299
Biesanz, Mavis, 114, 289, 299
Birds of Oaxaca, 303
Bolaños Cacho, Räúl, 72, 227
Bonilla y Segura, Guillermo, 263, 302
braceros, progress as a result of their work, 19, 50, 139
Brena, Guillermo, 136, 137
Brenner, Anita, 29, 134, 150, 288, 290, 291
Broken homes in the Federal District, 289
Browning, Clyde Eugene, 286
Burgess, Ernest W., 284
Bustamante, M. E., 300

Calderón de la Barca, Madame, 17, 254, 300
Calvo de la Torre, Angel, 250, 251
camión, defined, 290
Camohmila Center, a Y.M.C.A. camp near Tepoztlán, 223
Candano, Antonio, 248, 249, 250
Caplow, Theodore, 284

307